Leeds

D0321284

PEVSNER ARCHITECTURAL GUIDES

Founding Editor: Nikolaus Pevsner

PEVSNER ARCHITECTURAL GUIDES

The Buildings of England series was created and largely written
by Sir Nikolaus Pevsner (1902–83). First editions of the county
volumes were published by Penguin Books between 1951 and 1974.
The continuing programme of revisions and new volumes has
been supported by research financed through the Buildings Books
Trust since 1994.

The Buildings Books Trust gratefully acknowledges
Grants towards the cost of research, writing and illustrations
for this volume from

THE HERITAGE LOTTERY FUND

Assistance with photographs from

ENGLISH HERITAGE

Leeds

SUSAN WRATHMELL

WITH JOHN MINNIS

with contributions by

JANET DOUGLAS

ELAIN HARWOOD

DEREK LINSTRUM

CHRISTOPHER WEBSTER

ANTHONY WELLS-COLE

STUART WRATHMELL

PEVSNER ARCHITECTURAL GUIDES

YALE UNIVERSITY PRESS

NEW HAVEN & LONDON

For Richard Taylor and Phil Ward, and for my family.

The publishers gratefully acknowledge help in
bringing the books to a wider readership from
ENGLISH HERITAGE

YALE UNIVERSITY PRESS
NEW HAVEN AND LONDON
302 Temple Street, New Haven CT06511
47 Bedford Square, London WC1B 3DP

www.pevsner.co.uk
www.lookingatbuildings.org
www.yalebooks.co.uk
www.yalebooks.com

Published 2005
Reprinted with corrections 2008
10 9 8 7 6 5 4 3 2

All rights reserved. This book may not be reproduced in whole or in part, in
any form (beyond that copying permitted by Sections 107 and 108 of the U.S.
Copyright Law and except by reviewers for the public press), without written
permission from the publishers

Copyright © Susan Wrathmell

Set in Adobe Minion by SNP Best-set Typesetter Ltd., Hong Kong
Printed in Italy by Conti Tipocolor

Library of Congress Cataloging-in-Publication Data

Wrathmell, Susan.
Leeds / Susan Wrathmell with John Minnis; and contributions by Janet
Douglas . . . [et al.].
    p. cm. – (Pevsner architectural guides)
    Includes bibliographical references and index.
    ISBN-13 978–0–300–10736–4 (pbk. : alk. paper)
    1. Architecture – England – Leeds – Guidebooks. 2. Leeds
(England) – Buildings, structures, etc. – Guidebooks. I. Minnis, John.
II. Title. III. Series.
    NA971.L38W73 2005
    720´.9428´19–dc22
                                        2005000717

Contents

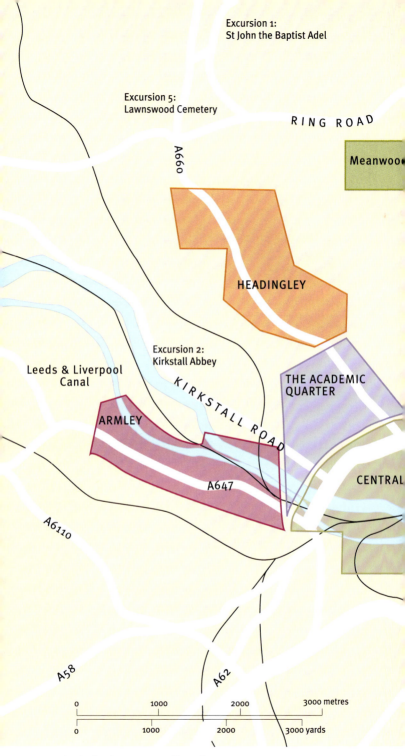

Excursion 1:
St John the Baptist Adel

Excursion 5:
Lawnswood Cemetery

RING ROAD

A660

Meanwood

HEADINGLEY

Excursion 2:
Kirkstall Abbey

THE ACADEMIC
QUARTER

Leeds & Liverpool
Canal

KIRKSTALL ROAD

ARMLEY

CENTRAL

A647

A6110

A58

A62

| 0 | | 1000 | | 2000 | | 3000 metres |

| 0 | | 1000 | | 2000 | | 3000 yards |

1. Leeds, showing areas covered by walks

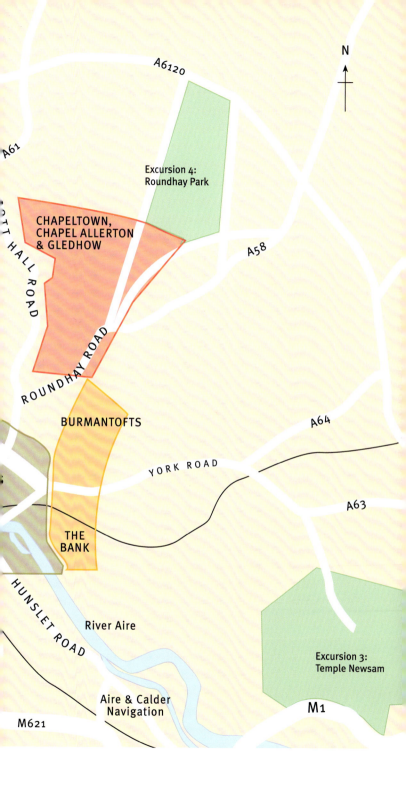

N

A6120

A61

Excursion 4:
Roundhay Park

CHAPELTOWN,
CHAPEL ALLERTON
& GLEDHOW

...OTT HALL ROAD

A58

ROUNDHAY ROAD

BURMANTOFTS

A64

YORK ROAD

A63

THE
BANK

HUNSLET ROAD

River Aire

Excursion 3:
Temple Newsam

Aire & Calder
Navigation

M1

M621

How to use this book

The book is designed as a practical guide for exploring the buildings of central Leeds and its inner suburbs. The first section of the gazetteer, following the Introduction, covers nine major buildings all of which can be found in the city centre. This is followed by coverage of the central area, mostly within the Inner Ring Road, for which five walks explore phases of the city's development up to the present day. Each walk starts with a map which indicates the area covered and the route of the walk(s) to be followed. A section follows, devoted to the area including the suburb of Little Woodhouse which has been developed for the Universities. Walks are also provided for a selection of suburbs in outer Leeds. From the w, clockwise: the cloth-making village of Armley, Headingley's ancient centre and C19 suburbs out to Beckett Park; Chapel Allerton, Chapeltown and Gledhow and, to the E, the Bank and Burmantofts. The final section provides a series of suggested excursions, including St John the Baptist, Adel, Kirkstall Abbey, Temple Newsam, the great park at Roundhay, and Lawnswood Cemetery. The wider Leeds area will be covered in the forthcoming revision of *The Buildings of England: Yorkshire West Riding* (*North*).

Throughout the book, certain topics are singled out for special attention and presented in separate boxes:

Lost Buildings: The 'Castle' and Manor House p. 6, The Old Infirmary p. 84, The Cloth Halls p. 104, Lost Buildings of the early C19 p. 119, The Quarry Hill Flats p. 171

Leeds Architects, Artists and Patrons: Ralph Thoresby, antiquary, 1658–1725 p. 4, John Harrison (1759–1656), an early benefactor p. 10, John Barran and Thomas Ambler p. 21, John Atkinson Grimshaw (1836–93) p. 23, Bedford & Kitson, architects p. 249

Manufacturers: William Potts & Sons, clockmakers p. 158, The Burmantofts Pottery p. 225

Transport and Industry: Leeds–Liverpool Canal p. 128, Gott's Bean Ing Mills p. 138, Aire & Calder Navigation p. 142

Religious Buildings: Hook and the Choral Service p. 47, Planning and Liturgy at St John p. 50, Decorative Tiles at Kirkstall Abbey p. 278

Materials and Methods: The Roof of the Victoria Hall p. 67, Fire-proof Construction p. 206

Styles: The Leeds Look p. 36

Acknowledgements

First, a great debt is owed to Nikolaus Pevsner, whose visit to Leeds, for the first edition of *Yorkshire: The West Riding*, 1959, provided the foundation for Enid Radcliffe's second edition of 1967 and for this volume of the City Guides series.

Particular thanks are due to Derek Linstrum who gave advice on all aspects of the work at the early stages. His agreement to write the text for the Town Hall, Corn Exchange and Mechanics' Institute enhances this guide enormously. I am equally grateful to all the expert contributors: Janet Douglas (St John's church); Elain Harwood (Leeds University campus); Christopher Webster (the Parish Church); Anthony Wells-Cole (Temple Newsam House) and Stuart Wrathmell (Kirkstall Abbey). I must especially thank John Minnis, co-author of the Sheffield volume, for his work on the Leeds suburbs and his generous help and advice.

I owe a major debt to the Leeds City Council staff, in particular the Conservation Team, including Richard Taylor, Phil Ward, Rob Murphy, Chris Bateman, Peter Vaughan and Helen Saunders. They gave expert advice throughout, checked text and advised on the walks. My appreciation is reflected in the dedication. Angie Rycroft provided illustrations; thanks also to Chris Clarke and members of the Plans Section. Kevin Grady, Director of Leeds Civic Trust, gave valuable information and advice; his support has been greatly appreciated. Thanks also to Peter Baker, Peter Brears, Stephen Burt, Ann Clark, Michael Devenish, Arthur Hopwood, Colin Price, and Joan Newiss. Freda Matthews generously made her research on Little Woodhouse available and commented on the draft.

Thanks to Tom and Josephine Wesley who devoted much time to text corrections, also to Anna Craven, Diana Hill and Chris Hammond. Robert Sladdin, Director of Estates, assisted with the University text. David Boswell read the entries on Bedford & Kitson, Headingley and Chapel Allerton, while Helen and Andy Guy gave expert advice on industrial archaeology. Kate Minnis, Tom and Josephine Wesley, and John Claxton kindly checked proofs.

The author and contributors are indebted to church custodians and clergy, including the Rev. Timothy Lipscomb at St Bartholomew's, Barrie Pepper (St Aidan's), Christopher Tyne (St Saviour's), Stephen Savage (St Hilda's), and Ann Clark (St Peter's). Robert Finnigan, the

Roman Catholic Diocesan Archivist, kindly discussed his researches and was my guide to the cathedral. Information about stained glass was supplied by Michael Kerney and Michael G. Swift. I also thank all those who allowed myself and the contributors access to buildings and answered queries, including Pat Egan at the Municipal Buildings, Peter Foy and Christine Lindley (Leeds General Infirmary), and the office of the Lord Mayor (Civic Hall).

I would like to thank librarians and archivists for their professional support, especially the staff of the City Library, the Leeds Library and Bryan Sitch of the Leeds Museum Service. Alexandra Everely and the staff of the West Yorkshire Archives, Sheepscar were always helpful, and the Brotherton and the Leeds Metropolitan University libraries kindly gave permission to use their facilities. Geoffrey Forster, librarian of the Leeds Library, advised on the interpretation of buildings in Commercial Street. Study facilities were willingly made available at the Leeds Library, the Civic Trust Headquarters where Dorte Haarhaus was always welcoming and, during the last year of work, the RIBA Yorkshire Region's headquarters was a haven, where Rachel Hughes and Emma England gave enthusiastic support. Architectural information was generously given by John Thorp, Civic Architect, Gordon Carey and Chris Jones (Carey Jones Architects), Maurice Lyons (Bauman Lyons) and Laurence Teeney (Bowman Riley Architects). I am indebted to the West Yorkshire Archaeology Service: Ian Sanderson for advice about current thinking on Leeds' origins, and Helen Gomersall for expertise on industrial history. David Robinson of English Heritage kindly commented on the text for Kirkstall Abbey at a late stage. Special thanks also to the City Guides authors, especially Clare Hartwell, Ruth Harman and Andy Foyle.

I am very grateful to those who have given help and encouragement, including Pippa Bramham, Peter Bramham, Jane Devenish, Doug Grant, Mary Rose Millin, Keith Stephenson, Deborah Taylor, Jane Taylor, Gwynne Walters and John and Peter Wrathmell.

This volume was funded by the Buildings Books Trust with support from the Heritage Lottery Fund. Thanks are due to English Heritage, who provided many of the photographs, through the skills of their photographer, Tony Perry. Particular thanks go to the editorial team at Yale University Press. I am greatly indebted to Charles O'Brien, the editor, who showed great patience and understanding throughout. Simon Bradley and Gavin Watson advised on parts of the text, Gavin also providing administrative support. Emily Winter, assistant editor, guided it through the final stages, and Emily Lees researched the pictures. Touchmedia produced the maps, Sue Vaughan was the copy editor, Charlotte Chapman the proofreader and Judith Wardman the indexer; Sally Salvesen was the Commissioning Editor.

It remains to appeal to all users to draw my attention to errors and omissions through the publishers.

Introduction

Introduction

Leeds is the largest city in Yorkshire, with a population of 715,000. Its boundaries extend far beyond the built-up area into still-rural districts of West Yorkshire, providing the explorer with buildings of great variety and interest. The centre lies on the N bank of the river Aire, whose valley cuts through the Millstone Grit of the Pennines. The warm s-facing slope encouraged early settlement, and the proximity of the Yorkshire Coal Measures, with layers of sandstone and clay for brick-making, provided the materials for the burgeoning town of the C18 and early C19. In the Victorian and Edwardian boom years, polychrome brick, richly moulded terracotta and coloured faience became the predominant materials for grand buildings and continue to define the vibrant architectural character of the modern city. Leeds was fortunately spared the need (if not the desire) for major Postwar rebuilding and the architecture of the later C20 is, for the most part, not over-represented.

For first-time visitors arriving by train tantalizing views unfold on the approach to City Station. From the s towers invigorate the skyline, none more so than the Town Hall, that symbol of Leeds at the height of Victorian confidence, and beyond, the Civic Hall and University buildings of the 1930s in gleaming Portland stone. Nearer the centre the traveller comes close to the river, canal and the web of railway lines that shaped the city's development over several centuries. They attracted industry, and the eye is instantly caught by the extraordinary cluster of campanile at the Tower Works, Holbeck, but in the C21 they must compete for attention with a screen of brash new riverside apartment blocks. From the E the railway passes between the Perp tower of the C19 parish church and the solid and muscular Corn Exchange, unforgettable landmarks among the busy streets of the old town.

Leeds has large, attractive suburbs appropriate to a prosperous manufacturing city, but its extensive boundaries also encompass several former villages and even a scatter of mansions associated with the landed society of its pre-industrial age. This guide, however, makes no pretensions towards comprehensiveness and concentrates on the city centre and the principal w and n suburbs, with selected excursions to buildings of major interest.

2. Civic Hall, by E. Vincent Harris, 1931–3; detail of clock. Owl by John Thorp, 2000

Early and Medieval History

Bronze Age finds have been made throughout Leeds, not only scattered objects but also two barrows on Woodhouse Moor (recorded in the mid-C19); earthworks nearby (Rampart Road) are possibly the remains of an **Iron Age** fortification. This was the country of the Brigantes, who strongly resisted the **Roman** occupation of the north, which lasted into the C5. Leeds may have been the site of *Cambodunum*, mentioned in the *Antonine Itinerary*. Finds of Roman material and the line of a road running through the town E of Leeds Bridge suggest a *mansione* here (where travellers could break their journey), while earthworks at Quarry Hill (mentioned by historians in the early C18 and mid C19) may have been the remains of the 'fort by the river-bend' on the Manchester–York road, overlooking a crossing on the Aire. Leeds was probably a major early **Anglo-Saxon** settlement in West Yorkshire. Bede in 730 mentions 'Campodonum', and 'the region known as Loidis' from which the city's name derives. Bede also notes the monastery of Abbot Thrythwulf here in the early C8, which fell out of use during Viking incursions in the later C8. The discovery in the early C19 of an apparently Anglo-Saxon flexed burial suggests evidence for pagan occupation. Firmer proof of Leeds' importance as a religious centre by the C9 and C10 is provided by fragments (now in the City Museum collection) of at least six Anglian preaching and memorial **crosses** with Scandinavian-influenced decoration, discovered in 1838 amongst the building rubble of the parish church's C14 tower. The best preserved, displayed in St Peter's Church, has a shaft depicting haloed figures and Weland the Smith; its wheel-head stone is probably from another cross [3].

In the mid C10 or C11 Leeds may have been known further afield. The *Life of St Cadroe* refers to the saint passing through 'the *civitas* of Leeds',

Ralph Thoresby, antiquary, 1658–1725

Much of the early history of Leeds was recorded by Ralph Thoresby, a wealthy merchant, in two volumes; one on the history of the town, *Ducatus Leodiensis* (1715), the other on the history of the church, *Vicaria Leodiensis* (1724). His diaries, covering the period 1677 until his death in 1725, were first published in 1830 and provide a unique account of the developing town and its environs. Thoresby was a member of the Corporation from 1698 and an avid collector of scientific and archaeological objects. His large house on Kirkgate (taxed for five hearths in 1672; destroyed in the late C19) had a turret and observatory; there was a well of 'spa water' in the garden. His collection of curiosities became the basis of the town's first museum and he is commemorated by the Thoresby Society (founded 1889).

3. Weland cross, C10.
Drawing

a term sometimes used for a cathedral centre. It is thought that Leeds escaped the harrying of the North following the Conquest. The manor was gifted to Ilbert de Lacy and the Domesday Book of 1086 mentions a mill, a church (dedicated to St Peter) and a priest. The settlement was compact, centred on a single street, now Kirkgate, which extended uphill NW from the church towards the cultivated open fields of Woodhouse. Upriver to the W, standing on a slight rise, was the manor house (*see* topic box, p. 6) and its park. It was linked to the village by paths along the N bank of the river, now the line of The Calls, Call Lane and Sovereign Street. The Headrow and Lady Lane follow the line of ancient routeways on the edge of the open fields. The extensive manor was broken up in 1089 when the house and manorial corn mill were divided from 'Leeds Kirkgate-cum-Holbeck' (comprising the parish church and village) which was granted to Holy Trinity Priory, York. In 1180 the manor of North Hall, in the area of Lady Lane and Vicar Lane was also separated. The Knights Templars were given small parcels of land throughout the village and in 1155 acquired the manor of Newsam, SE of the town.

Early buildings are scanty, the major medieval survivals confined to the once rural districts now within the city boundaries. The arrival in the early C12 of the Burgundian Cistercian order produced a string of houses in Yorkshire, whose sequence begins with Rievaulx.

Kirkstall Abbey, founded in 1152 in a typically secluded setting W of Leeds along the Aire, remains one of the most complete, though ruinous, testaments to the architecture of this prodigious order [145–50]. It also marks a transition from Burgundian Romanesque to a native form of Gothic in the early use of rib-vaulting. The Abbey's estates expanded to the N and E, with interests in Armley, Chapel Allerton, Gledhow and Headingley. It transformed the local economy, both through the availability of wool (the Abbey owned around 4,500 sheep by 1301) for the burgeoning cloth-making industry and through trading links with northern Europe and Italy. At Adel is one of the most rewarding Norman parish churches in Yorkshire, indeed nationally [4, 144]. Built between 1150 and 1170, it is small, of nave and chancel only, but with sumptuous decoration both inside and out, including rare figurative sculpture.

In 1207, the lord of the manor Maurice de Gant (also known as Paynel) founded the Borough of Leeds. He rebuilt in stone the bridge across the Aire, perhaps using skilled masons from Kirkstall Abbey, and laid out the new street of Briggate from the river N to Kirkgate. This had thirty plots on either side and space for a market, in operation by 1258. Occupants paid fixed rents for a house plot and an allotment (toft) at Burmantofts, E of the town; income was to come from trade or a craft, which fostered the growth of the domestic cloth-making industry and a rise in the town's population. York and Hull

The 'Castle' and Manor House

The group of buildings enclosed by Mill Hill, Boar Lane and Bishopgate Street stand on the site of the medieval manor house. A fortified stone 'castle' was erected in 1069, but reputedly demolished in the early C13, and replaced by a farmstead, with a grange and 'great garden'. By 1341 there was a complex of three enclosures: a moated site, a courtyard, and a group of farm buildings including a grain store. The site is still shown as 'Castyll hill' on a plan of Leeds made in 1560, which includes a drawing of the house, showing a close-studded timber-framed hall with gabled end. Cossins' map of c. 1726 [6] shows it as rebuilt in the later C16 by the lord of the manor, Richard Wilson: a symmetrical U-plan hall house with cross-wings and storeyed porch. In 1765 the Wilsons built a new mansion, leaving an earlier wing standing. By the early C19 the mansion was tenanted, the industrial town having become a place that was 'odious to inhabit'. The old wing was purchased in 1815 by Henry Scarbrough who converted it to The Kings Arms Inn. He later acquired the mansion for use as The Scarbrough Hotel. This was demolished in the 1930s. The inn, now The Scarbrough pub, was remodelled, but roof timbers appear to be of C16 origin. Building work nearby in the mid C19 revealed sections of the 'castle' moat.

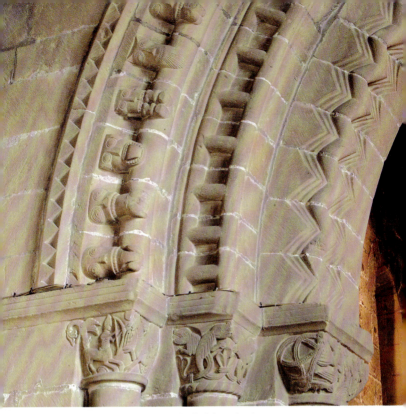

4. St John the Baptist, Adel, *c.* 1150–70, detail of chancel arch

remained the important provincial centres, however, and until the late C17 Leeds remained small, its character still rural and dominated by St Peter's. This was rebuilt, after a fire in the C14, to a cruciform plan with a 96 ft (30 metre) high tower (dem. 1838). As the population expanded during the C15 and C16, urban interests proclaimed their importance with monuments in the parish church (the tomb of Thomas Hardwick d.1577 survives with a fine fresco panel), the erection of chantry chapels in town, and the building of new **timber-framed houses**. Of Rockley Hall, built by the town bailiff Henry Rockley (d.1502), only roof timbers are thought to survive in buildings in Rockley Hall Yard. A small clue to external appearance is given by the fragment of a jettied, gabled cross-wing from a large house in Lambert's Yard, off Lower Briggate. A house on North Street, demolished in 1896, had pargetting on the gable, common to vernacular buildings in eastern England. The most important relic of the late medieval period, however, is the surviving part of the immense mansion at Temple Newsam [151], begun after 1488 by Thomas Darcy – a courtier, mercenary and future crony of Thomas Wolsey. It was built of brick, with diaper patterning, on four sides of a courtyard with the gatehouse in its N range.

The Seventeenth Century

The ambition of Leeds' cloth merchants to become a self-governing body was realized in 1626 with a Charter of Incorporation creating a free borough governed by a self-electing Corporation, whose members inspected and controlled cloth produced in the town. Three years later the Corporation, led by Richard Sykes, purchased the manor from the Crown. In the survey drawn up in 1628 a good picture is provided of the town's buildings: 'The houses . . . are very thick and close compacted together, being ancient mean and low built; and generally all of timber; though they have stone quarries frequent in the town, and about it, only some few of the richer sort of the inhabitants have their houses more large and capacious; yet all low and straightened on their backsides.'* The wealthiest merchants, however, now began to build (or rebuild) on a grander scale and increasingly used brick. Alderman Thomas Metcalf's aptly named 'Red Hall' of 1628 on Upperhead Row (dem. 1961) was probably the first to be built in this material. Stone was used for its quoins and dressings, carved with an elaboration comparable to that of the great stone houses of the clothing districts around Halifax. Several new brick houses were built near to the new church of St John, consecrated in 1634 at the N edge of the town with an endowment by the cloth merchant, John Harrison (*see* topic box, p. 10). This is the first major survival within the town and one of national interest both architecturally and historically [25–6]. Though entirely Gothic in detail it has a remarkable double nave and wonderful Jacobean woodcarving [5]. There was a pressing need for a new church as St Peter's was overcrowded, tiers of wooden galleries having been

* The manor had been acquired by the Crown in 1399. To pay off debts it seems Charles I sold the manor to the Corporation of London, who surveyed it before selling it on.

Cloth-Making

Cloth production began early in Leeds. The first recorded water-powered fulling mill in England was built at Temple Newsam by 1185 and such mills proliferated during the C13. It was during this period that the bulky horizontal loom (powered by two weavers) for making broadcloth was introduced. The expansion of the industry was encouraged in the C16 as the availability of small plots of land, fulling mills and dyehouses drew skilled clothmakers to Leeds and away from ancient centres such as York and Beverley, where the guild system prolonged apprenticeships and living costs were high. Leeds and its surrounding villages produced broadcloths of many colours, together with highly specialized work such as that by Randall Trenche and his assistants, who made tapestries using wool, silk, silver and gold thread for Sir Francis Willoughby of Wollaton Hall, Nottingham, from 1589.

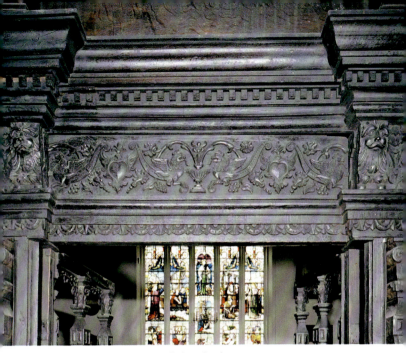

5. St John the Evangelist, *c.* 1634, detail of woodwork

built to accommodate its congregation of 3–4,000. St John appears to have been some years in the planning, indicated by coats of arms in the church, dating to before 1625. The woodcarver, *Francis Gunby* was also engaged in the contemporary remodelling of Temple Newsam House for the London merchant and courtier, Sir Arthur Ingram. His fortune from the sale of Crown lands paid for alterations carried out in the style of Hatfield House with a series of lovely canted bay windows, displaying Ingram's wealth in leaded glass.

Leeds was divided socially by the Civil War between merchants for the King and clothmakers for Parliament. From the Restoration the merchants were once more in the ascendant. Woollen cloth made in the West Riding became a major export and was sent through Hull to markets in Holland and Germany; merchants' sons were also sent to learn their business in northern Europe. Prosperity paid for rebuilding the war-damaged town. In 1698 Celia Fiennes described Leeds as 'a large town, several large streets clean and well pitch'd and good houses, all built of stone, some have good gardens and steps up to their houses and walls before them'. The principal houses were even supplied with water through pipes from a reservoir near St John's which was filled using a pumping engine built on the river in 1694 by *George Sorocold*. An even more impressive feat was the Corporation's construction of the **Aire & Calder Navigation**, opened in November 1700, which enabled transport of cloth and other goods in large cargo boats to Hull for export to the European markets.

John Harrison (1579–1656), an early benefactor

John Harrison, cloth merchant, was one of the most influential figures in early C17 Leeds. He acquired the North Hall and Rockley Hall estates in the northern part of the town, built a house at the N end of Briggate and established the ancient pathway N from Briggate as 'New Street', now New Briggate. The rents from his houses there were redistributed amongst poor cloth-making families for whom he stored provisions at Rockley Hall. In 1611 he became joint bailiff (the king's representative in the town), receiving market stall rents in competition with the owners of the buildings fronting the street. He owned several burgage plots, cottages and tenements in Vicar Lane, and a number of closes scattered throughout the old manor. He also owned the dams and ditches known as Great Mill and Little Mill Dykes and a fulling mill, which he extended to grind imported redwood for dyeing. In 1615–18 he paid for the building of a new Moot Hall on the market place in Briggate, followed in 1619 by a new Market Cross. Harrison founded a new grammar school on his 'New Street' in 1624. It was small and in a conventional Jacobean style but built of stone, an early use for secular buildings within the town. His greatest legacy, however, was the endowment of the church of St John, opened in 1634. By that year he had built almshouses close to the church (for forty poor women) and became Alderman of the town.

Georgian Leeds, 1725–1840

John Cossins' map of *c.* 1726 [6], the first accurate plan of the town and its buildings, illuminates contemporary descriptions. It shows Briggate, the closely built-up Head Row and New Street areas to the N developed in the C17, the increasing settlement s of Leeds Bridge, the Aire & Calder Navigation warehouse and wharves and tenter grounds. Several major new houses are shown on the map and in the margins. They were mostly of brick with stone dressings, with three-storey and five-bay symmetrical façades and some Baroque details, including the domed house for John Atkinson on Call Lane and Hugh Sleigh's house in Briggate which displays such details as graceful pilasters, and a parapet with urns but also shops to the ground floor. Others have features relating to commercial use: Mr Dixon's on Call Lane has a tier of wide loading doors and a cellar, while two large properties, with closely spaced windows, are of a size suggestive of use as warehouses and workshops. Robert Denison's fine mansion in North Street,* possibly designed by *William Thornton*, showed in its detail a sophisticated acquaintance with contemporary Roman sources. Only Matthew Wilson's house in New Briggate, close to St John's, survives [84], but early C18 relics are the

* Recorded in a photograph of the 1880s

minor houses on Briggate (Nos. 3–5 and Queen's Court, both with workshop yards behind) and Bridge End and Dock Street (close to the Aire & Calder Navigation). Three other buildings in Cossin's map reflect the growing confidence of the early C18 mercantile class. In Kirkgate is the first Cloth Hall, built in 1711 by merchants trading in 'white' or undyed cloth brought in from Calderdale (*see* topic box, p. 104); on Briggate is the Moot Hall, rebuilt in 1710 (dem. 1824) by *William Etty* of York with ground floor shops. It had giant pilasters, open pediment and cupola. A statue of Queen Anne by *Andrew Carpenter*, 1713 (preserved in the City Art Gallery) is shown within an elaborate carved surround with swan-neck pediment. *Etty*'s Holy Trinity Church [45] still stands on Boar Lane as testament to the urbane taste and sophistication of early C18 Leeds. The style is still Baroque but closer to that of Gibbs, made more so after 1839 by the replacement of its original spire with a tower by *Chantrell* firmly in the manner of Wren.

From the mid C18 onwards the open yards behind properties in the older part of town were built up with artisan housing, as at Queen's Court and Blayd's Yard off Briggate. In 1757 the building of the large Coloured Cloth Hall signalled the beginning of expansion to the w. The first **planned developments** of superior housing, on the Wilson's Park Estate, began with the laying out of Park Row in 1767–76. The centrepiece was Park Square (begun in 1788) [57] with St Paul's Church (designed in 1791–3 by *William* or *Thomas Johnson*, dem. 1905) on the s side. But its position close to the river, where polluting dyehouses and

6. Map of Leeds, by John Cossins, *c.* 1726

mills were built from the 1760s, caused development to terminate in 1797 with less than ten of the fifty fields disposed of. The completed parts were not exclusively residential and several houses had workshops and warehouses as well as stables and coach houses.

For those who could afford it, the ideal was a home at some remove from the town. Two such houses are the work of Yorkshire's principal mid-C18 architects working in the Palladian tradition. At Far Headingley, Kirkstall Grange [140], rebuilt for Walter Wade in 1752, is attributed to *James Paine*; Gledhow Hall, built soon after 1766 for the merchant Jeremiah Dixon, is probably by *John Carr*, who designed a town house for Dixon in 1753. Carr went on to erect the town's Infirmary in 1768. Palladian too are the stables [156] and other additions made at Temple Newsam House after 1738, probably by *Daniel Garrett*, but the remodelling of the interiors of the N wing are in a lively Rococo style [155]. In time smaller suburban villas were erected closer to town. The best such houses survive at Little Woodhouse, close to or within the modern Leeds University campus, among them Claremont (1772), Springfield House (1792), Belle Vue House (1792) and Beech Grove House (1799). Most splendid is the Neoclassical Denison Hall, built in 1786 by Carr's pupil *William Lindley,* with fine Adam-style interiors.

The early C19 town was transformed to meet the needs of its expanding population, its trades, and its interests both financial and intellectual. New **public buildings and institutions** now appeared, amongst them a court house and commercial buildings, while new cloth halls and market halls were built to replace the overcrowded market areas of the old town. Additional bridges were also made across the Aire to outlying villages. Much from this period has been destroyed (*see* topic box, p. 119); only the Leeds Library, by *Thomas Johnson,* rebuilt on a new site on Commercial Street in 1808, survives to indicate the wealth and taste of the time. Johnson was a local architect but within a few years Leeds businessmen were extending their patronage to architects from outside who played a role in establishing a fashion for the **Greek Revival**. This style appears in the domestic architecture of West Yorkshire with the remodelling of Benjamin Gott's villa at Armley by *Robert Smirke* after 1816 [116]. Its innovative construction made use of cast-iron framing and doors. Also of this period, and also fashionably Grecian, is Roundhay Mansion, complete by 1816 and attributed to *Thomas Taylor.* Taylor has been described as the town's first true professional architect, having worked in London for five years with a builder and eight years in James Wyatt's office. He settled in Leeds *c.* 1810 and designed the new Court House in 1811 (dem. 1901). He was followed by *R.D. Chantrell* who came to Leeds from Sir John Soane's office in 1819 and made his career in the town until 1847. Amongst his earliest works was the Neo-Grecian Philosophical Hall (1819–22, dem.) for the newly-founded Philosophical and Literary Society. Chantrell progressed from the graceful classical style of this early building to the addition of a Baroque tower to Holy Trinity Church in 1839 and the Gothic rebuilding of the parish church in 1837–41 (*see* below). *John Clark* of Edinburgh worked for the mill owner John Marshall in the 1820s and it is likely that Marshall introduced him to other industrialists, including Hives and Atkinson for whom Clark designed the great Bank Flax Mills [73] between 1824 and 1833 and John Hives' own house at Gledhow Grove in 1835–40. This is in a Greek style with Egyptian details to the stables. Several other notable Neoclassical suburban survivals are Harehills Grove of *c.* 1817; Meanwood Hall of *c.* 1834, also by *Clark* for Christopher Beckett [142]; Headingley Hill House of *c.* 1836; and Roundhay Hall, Gledhow of 1841–2 by *Samuel Sharp* for the stuff merchant William Smith [131]. Grand houses were still built closer to the town at Woodhouse, for example Woodsley (now Fairbairn) House, 1840 [104]. Alterations were made to Little Woodhouse Hall in 1847 [97], where *Owen Jones* advised on the enrichment of the staircase hall. But the houses in this area were now neighbours to streets of modest terraces. The Georgian taste for residential garden squares persisted with Queen Square, 1806–22, but the ambitious plans for Hanover Square and Woodhouse Square were never fully realized. Similarly ill-fated was the proposed development of Earl Cowper's estate in Chapeltown as 'New Leeds', which produced only a few, though fine, terraced houses and villas in the late 1820s and 1830s.

New Anglican **churches**, all Gothic, were erected for the growing town under the 1818 'Million Act'. *John Clark*'s austere St George was erected in 1836–8 to serve the western suburbs. But early C19 Leeds was also 'a stronghold of dissent', with numerous **chapels** in the town. Alas, most have been demolished, including *Joseph Botham*'s Brunswick Methodist Chapel of 1824–5 with its semicircular ended gallery and monumental organ. Two survivals are more typical of plain chapel design: the Salem Chapel, Hunslet Road (1791) and the former Methodist Chapel in Lady Lane by *James Simpson* (1840).

Industrial Leeds

The background to the changes in Leeds of the late C18 and early C19 is the transformation of its economy by the industrial revolution. Cloth-making in the West Riding was still a domestic industry in the mid C18 with goods supplied from Pennine villages to the markets in Leeds and elsewhere via a network of roads and stone-paved packhorse routes. Desire for access to colonial trade led Leeds and Bradford merchants to promote the Act, passed in 1770, for the **Leeds–Liverpool Canal**, opened from Leeds in 1777. By 1816 it provided a continuous link between the Mersey and the Ouse, via the Aire & Calder Navigation.

By the date of the canal's opening, the cottage industries of cloth weaving and spinning were being superseded by factory production in cloth **mills**. A merchant visiting Leeds in 1776 saw at Armley 'a scribbling mill by which more wool is discharged at once than ten hands can do; tis performed by an horse, its peculiar construction cant be described as it is not exposed to view'. By 1800 there were many mills, as described by the artist John Russell, 'both of wind and water. They grind corn, oil, dyer's materials etc. The river is large, black, and nasty, which arises most probably from the dyes and filth from manufactories.' At Armley Mills (now Leeds Industrial Museum), Colonel Thomas Lloyd rebuilt an existing fulling mill as an enormous woollen mill in 1788. Merchant-turned-manufacturer Benjamin Gott began construction in 1792 of his even greater riverside mill on open ground at Bean Ing, w of the town (*see* topic box, p. 138), where he was able to develop steam-powered machinery in privacy. The mill was conceived as a huge fully-integrated woollen factory, developed in stages and complete by the 1830s. To improve access to his mill, he also built the elegant Wellington Bridge across the Aire in 1817–19, designed by *John Rennie*. Winker Green Mills, Armley, is another important survivor from this early period, built in 1803 and developed by William Eyres from 1825. By the mid C19, mills extended far along the canal into the Kirkstall valley and and E along the Aire, including the mighty ranges of the Bank mills built for Hives & Atkinson, 1824–33.

Flax-spinning mills were promoted by John Marshall of Scotland Mill, Adel, who established a subsidiary mill at Holbeck by 1794, before moving his entire business to Leeds in 1806. Marshall was an innovator. His flax warehouse of 1808 in Water Lane uses 'fire-proof' construction (*see* topic box, p. 206) of cast-iron columns, beams and brick vaults, of the type first experimented with by Marshall in his flax mill at Shrewsbury in 1796. The apogee of improved methods of industrial production was Temple Mills, the final expansion of the Marshall flax-spinning empire, designed in scholarly Egyptian style by *Joseph Bonomi Jun.* in 1838–43 [7]. The choice of style, alluding to historic connections between flax and Egypt, and the decision to build in stone to ensure the vast building's stability, speaks volumes about the dominance of Leeds' flax industry. The stylistic novelty was matched by the sophistication of its planning and design by *James Combe*, engineer, notably its vast single-storey workshop covered by brick vaults carried on iron beams and columns and pierced by glass domes [66]. Pioneering methods for controlling humidity in the factory were another novel feature. It was celebrated as a wonder of the age, the *Penny Magazine* in 1843 describing it as 'among the largest factories in the empire'.

These innovations were made possible by contemporary developments in **engineering.** During the C19 Leeds was established as one of the world's most important engineering centres, with numerous foundries in Holbeck and Hunslet, and engineering overtook the textile trade to become the city's largest employer. *Boulton & Watt* of Soho, Birmingham supplied engines and gas lighting for Gott's mills, while from 1789 Marshall collaborated with the engineer, Matthew

7. Temple Mills, 1838–43, by Joseph Bonomi Jun., detail

Murray in developing machinery for his works. From 1795 Murray established a large foundry complex alongside Marshall's mills in Water Lane, Holbeck, making structural ironwork, machines, tools and steam engines. Such was the intensity of the rivalry between Murray and James Watt that Halligan, a former employee at the Soho Foundry, was persuaded to act as a spy at Holbeck and report on the processes used by Murray. This, perhaps the world's first integrated engineering works, still forms an outstanding group of former casting shops, foundries and fitting shops. Another fortunate survivor is the much smaller Midland Junction Foundry in Silver Street of 1793, established as a brass and iron foundry by Joshua Wordsworth for making textile machinery. Machine production for textile mills increased through the c19. At Tower Works, Globe Road the Harding family made a fortune producing steel pins for carding and combing machines, funding elaborate additions to the premises from 1864 until the 1920s and creating the unforgettable skyline of Italianate chimneys which greets the train traveller to Leeds today [65].

In 1811–12 Matthew Murray designed and made a steam locomotive at his Round Foundry for John Blenkinsop's Middleton Railway. Murray lived to see the coming of the public **railways**. The first two lines terminated outside the town: at Marsh Lane (the Leeds & Selby Railway of 1834, which made a direct challenge to the Aire & Calder Navigation's dominance of eastwards trade), and in Hunslet (the North Midland Railway line to Derby and London, 1840). The earliest incarnation of the present City Station was the Leeds & Bradford

8. Dark Arches, by T.E. Harrison, consulting engineer, 1864–9

Railway's Wellington Station of 1846; the line was soon leased by the Midland Railway who built new platforms and a hotel. In 1849 the Leeds & Thirsk Railway opened Central Station just to the w with a large goods station (both demolished) served by the magnificent viaduct across the Leeds–Liverpool Canal and the Aire erected by *Thomas Grainger*, engineer. He also designed the important group of surviving engine sheds and repair shops for the L&TR on the s bank of the canal. The Great Northern Railway, whose chairman was Edmund Beckett of the Leeds banking family, ran trains into Central Station from *c*. 1850. They built a hotel by the station and greatly expanded the huge complex of goods sheds in the area between Wellington Street and the river. By 1860 the London & North Western Railway and the North Eastern Railway (which had absorbed the L&SR and the L&TR) were running trains to Leeds. In 1864–9 the two collaborated to build a connecting line with a 'New' Station alongside Wellington Station. This was reared upon the sublime Dark Arches [8] 'which bridge the Leeds and Liverpool Canal and a weir from the Aire . . . those who have not penetrated to the cavernous regions which constitute its basement, can hardly picture to themselves the magnitude of the enterprise, and the vast labour and skill which had been exerted in its completion'. They survive as one of the grandest sights of the city today.

Victorian & Edwardian Leeds

During Victoria's reign, Leeds became the fourth largest town in England, earning it the title of 'Capital of the North'. The Borough's population boomed from 53,000 in 1801 to 429,000 by 1901, swollen by the influx of Irish immigrants employed in the flax trade and Jews from Eastern Europe who found work in the booming mass clothing industry. City status was granted in 1893. Emblematic of these changes was the transformation of its streets by new buildings not only for trade and industry but increasingly for commerce and the entertainment.

The reconstitution in 1835 of the corporation as an elected body with a town council began a transformation of the town's government, followed by construction of a large group of **civic and public buildings** during the middle decades of the C19. Foremost among these are the trio by the youthful *Cuthbert Brodrick* of Hull who set his unique architectural stamp on the character of Victorian Leeds, beginning with the Town Hall (1852–8) [29, 30]. This was conceived by the new council as a display of the town's wealth and ambition and intended to place in the shade Bradford's recently completed St George's Hall (1852, by Brodrick's master Herbert Lockwood). Its closest counterpart is rather Elmes' St George's Hall, Liverpool (1839–41), with which it shares a plan focused on an extravagantly large concert hall surrounded by courtrooms, but expanded to include council meeting rooms and municipal offices. Setting it apart architecturally from Bradford and Liverpool's buildings is the mighty tower, a late change to the design but now its most recognizable feature. One would hardly disagree with Pevsner's view that 'Leeds can be proud of its Town Hall, one of the most convincing buildings of its date in the country'. Brodrick's skill was displayed not only in the scholarly adoption of French Neoclassical models but also in his expert handling of local gritstone into solid decorative motifs, a feature also of his extraordinarily original oval plan Corn Exchange (1860–2) with its casing of rugged diamond-pointed rustication [32]. Brodrick was also a creative and skilled engineer, making an early use of laminated timber arches in the roof of the Town Hall and creating a complex gridded structure for the domed roof of the Exchange. Brodrick's third major building was the Second Empire-style Mechanics' Institution now City Museum in Cookridge Street, which has an unusual supporting structure for the floor of the circular lecture hall.

Brodrick's choice of style occasioned criticism from George Gilbert Scott* and it was he more than anyone who created an enduring taste for Gothic in Leeds. Although castellated Gothic was the choice for the Borough Gaol at Armley, completed in 1847 by *Perkin & Backhouse* [117], and an appropriately ecclesiastical style was used by *E.M. Barry* for Leeds Grammar School, Moorland Road (1858–9) it was *Scott*'s rebuilding of the General Infirmary of 1863–8 that confirmed Gothic as an appropriate

Remarks on Secular and Domestic Architecture, 1857.

style for secular buildings. It is a building of absolute modernity in plan and function but externally is in the richly polychromed style of Scott's later Midland Hotel, St Pancras [41]. A tension between the classical and Gothic is best expressed by *George Corson's* design for the Municipal Buildings, 1878–84, where the façade defers to the Town Hall but whose interior resembles the Byzantine style of William Burges.

The Gothic Revival was led by new **churches** in the town. It began with the rebuilding in 1837–41 of the parish church of St Peter [23, 24], which was promoted by the dynamic Vicar of Leeds, Walter Farquhar Hook and funded by private subscription. This was the major work of *R.D. Chantrell*, undertaken at the same time as his restoration of St John, Adel. It occupies an important place in the history of Anglican architecture, representing an unusually scholarly understanding of c14 Gothic architecture for its date, and a setting for the limited revival of certain forms of ritual. The new church followed the foundations of the old and included a large chancel, which Hook justified for use by a choir. Such innovations were important but the church was too early to reflect the influence of the Ecclesiological Movement and inside, the older traditions of the preaching box were still adhered to. It is instead among the new 'town' churches in the slum districts that the influence of Anglo-Catholicism can be seen. St Saviour's, 1842–5 by *John Macduff Derick* [119] was built for the working-class area of the Bank at the town's E edge. The cost was met by E.B. Pusey, posing as 'Mr Z', who advised on the design for a church with nave, aisles, transepts and chancel. Its prominence within its squalid surroundings was to be enhanced by a tower and spire. These were not executed but the interior was enriched with stained glass designed by *A.W.N. Pugin* [9]. Its daughter church, St Hilda of 1876–82 by *J.T. Mickelthwaite* also has an interior of spectacular High Anglican style [120]. For the Roman Catholic community of the Bank, largely composed of Irish immigrants, there was Mount St Mary, begun in 1853–7 by *Joseph Hansom* and *William Wardell* with chancel and transepts by *E.W. Pugin*, 1866. Erected on even higher ground than St Saviour's and also intended to have a landmark spire, the church's special qualities have been the sad victim of neglect in the last decade. Enthusiasm for revised forms of Anglican worship also led the trustees of St John, New Briggate to plan its demolition, thankfully prevented in 1865 by *Richard Norman Shaw* who drew *George Gilbert Scott* (then working on the Infirmary) into the argument for its retention. Scott also contributed the monument to Dean Hook at the parish church in 1875.

The influence of the Gothic is further apparent in the **Nonconformist churches** of the mid c19. The rebuilt Mill Hill Unitarian Chapel of 1847–8 by *Bowman & Crowther* of Manchester established Gothic as a permissible style for Dissenters too [52]. The design is serious and scholarly. Its form of nave and chancel of equal length and height

9. St Saviour, 1842–5, w window designed by A.W.N. Pugin

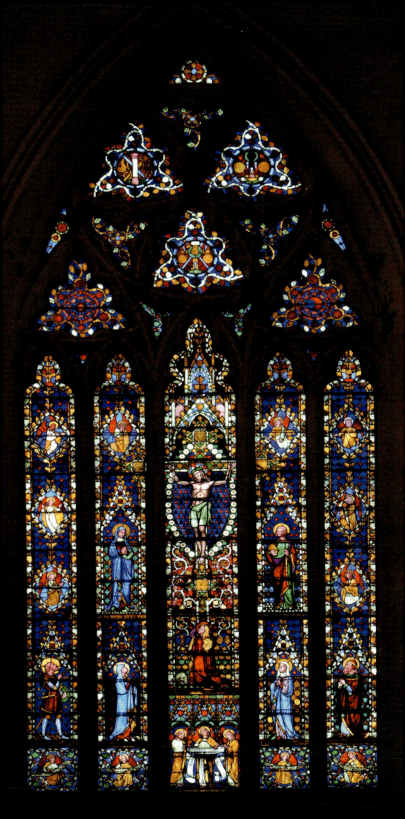

10. Former Headingley Hill Congregational Church, by Cuthbert Brodrick, 1864–6

and an entrance at the centre, is derived from the parish church but without the tower. The new chapel was given the name 'the mayors' nest' early on, when it provided the town with four Dissenting mayors in five years. *Cuthbert Brodrick*'s only church is the Headingley Hill Congregational Church, of 1864–6 [10], Gothic in detail but with some of Brodrick's usual inventiveness including rosette emblems and remarkable carved beasts. At the end of the century the Methodists in the town remodelled Simpson's 1830s Oxford Place Chapel in a sumptuous Italian Baroque style [75]; richly striped in pressed brick with bell-tower and adjoining chambers.

The **warehouses** of mid-C19 Leeds are in aggregate as impressive and interesting as the Town Hall. Their greatest concentration is in the streets closest to the railway station, and the demolished large Cloth Hall in King Street. The warehouses provided cloth manufacturers and merchants with offices, stores and showrooms in one building.

John Barran 1821–1905 and Thomas Ambler

John Barran, the son of a London gunmaker, set up in Leeds in 1842 as a tailor and clothes dealer. By 1851 he had premises in Briggate, producing made-to-measure and ready-made clothes, and he opened a small factory in Alfred Street in 1856. The adoption of new technology was critical to Barran's success; on a visit to the 1851 Great Exhibition he viewed a band saw for cutting furniture veneers and subsequently applied this to cutting several layers of woollen cloth at once. His factories also employed the new Singer sewing machines. From *c.* 1870 Barran speculated in property development and in 1870–1 he was mayor. He promoted the reconstruction of Boar Lane, including new premises for himself, for which he commissioned *Thomas Ambler*. Ambler, the son of an engineer, was articled to George Smith and set up his own practice in 1860. He was associated with the Leeds Permanent Building Society throughout his career. During the 1870s and 1880s he designed numerous commercial buildings in the city but his career is distinguished by his work for Barran, notably the exotic Moorish factory in Park Square (now St Paul's House) of 1878, where cutting rooms had band saws powered by gas engines. Also by him is the Golden Lion Hotel of 1879, on the site of Barran's first Briggate workshop. Barran's success in the clothing business led to construction of an even larger clothing factory in 1888–1904 (now Joseph's Well, Chorley Lane) and an enormous warehouse on St Paul's Street in 1892. By this time Barran's workers produced thousands of finished garments each day. Ambler's association with the Barran family extended to the next generation, designing a villa (Parcmont) for John Barran Jun. in 1883, close to Roundhay Park, which the elder Barran had purchased for public use in 1871.

Nos. 17–19 Wellington Street are early examples, 1859–60, displaying Italianate, Greek, Gothic and Moorish motifs; by *George Corson*, who followed his brother William from Dumfries in the later 1840s. *Brodrick*'s demolished King Street warehouse of 1862 was again in his own individual style, this time Italianate and richly polychromatic in red, blue and black brick. These buildings established a pattern for warehouse design for the rest of the century. As the mass clothing industry grew in the 1860s warehouses were often designed to double as factories. The industry's pioneer was John Barran for whom *Thomas Ambler* designed the outstanding Hispano-Moorish factory and warehouse in Park Square in 1878 [56].

Office buildings proliferated as Leeds became a centre for banking and insurance. Leeds' first bank was Lodge & Arthington, founded in 1758. In 1770 it came under the control of John Beckett, making the Becketts one of the town's most powerful families, with interests extending to politics and railway speculation by the 1840s. In 1827 a branch of the Bank of England was opened in the town and six new joint stock banks were set up between 1832 and 1836. They colonized the new streets in the neighbourhood of Park Row with buildings in an Italianate style. The earliest purpose-built office block in the city, the Leeds & Yorkshire Assurance Company (1852–5) on Albion Street is a magnificent Venetian palazzo by the Bristol architect, *W. Bruce Gingell*. Italianate was adopted too for the rebuilding of the Bank of England in Park Row (*P.C. Hardwick*, 1862–4) [59] and continued in favour even into the 1890s. But Beckett's patronage of *George Gilbert Scott* for its Park Row bank in 1863–7 (dem. 1965) also suggested Venetian Gothic as a symbol of commercial trustworthiness. Mixed Renaissance styles were adopted with enthusiasm by the major financial institutions in the 1890s, replacing the buildings along Park Row so memorably recorded by the painter *John Atkinson Grimshaw* [11].

The warehouses and office buildings provide a good opportunity for evaluating the changes in **building materials** in the later C19 and early C20. As in the early C19, local sandstones, and in particular Millstone Grit, continued to be used for prestigious buildings. The railways brought stone from further afield and buildings of the 1860s, such as Corson's Hepper House in East Parade [58] and the Branch Bank of England, South Parade, introduced imported granites for decorative details. The abundant supply of good local clay meant brick, which was now produced on an industrial scale, enjoyed a renewed popularity and was much favoured in combination with sandstone dressings. Scott's General Infirmary demonstrated its appropriateness for polychromed Gothic, which found wider expression in warehouses of the 1860s and after. From the same source as bricks came **terracotta**, which was pioneered as an alternative architectural material and seized upon with invention in Leeds. The market was dominated for several decades by the Leeds Fireclay Company at Burmantofts (*see* topic box, p. 225), whose products were first choice for all architects at work in the city from the 1880s onwards. *Alfred Waterhouse* enthused over terracotta's smoke and soot-resistant properties, using it for two buildings in Park Row: the Prudential Assurance Building (1890–4) and Greek Street Chambers (1898). The main rival to the Leeds Fireclay Co. was J.C. Edwards of Ruabon, North Wales, who supplied *Chorley & Connon* with fiery red terracotta for the Liberal Club, Quebec Street in 1890 and rich pink and oranges for their Hotel Metropole, King Street [54], in 1897–9. Detailed decorative work in terracotta was often of great skill, whether supplied by the producer (the chief modeller at Burmantofts was *E. Caldwell Spruce*) or executed separately. *Thewlis & Co.* provided the sculpted detail in sandstone at the former West Riding Union Bank, Park Row (1902) and in Marmo faience at King Street's Atlas House (1910). Superb decoration, inside and out, also distinguishes *G.B. Bulmer*'s Baronial Gothic Yorkshire Penny Bank of 1894 in Infirmary Street.

John Atkinson Grimshaw (1836–93)

11. Park Row, by J. Atkinson Grimshaw (1882). View N showing Beckett's Bank, by G.G. Scott, 1863–7 (right) and old St Anne's Cathedral, by J. Child, 1837–8

The atmospheric paintings of *J. Atkinson Grimshaw*, romantic street scenes shrouded in rain and lit by diffused moonlight, provide a romantic evocation of Leeds at the height of its industrial development. Leeds Bridge [44], Park Row and Boar Lane are amongst his many depictions of the city in the 1880s. Grimshaw was born in a back-to-back house in Park Street. His father was later an employee of the Great Northern Railway. Strongly influenced by John Ruskin's *The Elements of Drawing*, published in 1857, Grimshaw made many close studies of nature in Hyde Park, Woodhouse Moor, Adel Woods and Woodhouse Ridge before becoming a professional painter in 1861. He also drew inspiration from the work of the Leeds Pre-Raphaelite painter James William Inchbold and painted landscapes of Yorkshire and the Lake District as well as the streets of London.

Alongside the building activities of individual companies, the corporation initiated improvements for the city centre as a whole with the clearance of insanitary property for speculative redevelopment for **mixed-use buildings**. These are exemplified by the commanding range along Boar Lane, whose redevelopment was first urged in 1845 by the Chartist Joshua Hobson but eventually undertaken in 1869–76 by *Thomas Ambler*, with the patronage of the clothier and then mayor, John Barran (*see* topic box, p. 21). The buildings included warehouses, workshops, hotels and offices executed in a variety of styles. Commercial Street, Duncan Street, Vicar Lane and Briggate were all transformed in the later C19; so much so that by 1909 one description noted that 'the centre of Leeds has been practically re-carved and polished'. This boast was made, significantly, in a guide for shoppers, for whom later C19 Leeds now catered with a dazzling array of emporia.

Foremost among these were the numerous and celebrated **arcades**. The building of arcades in urban centres was an enthusiasm of the 1870s and later, taken up with relish in Leeds. All are found along Briggate, where the medieval layout of narrow burgage plots with long yards recommended itself for creating the traditional top-lit covered passage with entrance frontages at either end. The Gothic-style Thornton's Arcade [81] was the first, built in 1877–8 over the Old Talbot Inn yard. The parallel Rose & Crown Yard was built over in 1889 for the Queen's Arcade by *Edward Brown* of London, with a hotel in the upper storey. Nearby on Lands Lane was the Victoria Arcade (dem. 1959) and further N, on New Briggate, the Grand Arcade of 1897 by the local architects *Smith & Tweedale*. Extravagantly decorated outside with Burmantofts glazed terracotta, the interior is surprisingly plain. On a far grander scale are the two principal developments conceived by the Corporation as part of improvements of the decaying and unhygienic market area. Between Briggate and Vicar Lane land was sold to the Leeds Estates Company, who cleared the existing 'shambles' and erected the County and Cross Arcades (now Victoria Quarter) between 1898 and 1904. Their architect was *Frank Matcham*, who celebrated the opening of the C20 by designing possibly the most opulent arcade in England, its broad passages top-lit by glass barrel vaults and every surface enriched with colourful Burmantofts faience and mosaics [12, 82]. At the same time the Corporation erected the crowning glory of Edwardian Leeds, the ostentatious City Markets of 1904 [49], designed to replace the long established market on Kirkgate and Vicar Lane. Won in competition by *Leeming & Leeming*, architects of Halifax Market Hall (opened 1898), the market was executed in an even grander, endlessly inventive Free Style with an outer range of shops and offices, under a romantic skyline of domes and pinnacles, masking the breathtaking cast-iron market hall [49]. Equally opulent is the jewel-like interior of Whitelock's pub, off Briggate [48].

12. County Arcade, by Frank Matcham, 1898–1904, detail

Individual shops of this period survive only rarely. A notable exception is John Dyson's jewellery shop in Lower Briggate; with the type of showy front so characteristic of this trade, including a large clock [47], and an exceptional interior of 1910, replete with counters, display cases, suites of offices and workshops.

Theatres should be mentioned alongside arcades, with which they were often associated. Thornton's Arcade was built with the proceeds of the lease of his 'New Music Hall and Fashionable Lounge' at the White Swan, rebuilt in 1865 by *George Smith*. Now the famous City Varieties, its rectangular auditorium is a rare survivor of its type in England. A more highbrow 'temple of drama' was provided in 1877–8 by the Grand Theatre, New Briggate [83], with seats for 2,600, an assembly room for over 1,000 (converted to a cinema in the early C20), supper room and six shops. The design of the hybrid Gothic facade is commonly given to *George Corson* but the principal work, and certainly the glorious interior, is the work of his chief assistant, *J.R. Watson*. It is of a quality equal to London theatres of this date. The Coliseum Theatre, designed for mass spectaculars in 1885 by *William Bakewell,* masquerades as a Gothic basilica with gabled front and large rose window. *Matcham*'s Empire Theatre in the Cross Arcade was destroyed in the 1960s.

The diversions of the Victorian and Edwardian city centre were intended largely for an expanding, and wealthy, middle class. **Suburban development** after the 1840s produced numerous small middle-class **villas** at Headingley Hill. Most remained in the classical taste of the early C19 but an unexpected enthusiasm for Perp Gothic can be seen at North Hill House of 1846. The majority of villas in Headingley and Chapeltown date from the 1850s, 60s and 70s, including a small group designed by *Brodrick* e.g. No. 7 Alma Road [134]. Major planned developments include the Newton Park Estate (Chapel Allerton) begun in the 1880s. Houses by *Chorley & Connon* in Domestic Revival style. The best **Arts and Crafts** housing of *c.* 1890–1914 is by the local firm of *Bedford & Kitson* (*see* topic box, p. 249) ranging from individual houses in Headingley Hill such as Arncliffe (1892–4), and the Voyseyesque Lincombe (No. 7) for H.M. Hepworth [138], to the superb houses around Allerton Park, Chapel Allerton. The Edwardian suburbs are marked too by attractive public buildings such as libraries and several early cinemas. The wealthiest, as always, moved further out for space and privacy and erected **mansions** such as Meanwood Towers, a High Victorian Gothic fantasy begun in 1867 by *E.W. Pugin* for Thomas Kennedy, a partner in Fairbairns, engineers, and completed in 1873 by *Norman Shaw*. Shaw's pupil, *E.S. Prior* designed the nearby Carr Manor in 1881 in the style of a C17 Yorkshire manor house with excellent interior work in matching style [143].

The comforts of C19 industrialists and businessmen were not shared by their workers. Since the late C18 developers had rushed up terraces on the E edges of the town in the form of cheap back-to-back artisans' cottages planned around long, narrow courts. The scandalous state of Leeds' housing by the mid C19 made it the subject of attacks by *The Builder* in the 1860s and the 1866 Leeds Improvement Act laid down that back-to-backs should be built in blocks of four pairs, separated by privies. Reformers, such as James Hole, a native of Leeds,* demanded action from the Corporation and the erection of improved dwellings. Isolated efforts by William Beckett Denison to promote schemes of flats were ignored by developers who continued to build new slums. Back-to-backs continued to be built even into the 1930s. Though most have been cleared, examples remain in Little Woodhouse and Armley [115]. Until the 1870s the only public open space in the congested town

* Author of *The Homes of the Working Classes*, 1866.

13. Roundhay Park, drinking fountain, by Thomas Ambler, 1882

was Woodhouse Moor and this shortage led to the acquisition by John Barran of the grounds of the mansion at Roundhay, in spite of its distance from the centre, as a 'green lung'.

The northern and western suburbs have an exceptionally rewarding collection of **churches**. The elegant St Chad, Far Headingley, 1868, was largely executed by *W.H. Crossland* but *Edmund Beckett Denison* (the future Lord Grimthorpe) of the Leeds banking family, an amateur horologist and Scott's patron and 'friend and tormentor', gets the credit [139]. Similar in style but quite different in character is the grandest suburban church, St Bartholomew, Armley of 1872–7 [14, 113–4], the sole large-scale work of *Henry Walker & Joseph Athron*. The distinguished church of St Michael by *J.L. Pearson* of 1884–6 [133] is the principal ornament of Headingley, its soaring interior a convincingly spare essay in c13 Gothic. At the heart of the Newton Park Estate in Chapel Allerton is the little-known St Martin's Church of 1879–81 by *Adams & Kelly* with its fabulous early c20 decorative scheme and furnishings [123].

14. St Bartholomew, Armley, by Walker & Athron, 1872–7, view from the NE

15. St Aidan, Harehills, apse mosaics by Frank Brangwyn, 1916

Nearby is *G.F. Bodley*'s late and noble St Matthew, Chapel Allerton of 1897–9 [129]. The red brick basilica of St Aidan, Harehills [128], 1889–94, by *R.J. Johnson & A. Crawford Hick*, marks the shift towards Byzantine and Early Christian models for new churches. Inside are *Frank Brangwyn*'s stunning early c20 mosaics [15]. The last great ecclesiastical work in central Leeds was the replacement of the Roman Catholic church of St Anne (1837–8 by *Child* [11]) with the graceful new cathedral on Cookridge Street by *Eastwood & Greenslade*, 1901–4, in a Free Gothic with superb Arts and Crafts carving [27–8].

New schools for the town and suburbs followed the 1870 Education Act, which provided elementary schools at the discretion of elected School Boards. Sixty-one **Board Schools** were built, mostly outside the area covered by this guide. The Board was given splendid offices by *George Corson* alongside his Municipal Buildings in 1881 and he also produced designs for some of the early schools, before *Richard Adams* became the Board's architect from 1873–86. He designed thirty-five schools, in red brick, both Italianate and Gothic in style. Three schools within the area deserve mention: *Adams*' Italianate Armley Board School of 1878; the Leeds Higher Grade School by *Birchall & Kelly*, 1889–90 [79], and the grandest, Hillcrest Primary School, Cowper Street [16] by *Philip Robson* in Baroque taste, opened 1905. In the same style is *W.S. Braithwaite*'s Pupil Teachers' College of 1900. The Art School by *Bedford & Kitson*, 1903 is a clever design for an awkward site behind the Mechanics' Institute, from which it grew, and is distinguished by the splendid mosaic panel by *Gerald Moira* [78]. Leeds industrialists also saw the need for 'excellent technical education' to meet the competition from Germany by the 1870s. The Yorkshire College of Science was founded in 1874, with buildings erected from

16. Hillcrest Primary School, Chapeltown, by Philip Robson, 1905

1877 by *Alfred Waterhouse* in an increasingly mature Gothic style. It formed the nucleus of Leeds University after 1904 [91].

A final word is needed about Victorian and Edwardian **public sculpture**. The earliest example in Leeds is the statue of Sir Robert Peel by *William Behnes*, the first large-scale bronze to be cast in one piece in Britain. Unveiled outside the Court House in Park Row in 1852, but removed later to Woodhouse Moor [136]. Local merchants and engineers were also the subject for commemoration. Two early examples are in the form of church monuments, namely Michael Sadler, linen merchant, of 1837 by *Patric Park* (now in St George's Fields) and *Joseph Gott*'s reclining figure of Benjamin Gott (d.1839) in contemporary dress at St Bartholomew, Armley. The statue of engineer Sir Peter Fairbairn, 1868, is placed prominently in Woodhouse Square within sight of his works and home [101]. The sculptor was *Matthew Noble*, whose statues of Queen Victoria (1858) and Prince Albert (1865) adorn the vestibule of the Town Hall. *George Frampton*'s colossal monument, 1903, of the aged and enthroned Empress flanked by figures of Peace and Industry, was designed for the forecourt of the Town Hall, but is now at Woodhouse Moor [106]. Frampton was prominent among the 'New Sculptors' of *c.* 1900, whose work found at Leeds a civic prominence unique in England with the opening of City Square in 1903, when Colonel T. Walter Harding, mill owner, patron of the arts and Lord Mayor in 1898–9, made a gift of the mighty bronze equestrian statue of the Black Prince by *Thomas Brock*. He accompanied it with several pieces by *Alfred Drury*, from whom Harding had earlier commissioned a series of portrait plaques for his Tower Works [64], including graceful allegorical figures of 'Morn' and 'Even' holding electric lamps, and a statue of

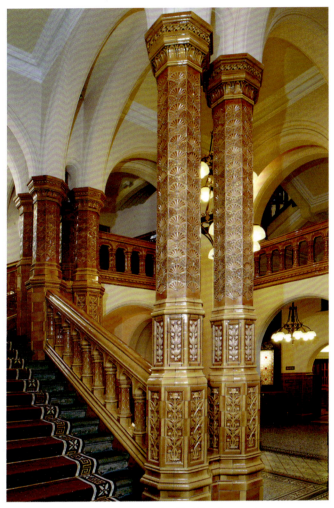

17. Leeds University, Great Hall staircase, by Alfred Waterhouse, 1890–4

Joseph Priestley. Figures of other Leeds notables, by *F.W. Pomeroy* and *H.C. Fehr*, complete the ensemble. The public cemeteries also provide showcases of important sculptural work. At Lawnswood Cemetery (opened 1875), there is *William Hamo Thornycroft*'s monument to the Currer Briggs family with his favoured motif of the Sower, and the macabre monument to Sam Wilson, patron of Alfred Gilbert, executed by *E. Caldwell Spruce* [160]. Defying categorization is the bizarrely realistic monument of 1911 to Ethel Preston [159], its sculptor unknown, showing her in the porch of her home, its front door left slightly ajar. A memorial to the 'wife of the oldest steeplejack in England', in the form of a chimney, is at Beckett Street Cemetery.

Between the Wars

Leeds' mass-clothing industries found prosperity in the manufacture of military uniforms during the First World War, witness to which is given by the large former Heaton's factory, North Street opened in 1916. The city's prosperity in the 1920s encouraged Charles Wilson, the charismatic Conservative Council leader, to pursue a policy of expanding the city's boundaries to encompass Adel and Temple Newsam. Road widening and tramway construction had followed by 1926 when the Outer Ring Road was begun with arterial roads linking suburbs to the city centre. The Edwardian heyday was over – pollution and overcrowding were major problems and the Council now embarked upon a major scheme of replanning and slum clearance. An Act passed in 1925 allowed for the purchase and demolition of properties on the N side of the **Headrow** and the making of an E–W traffic relief road between Mabgate and the Town Hall. In the Council's Tercentenary Celebration booklet of 1926 the world was informed that 'Leeds has taken . . . the unprecedented step of instructing the eminent architect, Sir Reginald Blomfield, to prepare an elevation of the buildings which will front the new street and of requiring those persons who will build to the new frontage line to conform to this elevation'. Local architects executed much of the scheme and in spite of interruption by the Depression, the Second World War and Postwar modifications, the street remains much as Blomfield intended. Its ambition, if a little unadventurous to Pevsner's eyes, was unusual in the major English cities outside London at this date. As an extension of the scheme's W end, Victoria Square was redesigned by *J.C. Procter* to form an appropriate setting for the city's War Memorial in 1936–7. The rebuilding of The Headrow was contemporary with the Council's major slum clearance programmes. The first part of the celebrated Quarry Hill flats (*see* topic box, p. 171) was completed in 1938, its design explicitly influenced by progressive housing on the Continent.

The most important undertaking of this period is the Civic Hall by *E. Vincent Harris*, 1931–3 [2, 39], built with government grants to provide work for the unemployed during the Depression. It had, Pevsner thought 'originality and some courage, even the courage of naughtiness in the details', including the memorably odd Wrenish towers of its front. The interiors are masterful, including a reprise of the design used for the entrance hall of Sheffield City Hall. The Hall was the first of a series of dazzlingly white Portland stone buildings for interwar Leeds, no doubt intended to improve the image of the city summed up by H.V. Morton in the *Daily Herald* in 1933: 'to be frank, the whole of Leeds should be scrapped and rebuilt . . . It is a nasty dirty old money box.'

In the major expansion of the University, *Lanchester, Lucas & Lodge* made monumental additions along Woodhouse Lane with a frontage dominated by the soaring clock tower of the Parkinson Building [18].

18. Leeds University, Parkinson Building, by Lanchester, Lucas & Lodge, 1936–51

Inside are lavish marble-lined rooms and the domed Brotherton Library [93], completed in 1936. Stripped classical of a more prosaic kind was used for the rebuilding of the London Midland & Scottish Railway's Queen's Hotel, City Square. Its smart fittings are the work of *W. Curtis Green* and at the rear there is a spacious new station concourse in streamlined Art Deco style [61]. This style otherwise finds little expression in interwar Leeds, even in the new shops of this period. Burton's, usually a reliable monument to natty taste, built most of its city centre stores after 1945. Even its expansive Hudson Road Mills, completed in 1934, have only a touch of the jazz-age decoration employed by the company architect, *Harry Wilson* on the store in Duncan Street. The one other eyecatching shop elevation of this period is the flagship store for Marks & Spencer (founded in Leeds in 1884), faced in polished black granite. Designed by *Robert Lutyens*, executed by *Norman Jones & Rigby* from 1939. Of a more eccentric style is the Neo-Byzantine of the former United Hebrew Congregation Synagogue by *J. Stanley Wright* on Chapeltown Road of 1929–32 [125].

1945–80

Leeds was spared the damage wrought among the industrial cities of England by the Second World War. Nine bombing raids, intended for the mills and factories of Hunslet and Kirkstall, caused only minor destruction to the centre: *Chantrell*'s Philosophical Hall on Park Row was the one significant loss. After 1945 the Council returned to its concerns of slum clearance and rebuilding, as at Saxton Gardens, E of the centre, where acres of back-to-backs were swept away. The Postwar period was one of prosperity as service industries expanded and the Council's Development Plan, issued 1951–5, set out a grandiose scheme for rebuilding much of the city's civic centre. *R.A.H. Livett*, appointed as the first City Architect in 1946, directed the programme but progress was fitful and the results at times disappointing. Modernism was introduced to Leeds after 1951 with the campus for the Central Colleges (now Leeds Metropolitan University) by *Yorke, Rosenberg & Mardall*. They planned a tight, coherent group of steel-framed, curtain-walled blocks of mixed heights, but delayed funding and a revised design in 1966 added new buildings of workmanlike appearance. In contrast, the University began with extensions of dispiriting economy before embarking on adventurous plans by *Chamberlin, Powell & Bon* from 1963, a monumental scheme for 10,000 students designed for flexibility. Its highlight, and the core of the plan, is the Roger Stevens Building (1968–70) [19] containing communal lecture theatres whose design acted as a prototype for the firm's Barbican Theatre in London.

To maintain a link between their expanding campus and the city, the University also lobbied successfully for the sinking of the new Inner Ring Road (in truth an inner city motorway), opened in 1964, which describes a curve around the N side of the centre. Associated with the traffic-oriented planning of this period is the large but unavoidable Merrion Centre, built close to the ring road in 1962–4. This was the first self-contained shopping centre in the city and incorporated office slabs, dance hall, cinema and multi-storey car parking. The effect of the new road was not as grievous as it might have been, effectively decanting traffic from the city centre and defining its limits, with benefits for the pedestrian. In 1963 the influential Buchanan Report used Leeds as a case study for the effect of traffic on cities and its findings inspired the thinking behind the review of the Development Plan in 1965–8. Proposals were now made for comprehensive redevelopment of much of the business and retail areas. Commercial Street was to be pedestrianized and connected to buildings of the surrounding streets by walkways across King Street and Boar Lane, pursuing a policy of 'vertical segregation' of pedestrians and traffic. Until quietly abandoned at the end of the 1970s, the plan did much damage with the building from 1974–8 of the dismal Trinity Arcade and the Bond Street Shopping Centre (now the Leeds Shopping Plaza) on the N side of Boar Lane.

19. Leeds University, Roger Stevens Building, by Chamberlin, Powell & Bon, 1968–70, detail of w façade

New buildings of the 1960s and 1970s in the city centre are generally disappointing and run contrary to the claim by the Council that Leeds in that period was 'a far cry from the grimy old city . . . new buildings born of new concepts are pushing their white rectangular columns into the sky . . .' The greatest activity, as it had been in the C19, was in the field of **commercial buildings** as offices for banks and insurance companies were erected along Park Row and its neighbouring streets. Slabs and towers became the norm, some of which pleased Pevsner in 1967, including the twenty-one-storey Exchange House by *Kitson, Pyman & Partners*, 1965, which replaced *Thomas Healey*'s Royal Exchange of 1872–5. This was the tallest building in the city centre and was soon followed by City House, the miserable slab adorning the rebuilt City Station, of 1967 by the notorious *John Poulson*, and the domineering

West Riding House. Of a higher order is *John Madin Design Group*'s bulky Yorkshire Post Newspapers headquarters, Wellington Street, completed 1970, alas at the price of sacrificing the Bean Ing Mills (*see* topic box, p. 138). The architectural record of the next decade is scarcely better, but two buildings stand out; the inverted ziggurat of the Bank of England, King Street, of 1969–71 by *Building Design Partnership* and the Brunswick Building (not completed, now Leeds Metropolitan University) of 1969–79 by the *City Architect's Department*. Both are, however, compromised by the need to include decks for never-completed walkways. In the suburbs, an interesting scheme is *Derek Walker Associates*' Newton Garth housing of 1969.

It was against this backdrop of insistent redevelopment that the Leeds Civic Trust was founded in 1965, originally to fight (unsuccessfully) against the demolition of *George Gilbert Scott*'s Beckett's Bank on Park Row. The Trust has been a forum for **conservation** issues ever since. The 1960s proved the need for vigilance and defence of the city's Victorian and Edwardian buildings, bolstered by the publication in 1969, sponsored by the Trust, of Derek Linstrum's *Historic Architecture of Leeds*. In spite of the growing recognition of the city's architecture, in 1974 the Secretary of State gave permission for the demolition of the s side of Boar Lane, against strong objections from the Trust and the Victorian Society's vigorous West Yorkshire group. Its retention and restoration was secured only by changing priorities and the developers' bankruptcy. Layers of grime were removed from soot-blackened buildings during the 1970s, most notably the Town Hall, to reveal once more the character of the native building stone. The more controversial practice of 'façadism' preserved other major buildings, including *Ambler*'s Moorish St Paul's House in Park Square [56]. Progressively, preservation by refurbishment has turned to more minor buildings, not only the well-to-do Georgian enclaves in the western part of the city, but also the considerable groups of surviving C19 back-to-back housing which residents' groups have lobbied to save in the suburbs.

The Leeds Look

The so-called **'Leeds Look'** was an attempt to restore visual coherence to the city by using traditional materials such as brick, terracotta, stone dressings and grey slate roofs in combination with Neo-historicist detail of a type associated with the city's Victorian and Edwardian heyday. One of the first buildings to be completed was the Jacob Kramer College, Blenheim Walk, of 1981–4 by *M. Thurmott*, City Architect, but the majority of new building was commercial and of a polite complacency that earned numerous criticisms locally and nationally. Westgate Point (*David Lyons & Associates*, 1987) is the best illustration [20].

20. Westgate Point, Westgate, by David Lyons & Associates, 1987

Leeds since 1980

Leeds' economy continued to do well in the 1980s and 1990s in spite of national recessions. It remained the largest printing centre outside London and the third largest manufacturing centre. An early addition to the city of this period is the Henry Moore Sculpture Gallery, with windowless walls of sandstone by *John Thorp*, Civic Architect, with *Neville Conder* [38]. This attempted to find a contextual form for modern architecture in an historic setting but the generally dispiriting legacy of Modernism seen in much commercial building in the 1960s and 1970s led instead to a reaction. The revival of historic styles which found favour nationally after *c.* 1980 became known in Leeds as the 'Leeds Look' (*see* topic box, p. 36). The more overt Postmodernism of the *Leeds Design Consultancy* 1994 Magistrates' Court with its colourful classical motifs introduced light-heartedness to the civic centre but the gargantuan 'design and build' project of Quarry House (*Building Design Partnership*, 1993) was a more dubious newcomer on the crown of Quarry Hill. There it overpowers the nearby West Yorkshire Playhouse of 1985–90 by the *Appleton Partnership,* with its conspicuous patterned polychrome brickwork and stubby fly tower.

The developments at Quarry Hill were intended as part of wider plans for **regeneration** of run-down areas of the city. The commissioning by the city in 1990 of a masterplan by *Terry Farrell* was intended at least in part as a riposte to the activities of the government-funded **Leeds Development Corporation**. This was established in 1987 to revive areas affected by industrial decline in s and Central Leeds and the Kirkstall Valley. It was given sweeping planning powers, but as in Bristol and Manchester there was local suspicion of this unelected quango. Its primary achievement was the regeneration of disused waterfront sites along the Aire and the canal, where the emphasis was on encouraging development of sites for businesses, spearheaded by Asda's dull offices on the s bank of the river. Other additions to the riverside opted for a warehouse style, sometimes with considerable success. The Calls in particular emerged as a popular mixed-use area, with sensitive transformations of listed warehouses and new build by *Allen Tod Architects*, begun in 1987. Access to the riverside was improved and a stylish footbridge by *Ove Arup & Partners*, erected 1992–3. Less certain was the masterplan for the area around Clarence Dock. Here, as had been achieved by the development corporations in Bristol and Manchester, the intention was to create a residential district around a tourist attraction, in the form of the Royal Armouries Museum [72] by *Derek Walker Associates*; completed 1996 after Leeds UDC had been wound up. The City continued the work begun along the riverside and canal but only since 2000 has much of the regeneration come to bear fruit. Dock Street is one of the best places to see a harmonious blend of infill [71], by *Carey Jones Architects*, among a rich mix of historic buildings, but there is justifiable concern elsewhere about over-development and the density of proposed new build. The future of the last piece of open ground, at Warehouse Hill, is being hotly debated as this guide is written. The former industrial area at Holbeck is gaining recognition with the conversion of the Round Foundry and Marshall's Mills.

Several important schemes for refurbishment were designed to restore the city centre as a major shopping area in competition with the out-of-town shopping malls. The Corn Exchange, White Cloth Hall, Thornton's Arcade, Queen's Arcade and City Markets were all revitalized during the late 1980s and 1990s. The outstanding enterprise was the refurbishment of the County and Cross Arcades as Victoria Quarter, by *Derek Latham & Co.*, where shopfronts were restored and the painted and decorated surfaces returned to their original brilliance.

Aspects of these developments pointed to a waning of interest in traditional forms and materials. This was in part the contribution of national architects of the High-Tech school. At the White Cloth Hall, the fabric was retained around a tubular steel frame inserted by *John Lyall*, and at the Victoria Quarter a similar structure became the centrepiece of the development in the form of a roof canopy over Victoria Street. A curious compromise between the historicist and functional traditions is *Abbey Hanson Rowe*'s No. 1 City Square of 1996–8 [21], full-blown Postmodern, but bisected by a glazed elevator shaft under a

21. No. 1 City Square, by Abbey Hanson Rowe, 1996–8

tensile roof canopy in the manner of Michael Hopkins. The conversion of mid-C19 warehouses on Cookridge Street for the Henry Moore Institute in 1993 was done with bold assertiveness by *Jeremy Dixon & Edward Jones,* with *BDP,* who decided to face its gable end in highly polished dark marble [86]. An easier symbiosis of traditional and modern was achieved by the insertion of a continuous glass façade for the Harvey Nichols store, Briggate, by *Brooker Flynn Architects,* 1997. Its influence was quickly felt in the elegant rebuilding of Nos. 15–16 Park Row, 1995, by the local firm of *Carey Jones Architects.* They have proved to be the dominant force in the best new build since the late 1990s. Much of this, as in the previous decade, was for offices as Leeds challenged Manchester for the title of fastest-growing financial centre outside London. New schemes for office building have concentrated on former railway lands including *Carey Jones'* excellent steel and glass Princes Exchange of 1999 [67].

Since 2000 the most obvious trend, however, has been towards luxury **residential and mixed use developments**, in particular along the canal and riverside and on a grand scale at Clarence Dock, where *Carey Jones* have picked up the baton. In several instances, the dreary 1960s office towers of the city centre have been imaginatively re-clad for apartments, sleekly so in the case of *Abbey Holford Rowe'*s 2002 refurbishment of Dudley House, Albion Street as 'K2 The Cube'. Towers are once more in vogue, and while *Foster & Partners'* office scheme for Criterion Place failed to materialize in the mid 1990s, *Ian Simpson* is planning a pair of striking angular towers of over thirty storeys for this site in 2005.

Every C21 city is a place of tension and change as differing interests are debated, and Leeds is no exception. It is a city of variety and delights, enjoying a buoyant economy and fortunate in having interested and committed conservationists, planners and architects, working to enhance its special character. Discussions must now seek to address the balance between a desire for a central 'iconic' building with the need for attention to the suburbs and rural areas. Private housing in Allerton Park by *Bauman Lyons Architects,* and social housing by *Levitt Bernstein Architects* at Caspar Apartments on North Street (2000) show the way, as does the restoration of Roundhay Park by *Purcell Miller Tritton.* Indeed the revival and restoration of **public spaces** has been amongst the most notable and encouraging improvements in C21 Leeds, including the creation of Millennium Square as a major public arena [77] and the laudable improvements made to City Square to rescue it from the disastrous replanning of the 1960s [51]. Both squares have been the work of *John Thorp,* the Civic Architect who since 1980 has done much to confirm Pevsner's view in *Yorkshire: West Riding* of 1967 that Leeds showed 'the blessings of civic pride and a certain orderliness'; an aspect of the city that the architectural traveller can still appreciate today.

Major Buildings

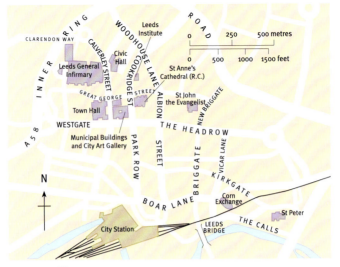

CLARENDON WAY

INNER RING ROAD

A 5 8

WOODHOUSE LANE

CALVERLEY STREET

COOKRIDGE ST

Leeds Institute

Civic Hall

Leeds General Infirmary

GREAT GEORGE STREET

ALBION STREET

St Anne's Cathedral (R.C.)

St John the Evangelist

NEW BRIGGATE

Town Hall

WESTGATE

THE HEADROW

Municipal Buildings and City Art Gallery

PARK ROW

VICAR LANE

BRIGGATE

KIRKGATE

N

BOAR LANE

Corn Exchange

St Peter

City Station

LEEDS BRIDGE

THE CALLS

0   250   500 metres

0   500   1000   1500 feet

22. Major Buildings

St Peter

Kirkgate

The parish church of Leeds [23]. 1837–41 by *R.D. Chantrell* for Dr Walter Farquhar Hook, who was vicar from 1837 until 1859. It replaced the medieval church at a cost of £30,000. Regrettably denied cathedral status in late C19 diocesan reorganization, but in its humbler and more specifically local role, regarded with much affection as '*the* Parish Church' of this huge city. St Peter's is of national importance in the history of Anglican architecture as, it has been claimed, the largest new church since St Paul's Cathedral. More importantly, it was the first great 'town church' – intended to minister to the increasingly disillusioned working classes of the Industrial Revolution – to be erected since the formation of the Oxford Movement had helped move Anglicanism in a 'higher' direction. The rapidly expanding literature on Gothic architecture also enabled the style to be treated with greater respect and scholarship. Remarkably, the church's architectural influence was severely limited. It was just too early to capitalize on the new ideas of church design initiated by the Cambridge Camden Society (founded in 1839) and within a few years of its opening was much criticized for its galleries, 'dishonest' plaster vaulting and the absence of a conventional chancel. Pevsner in 1959 was not enthused, not least by the fact that the railway in 1869 cut the church off 'from the centre of Leeds so effectively that it seems to stand at a half-commercial, half-derelict dead end'. Today the surroundings have been revitalized, the exterior cleaned and the interior much improved by *Martin Stancliffe*'s restoration and imaginative colour scheme of 1989.

Exterior

The cruciform **plan**, with an outer N aisle to the nave and chancel, follows the footprint of its medieval predecessor. Reconstruction and repair rather than rebuilding had been the first intention in 1837, but the older fabric was condemned as work progressed. Otherwise it seems inconceivable that Chantrell would not have reconsidered the plan. His main innovation was to move the tower from the crossing to the N transept, thus opening up the vista from nave to altar and, at the same time, giving the tower greater prominence when seen from the town centre. The choir vestry is of 1901 by *C.R. Chorley*, the Wesley Room, over the vestry by *Denis Mason Jones*, 1974.

23. St Peter, by R.D. Chantrell, 1837–41, view from the NE

Chantrell's chosen style of 'the transition from Decorated to Perpendicular . . . which has its peculiarities, though unnoticed by modern writers', is seen to effect in the tower's elaborate openwork battlements and pinnacles, so too in the w window's Perp tracery with a rich ogee hoodmould. The entrance is in the middle of the N side, under the tower. The chancel and nave are of equal length, four bays to the E, four bays to the w. They both have clerestories and tall aisles, and the chancel has a shallow apse. The outer N aisle, no higher than a cloister to allow light to pass over it and into the clerestory of the inner N aisle, has straight-headed reticulated windows.

Interior

Inside, the principles of formal classical planning that Chantrell acquired while a pupil of Soane are evident. One enters under the tower into a lofty, carefully contrived symmetrical space of almost Fonthillian proportions, with huge glazed doors to the left and right leading to the outer N aisles. Ahead on the N–S axis is the massive, sombre **organ** case, by *Chantrell*, occupying the whole of the s transept (*see* topic box, p. 47).

One passes between the ends of the E and W galleries to approach the crossing where the full E and W vistas open up to reveal this majestic interior, as well as the dichotomy of the design. The E **end** of the church has real dignity, with the altar raised on six steps, and with generous space in the sanctuary and in front of it for the new ideas of Victorian ritualism – claimed by Addleshaw and Ettchells* to be 'the first great instance of Catholic feeling in an Anglican church'. The W **end**, however, with its pews and galleries focused on the huge pulpit is still very much in the 'preaching box' tradition, a tradition despised by forward thinkers from the mid 1840s. **Crossing and transepts** are lierne-vaulted (in plaster), the apse is fan-vaulted (also in plaster). The nave and chancel ceilings have almost flat panels separated by substantial transverse beams embellished with arcaded decoration on their sides, actually the lower part of the largely concealed roof trusses. Piers of four shafts with fillets and four thinner shafts in the diagonals, and finely moulded arches. This is Dec, but the unusual panelling of the walls between the arches and the clerestory is Perp, and may have been influenced by similar features at Bruges Cathedral where *Chantrell* was working concurrently.

Galleries extend around three sides of the nave and into the first two bays of the chancel, looking down on the choir stalls. Richly-decorated gallery fronts, possibly papier mâché, with canopies like those of medieval chancel stalls. The galleries and congregation's pews below were to have extended to the E wall, giving the whole church a 'preaching box' appearance. They are supported on cast-iron columns and are slightly detached from the stone piers, to show, as *Chantrell* put it, 'they are merely furniture'. (Some of the apparently wooden decoration, for instance on pew ends, is also cast iron.) The **Lady Chapel** was created in the outer N chancel aisle in 1922. The **City of Leeds Room** was established in the former outer N nave aisle in 1975, by *Denis Mason Jones*, modified in 2000 by *Stancliffe*.

Furnishings

Reredos, marble, designed by *G.E. Street* with mosaics from cartoons by *Clayton & Bell*, executed by *Earp* and *Rust*. Unveiled 1888. **Mosaics** around the apse by *Salviati* of Venice, 1876. A comparison with the dull finish on the reredos confirms *Salviati*'s technical pre-eminence. **Statues of four Evangelists**, two at each side of the E window, by *Messrs Dennis Lee and Walsh*, 1861. Pair of free-standing, delicate wooden **sedilia**, designed by *C.E. Kempe*, 1891. Tall stone **cross** on the s side of the altar [3]; early C10, in the Anglo-Scandinavian style, including a panel depicting Weland the Smith in his flying machine. **Pulpit**, 1841, carved by *Fentiman*. **Font**, designed by *W. Butterfield*, erected 1883. **Old font**, by the s door, octagonal, C15, with later ogee-shaped, crocketed wooden cover. **Glass screen** in N transept, 'Jacob's Ladder' in etched glass, by *Sally Scott*, 1998.

*G. Addleshaw and F. Etchells, *The Architectural Setting of Anglican Worship* (1948).

24. St Peter, interior, looking w. Lithograph by Shaw and Groom (*c.* 1841)

Statue of St Peter, in wood, over the inside of N door, early C18. Brass **lectern**, currently at the rear of the church, by *Leaver* of Maidenhead, *c.* 1870. **Lady Chapel: Royal Arms** over entrance from tower, C18, altered, 1801; **reredos**, by *F.C. Eden*, with references to the style of his master, Comper, dedicated 1922. **City of Leeds Room:** former **Civic Pew front**, 1660, with coat of arms and Jacobean strapwork decoration.

Stained Glass

The following is a selection of the major windows. N chancel aisle E window: mainly C16 Flemish glass, collected by *John Summers* and assembled by *Thomas Wilmshurst*, 1841. Apse: 1846, by *Wilmshurst*. S wall of S chancel aisle 1862, designed by *E.M. Barry*, made by *W. Wailes*. S aisle: St Peter window, made by *Wright* of Leeds, designed by *Schwanfelder*, 1811, but still in the C18 tradition. W window, upper part: 1841, by *David Evans* of Shrewsbury, after a design by *Chantrell*, shows the coats of arms of the patrons. W window, lower part: 1856, by *Evans*. W end of N nave aisle: 1863, by *Heaton, Butler and Bayne*. City of Leeds Room: 'Penny Window', 1841, one of several windows in Geometric glass by *John Bower*. Several other good windows by *Michael O'Connor, W. Warrington, W. Wailes* and *J.B. Capronnier*, all mid C19.

Monuments

A large number, the important monuments are in chronological order as follows: S chancel aisle: effigy of knight, cross-legged, *c.* 1330, damaged. Close by: brass of Sir John Langton, d. 1459 and his wife; brass to Thomas Clarell, a former vicar of Leeds, d. 1469, with chalice but no effigy; table tomb to Thomas Hardwick, d. 1577, with fine fresco panel depicting Hardwick and his family. Lady Chapel: John Thoresby,

Hook and the Choral Service

For the past 150 years, robed choirs of men and boys occupying designated stalls in the chancels of parish churches have been the norm. In 1841, however, it was unprecedented. It was Rev. W.F. Hook's predecessor who introduced the robed choir; Hook's innovation was to place it prominently in the chancel on the cathedral model. At huge cost, he appointed S.S. Wesley – probably the foremost church musician of the age – as his organist and inaugurated daily choral services, another innovation for a parish church. A succession of eminent organists has continued that tradition to the present day. It is tempting to see Hook as one of the new breed of Victorian 'High Church' Anglicans, but his concern was not so much for ritualism as for 'order and decency' in his services. 'I will have a good service, even if I go to prison for it,' he apparently said. His biographer, writing in the mid C19, described the choir as 'unrivalled . . . for a union of delicacy with strength'.

d. 1679, tablet with bust by *Andrew Carpenter*; Captains Walker and Beckett, d. 1809, by *J. Flaxman*, 1811, with relief of Victory, mourning, under a palm tree; Thomas Lloyd, d. 1828, by *Joseph Gott*, frontal bust on a base with an inscription flanked by two Leeds Volunteers; Roger Holt Leigh, d. 1831, by *R. Westmacott Jun.*, relief showing Leigh seated on a Greek chair, with books on a table. s chancel aisle: Ralph Thoresby, the Leeds antiquary, d. 1725, inscription under a crocketed gable and between pinnacles, 1841, designed by *Chantrell* 'to exhibit a model of what a Gothic monument ought to be'. s of the altar: William Beckett, d. 1863, portrait on a high base on which stands an angel and two children, representing Charity, by *Baron Marochetti*. N of the altar: Dean W.F. Hook, d. 1875 (buried in Chichester), designed by *G.G. Scott*, executed by *Welsh* of Leeds with figures by *Keyworth Jun.* of Hull. Recumbent effigy on a tomb-chest with arched open sides. Naturalistic foliage in the spandrels. This shrine-like motif seems to be derived from the shrines of St Cantelupe at Hereford and St Frideswide at Oxford, two cathedrals restored by *Scott* in 1842 etc. and 1870 etc. There are many other good monuments from the late C17–C19, especially under the tower and in the City of Leeds Room.*

The **churchyard**, principally to the s of the church, is now an attractive and quiet corner of this bustling city, still crossed by several ancient paths. Although used as a graveyard since the Middle Ages, it is now paved with gravestones, all apparently from the late C18 or early C19. **War Memorial**. Cross, by Lutyens.

Christopher Webster

*The monument to Michael Sadler, recorded by Pevsner in 1959 is now in St George's Fields (*see* Academic Quarter, p. 183).

St John the Evangelist

New Briggate

Consecrated in 1634, St John's is Leeds' oldest surviving church [25] and something of an architectural rarity: a virtually intact C17 church, which juxtaposes a late Perp exterior with furnishings informed by Renaissance designs. The church was founded by John Harrison, a wealthy woollen merchant and philanthropist (*see* topic box, p. 10). Although it was widely acknowledged that the parish church was overcrowded, the Laudian Archbishop Neile of York was suspicious of the venture, suggesting that its proximity to St Peter's might become a cause of discord and further Puritan influences already well established in Leeds. By the early C19, St John's was regarded as old-fashioned and inconvenient: a local historian, the Rev. T.D. Whitaker, writing in 1816, described it as 'all gloom . . . without one vestige of dignity and grace', but it was not until 1861 that *John Dobson*, a local architect, was invited to design a new church. In 1865, the still youthful *Richard Norman Shaw* visited Leeds and while sketching the church was appalled to learn that it would soon be demolished. Acting alone, *Shaw* argued instead for restoration. George Gilbert Scott was called in to act as 'umpire' and supported the case for retention. Still unconvinced, the trustees appealed to the RIBA before reluctantly accepting the course of restoration.

Perhaps surprisingly after such bitter debate, *Shaw* was appointed architect for the restoration, but in his later years, even he spoke of his 'dismal failures' at St John's. Under constant pressure from the trustees, his severe treatment was not even in accordance with the points made in his own report. Between 1866–8, the walls were stripped of plaster, the important early furnishings altered, and several embellishments made in keeping with Victorian ritual. Much of this drastic work was fortunately undone or altered between 1884–98 during the incumbency of Canon John Scott, a cousin of the late Sir George Gilbert Scott, who pursued a policy of 'reparation', accepting many of Shaw's misgivings and re-engaging him to supervise the work. Between 1885–8, *George Gilbert Scott Jun.* was involved in the restoration and the work continued after 1888 under his pupil *Temple Moore*.

The **exterior** of St John's remains true to traditions of West Yorkshire church building: square mullioned windows, strong buttresses and battlements, all features that could have been found on churches built over a hundred years before. It has a rectangular plan, lacking a well-defined

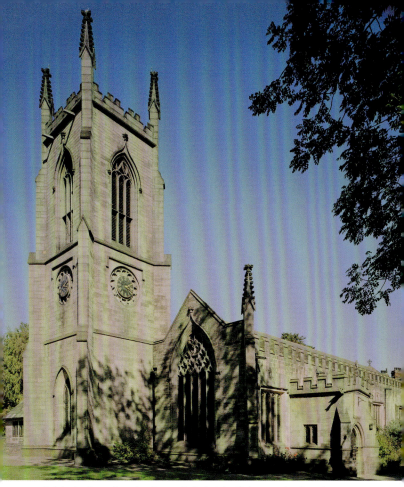

25. St John the Evangelist, 1632. Tower rebuilt by John Clark, 1838, view from the SW

chancel, and is outwardly largely Perp with W tower, nave and S aisle, chancel and S porch. Built of fine-grained sandstone quarried on Woodhouse Moor; Shaw's restorations are distinguished by coarse-grained sandstone peppered with quartz pebbles. The embattled tower is of three stages but only the base with a single window in each face is original. Its plain upper stages with small belfry windows were taken down in 1810 and replaced in 1838 by *John Clark*. Large three-light bell-openings with odd tracery and ogee hoodmoulds; twelve-foiled circular surrounds beneath them. Angle buttresses and tall corner pinnacles. The nave and aisle have straight-headed windows with cusped lights, but with odd little arch heads above the middle of each window. At the E end, twin gable ends with two Perp windows. Odd flamboyant tracery, more Dec than Perp, probably by *Shaw*. He added the N vestry and the C17 pastiche S porch and gates. A Renaissance-style porch existed in the C17, demolished in the C18.

The most remarkable feature of the **interior** [26] is that the church is of two naves rather than a nave and s aisle, divided by a central arcade and separated from the E end by a carved oak screen that runs across the entire breadth of the church. The arches of the central arcade, with two sunk-quadrant mouldings typical of the C14, are supported by stone piers, octagonal at the w end but then changing to a more complex moulded form with recessed quadrants in the diagonals and classical capitals with acanthus leaves and ball ornaments. The twin **roof** of the nave is of a basic truss construction and the lack of co-ordination between the arcade and the trusses is evidence of the piecemeal approach of C17 provincial builders. Suspended from the great oak ties are curious drop pendants, but even more curious are the carved corbels: most are angels with musical instruments, but in the corners are strange hermaphrodite figures. The pretty plaster panels of the ceiling (originally painted) contain strapwork and flowing naturalistic mouldings with various motifs: owls (the symbol of Leeds), Pan-like horn blowers, and peacocks with serpents in their beaks (the peacock was the Christian symbol of immortality). Later wooden battens securing the panels, ran straight across the central medallions, some of which were originally lion heads. Above the screen, semicircular wooden arches are infilled with strapwork spandrels.

The arrangements of the **chancel** and **chapel** are totally Victorian. *Shaw* was largely responsible for the present chancel. Separating it from the Harrison Chapel is an oak gate added in 1890 by Moore who re-organized the chapel for weekday services. For the first time, the church was given a second altar.

Planning and Liturgy at St John

The curious double-nave arrangement of St John's much exercised C19 critics who complained that the church was unsuited to 'modern' forms of worship and continues to be the subject of debate. Originally the church was orientated N–S with pews facing the pulpit on the N wall (reorientated to a traditional liturgical axis in 1807). This form has led some historians to argue that St John's embodied prevalent Puritan beliefs, yet there was also a chancel with benches for communicants. Less certain is the original position of the communion table, which in 1787 was recorded as being moved from s of the arches (i.e. the present Harrison Chapel) to a new position to the N. The profusion of richly decorated woodwork, not to mention the nature of some of the carved imagery, also sits uneasily with Puritan sentiments and has suggested, to some, support for the reforms of Archbishop Laud. These diametrically opposed interpretations might either reflect a search for coherence in a period when little existed or perhaps a post-Reformation desire to reconcile the new with the old.

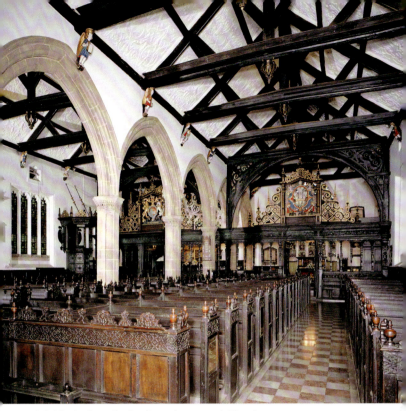

26. St John the Evangelist, interior, *c*. 1634, restored 1884–98

Furnishings. Nave: The great glory of St John's is its carved Jacobean **woodwork**, without doubt the work of *Francis Gunby*,* none of it particularly ecclesiastical in character and modelled on the domestic interiors of the period. The most important item in the church is the sumptuous oak **screen** [5]. Above a solid panelled dado, an arcade of tapering pillars with Ionic capitals and delicate filigree arches, over which runs a richly carved frieze of hearts, rosettes, tulips, vine leaves and animal grotesques. Human and lion heads support the projecting parts of the cornice. Above the screen, royal coats of arms are set within elaborate crestings. These were removed from the screen in 1866–8 but the crestings were brought back in 1890–1 to enclose religious symbols designed by *Temple Moore* (now on w wall). The **coats of arms**, reinstated in the 1970s, are curiosities. Over the N screen are the arms of James I who died in 1625, nine years before the consecration of St John's. The s screen bears the arms of Charles I as Prince of Wales. A possible explanation for this puzzling anomaly is that, although

*Francis Gunby produced a similar screen for All Saints, Wakefield (now the Cathedral). He was also employed by Sir Arthur Ingram at Temple Newsam House (*see* p. 282). There is also a close resemblance between the pulpit in the chapel there and that of St John's.

consecrated in 1634, the church was constructed and furnished well before that date.

Pulpit: equally sumptuous, also dismantled 1866–8 but reconstructed in the 1880s using original fragments skilfully blended with new steps, balustrade and back-board. The base comprises four tiers of panelling with pilasters, strapwork and carved heads; the eagles (the symbol of St John) to the sides of the back-board are original. Above, the canopy carries a carved frieze with some naked figures topped with strapwork and pinnacles. On the underside of the canopy is a sun face with rays. **Lectern** also 1880s, assembled from parts of the old reading desk. **Pews** retain their original bench ends with urn-shaped finials and strapwork panels but the doors were removed in the 1866–8 restoration (*see* below). **Mace-holder**: wrought iron. John Harrison, as the leading town councillor, frequently acted as Alderman and was in the habit of bringing the corporation mace into church. **Font** to the rear of the nave, by *Shaw*, a well-detailed octagonal bowl carved by one of his favourite craftsmen, *James Forsyth*. It originally stood beneath the canopy taken from the C17 pulpit; the ensemble was adorned with elaborate metalwork (whereabouts unknown).

Chancel: C17 **communion table** with bulbous legs ending with Ionic capitals and a strapwork frieze with carved heads with cavalier-type moustaches. One side is free of ornament suggesting that it once stood against the wall – an arrangement which the Puritans abhorred. **Reredos**, a composite piece: gold *Salviati* mosaics commissioned by *Shaw*, but in a setting by *Temple Moore*, reusing two angel corbels removed when the organ was rebuilt in 1885. The carved central panel, bought locally by Canon Scott, is probably the door of a tabernacle. It was claimed to be a medieval English piece but is probably Continental. **Altar rail** and **organ case** by *Shaw*, 1866–8; the **choir stalls** were introduced as part of his 'reparation'.

Harrison Chapel: **altar rail** from an old church in Kettlewell but the rest of the chapel is the work of *Temple Moore*, who panelled it with the pew doors removed in the 1860s. Moore also re-paved the chancel and chapel using marble slabs from Belgium and Carrara.

Stained glass: mostly undistinguished, from between 1868–1902. Clockwise from the porch: four small windows by *C.E. Tute*, 1897 and 1902. The windows on the w wall were all donated by Fairfax Rhodes and dedicated to family members: Scenes from the Life of John the Baptist by *Lavers, Barraud & Westlake* (1869); Tower window by *Hardman & Co.* (1901) and two small windows of Archbishop Neile and Dr Cosin, by *Victor Milner* who often worked for Temple Moore. N wall: late C19 commemorating local families. The fourth window by *Tute* (1894) shows scenes from the Acts of the Apostles, particularly charming are the owls which appear in the lower lights. E window: the Crucifixion with Saints by *Ward & Hughes* (1870). Harrison Chapel: memorial E window to John Harrison (d. 1656), by *Burlison & Grylls*,

1885. Paid for by local subscription after Canon Scott wrote to the local press complaining that there was no memorial to Harrison in Leeds. In the upper lights are scenes from the life of Christ and St John, in the lower tier is the life of Harrison. He is fancifully depicted with his market cross; helping aged people into his almshouses; at the building of the church and at prayer. The scene of Harrison with Charles I is based on a story handed down by Harrison's descendants. In 1647, the King passed through Leeds whilst a prisoner of the Scots. Harrison persuaded the guards to allow him to present a tankard of ale to the King; on lifting its lid, it was found to be brimming with gold coins. In the tracery of the Harrison window are the arms of the Archbishop of York, Charles I, the City of Leeds and Harrison's monogram, '*Templum pro Tumulo*'. Nave, s wall: mostly the work of *Lavers, Barraud & Westlake*, except for third window depicting Christ with the Woman of Samaria by *C.E. Kempe*.

Monuments. Three centuries of history have bestowed on St John's a rich array of tablets and brasses. Unfortunately the laying of new floors in the nave between 1866–8 destroyed many old floor monuments and in their place, brass plaques have been attached to the pew ends to mark the position of the vaults. Chancel. Harrison Memorial: the tomb of John Harrison (d. 1656) was moved to its present position in the 1860s with a new setting designed by *Shaw*. A large tablet without any figures. Classical forms without frills. It bears the inscription written on the original by Dr Lake, Vicar of Leeds between 1660–3. Set in the wall above is a simple brass plate to the Rev. Robert Todd, the first incumbent of St John's. The remaining monuments are largely of local interest, commemorating the lives of Leeds woollen merchants and incumbents of the church. **Painting**: w wall. A portrait of John Harrison was given to the church by his nephew, the Rev. Henry Robinson. In 1860, it was moved to the council chamber of the new Town Hall and later placed in the Art Gallery. It was finally restored to St John's in 1923.

The **churchyard** is paved with gravestones though few would agree with Pevsner's comment that this is 'a moving . . . and pleasing device'. The stone wall and arched E gateway are by *Shaw*. At the sw corner stands the Parish Hall and caretaker's house built in 1815 as a charity school on the site of the chapel attached to Harrison's almshouses.

Janet Douglas

St Anne's Cathedral (R.C.)

Cookridge Street

1901–4 by *J.H. Eastwood*, assisted by *S.K. Greenslade* [27]. Built by *William Cowlin & Sons* of Bristol, who had recently worked on J.L. Pearson's restoration of Bristol Cathedral.

The Roman Catholic Cathedral of St Anne,* built in a freely detailed Arts and Crafts Gothic style, replaced 'Old St Anne's' of 1838 by *John Child*, which stood on the E side of Cookridge Street, facing down Park Row [11]. It stood in the way of progress and was compulsorily purchased in 1901 for road widening for the city's tramway. The City gave a new plot on Cookridge Street to the N, an awkward trapezoidal site rising quite steeply to the E, tightly bound by Great George Street and St Ann's Street. Bishop Gordon's choice of possible architects was between *John Kelly*, the prolific local church architect who was nearing retirement, *J.F. Bentley*, architect of Westminster Cathedral, and *J.H. Eastwood*, former chief assistant to G. Aitchison and F.P. Cockerell. (Fellow Yorkshiremen working in London, Eastwood and Bentley were founder members of the Guild of St Gregory and St Luke, devoted to improving church craftsmanship.) Eastwood, working closely with Canon Charles Croskell, devised the ground plan of an aisled nave and chancel under a single roof, shallow transepts, choir, sacristy and presbytery, and an extensive basement housing other offices. Eastwood also contributed to the interior furnishings but *Greenslade* was responsible for the artistic flair of the detailed design work.

The original design anchored the church with an entrance tower at the sw corner to Cookridge Street; a strong landmark designed to be visible from the city centre. But the occupants of the warehouses opposite (*see* p. 151) threatened litigation over loss of light, resulting in the tower's less imposing position on the N side. Building began in 1901 and the first mass was held on 1st May 1904, before either high altar or tower were finished. Eastwood's decorative scheme for the sanctuary was completed in 1907 but work was delayed while further funds were raised. The cathedral was consecrated in 1924 and has been subject to two major reorderings; in 1954 in anticipation of the first televised high mass and again in 1960–3 by *Weightman & Bullen* of York.

*This account is much indebted to the work of Robert E. Finnigan, Diocesan Archivist.

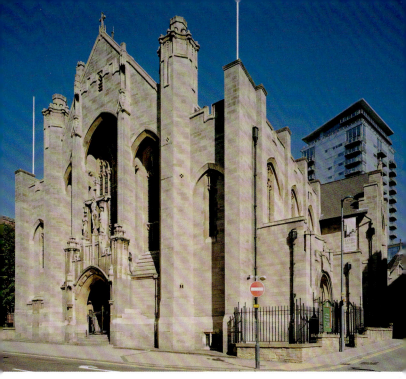

27. St Anne's Cathedral, Cookridge Street, by J.H. Eastwood & S.K. Greenslade, 1901–4

Exterior

In spite of the loss of the intended tower on the main w front, the cathedral makes a strong impact to the street, enhanced by finely jointed courses of large blocks of Weldon stone. Carved details are in beautiful, buff-coloured Ketton limestone. The w **front** is compact and impressive, a tripartite composition of tall gable flanked by bulky chamfered buttresses terminating in Gothic turrets with freely carved panels and squat truncated finials; lower side aisles. Deeply recessed ceremonial entrance carved with symbols of the Passion on the arch-moulding and traceried panels in the reveals. Greenslade's delightful ornament is richly carved in the Gothic tradition, reflecting the craftsmen's skills, while paired panelled doors behind low wrought-iron gates with cross and scroll motifs proclaim the high standard of work in all materials. A large Calvary sculpture dominates this façade, set on a stepped and moulded stone parapet. w windows of three, six and three lights, each with slender mullions and lace-like tracery, set deep in arched recesses. Statue niches are carved in the central window's mullion and terminate slim buttresses below the gable.

The s **front** has a round-arched porch, tightly confined behind railings with flared terminals, replacements of 1987. Two tiny three-light windows illuminate the s aisle chapels and, stepping back above, three two-light clerestory windows, elongated and with sinuous tracery, in wide segmental arches. Plain square buttresses project above the moulded parapet. s transept gable with paired windows and, high up, elaborate ribbon-like carving round a louvre panel. The e end stands higher but the roof-line is continuous, with more tall windows lighting the choir gallery. Neat octagonal sacristy projecting like a miniature medieval chapter house, with single-light windows and a pointed roof finished with stumpy lead finial. Uphill, **Cathedral Hall** by *Damond Lock Grabowski & Partners* completed 2003, a sympathetic Arts and Crafts design.

The N **side** is dominated by the massive projecting three-stage tower rising almost directly from the street. Square buttresses, battered lower stage, high plain middle stage, and upper belfry with pairs of traceried and louvred windows, modest pyramid roof (an early design shows it taller, but there were cost constraints).

Interior

The **interior**, although almost square on plan and with a short nave, has an illusion of depth ingeniously created by the uncluttered view to the high altar and the use of wide arches to the narrow side aisles; delicate carving is set high up, appearing far away. The spacious effect is partly due to the removal, in 1964, of a low screen wall between nave and sanctuary and its replacement with wide steps. Also of this date (when pews replaced the original chairs), the marble floor with cream and green tile paving. The walls are of Bath stone, made luminous by the opaque glazing of the w windows, through which natural light bathes most of the nave. The central window and inner porch are flanked by buttresses carved with statue niches and holy water stoups; the cross from 'Old St Anne' is on the wall above. The high **nave** is of three bays, the arcade piers having heavy roll or chamfered mouldings carried up to niches, then stretching across the shallow-pointed tunnel roof as heavily moulded ribs. The eye is drawn to intricate carving high up on the plain walls – Art Nouveau and Gothic forms around niches. Statues were placed in those flanking the chancel arch in 1934–7. Shallow, cross-vaulted side aisles with windows set above the side chapels. Slender attached columns rise up between the windows, breaking the line of a horizontal moulded band screening the window sills. The band is pierced by paired ogee-arched niches with stylized leaf carving. On the N side in the base of the tower (formerly baptistery) is a war memorial chapel. The short transepts are entered from a wider fourth bay, that on the N has shallow e chapels.

The illusion of length is continued into the four-bay **sanctuary**, set at a higher level and enclosed by an arcaded ambulatory. No choir stalls, instead a gallery over the ambulatory houses choir and organ. On the N side is an oriel window from the presbytery and in the angle with the N

28. St Anne's Cathedral, Lady Chapel, reredos by A.W.N. Pugin, 1842

transept, the organ chamber. This clever manipulation of the space was a late change to Eastwood's plans at the suggestion of Bishop Gordon and Canon Croskell. The **Lady Chapel** on the s side of the sanctuary is entered from the transept [28]. Above the entrance arch a beautiful statue niche with elaborately carved panels. Three bays with a shallow two-bay s aisle, the panelled capitals of the arcade pillars elaborately carved. Glazed panels between the ribs of the blue-painted timber ceiling were introduced in 1964, a clever device to light the reredos (*see below*).

Decoration and Furnishings

The decoration and furnishing of the cathedral was largely complete by 1924 with some embellishments in the 1930s, but in 1954 statues, furnishings and the pulpit were re-sited, the sanctuary whitewashed and new lanterns fixed in the nave. Other lavish early c20 fittings were removed in 1964, including Eastwood's fine cathedra and canons' stalls.

Sanctuary: **reredos** by *S.K. Greenslade*, 1901, made by *Flint Brothers* of Clapham. Similar to Pearson's work at Truro and Hove. Eight saints associated with the cathedral and the early Yorkshire church flank a low-relief carving of the Coronation of Our Lady. Ornate baldacchino with elaborate frieze of fruits symbolizing the Resurrection. – On the E wall are Venetian **mosaics** of 1928, by *Cesare Formilli*; St Francis looks up to the Ascension; St Patrick blesses the altar; the Assumption and brightly clad angels above. These replaced a series of encaustic paintings on the same themes, executed by Formilli to designs by Eastwood. – The Italian marble forward **altar** is of 1964 by *Weightman & Bullen*, incorporating from the original its alabaster centrepiece, inlaid with porphyry and lapis lazuli. – Also of 1964 the travertine and green marble paving and the plain oak **canons' stalls** by *Cawley* of Nottingham incorporating seven carved angels made in 1930 by *Boulton & Sons*; graceful **cathedra** with traceried side screens carved by *David Hardy*. – **Organ** by *Norman & Beard*, 1904. – Ornate **pulpit** by *J.F. Bentley c.*1895. Traceried alabaster side panels, on the front 'Feed my sheep' in *opus sectile*.

The **Lady Chapel** has furnishings from 'Old St Anne', in particular a distinguished Dec **reredos** by *A.W.N. Pugin*, 1842 [28], made by *George Myers*. Commissioned by the Rev. Father Walmsley at the request of the donor, Miss Grace Humble, daughter of one of Leeds Pottery's founding partners. SS Anne and Wilfrid flank Our Lady and six smaller figures, all richly painted in red, blue and gold. The altar is older (from St Mary's chapel, Lady Lane, 1794) encased and enriched by Pugin with large panels of quatrefoil tracery. Oak **benches** designed by *Canon Thomas Shine* (later the bishop of Middlesbrough), and made in 1915 by *Arthur Walker*, a local cabinet-maker. **Statue** above entrance arch of Our Lady Immaculate sculpted by *Boulton* of Cheltenham, 1933. Outside the Lady Chapel, *J.H. Eastwood*'s confessionals and **Shrine of**

Our Lady of Perpetual Succour, executed by *H.H. Martyn & Co.* of Cheltenham, 1913 and incorporating an earlier icon. Statue of St Charles Borromeo.

The skills of the architect and designer are set side-by-side in the two small N **transept chapels** which are embellished with gilded coved ceilings and warm brown tiling. The Sacred Heart Chapel by *Greenslade*, 1903, has reredos carving by *Nathaniel Hitch*; marble altar with carving of the Last Supper, a vein of brown marble linking the head of St John with Christ's heart. Large Sacred Heart statue by *Formilli*, 1922. In St Joseph's Chapel, 1904, *Eastwood*'s elaborate reredos with gilded canopy and statue; altar with St Joseph on his deathbed carved by *H.H. Martyn & Co.* of Cheltenham.

The **War Memorial Chapel**, in the base of the tower has fittings by *Formilli*, 1920: grey stone memorial high on the N wall inscribed 'Orate pro animabus' with 180 names crowded onto three circular marble plaques surrounded by plaster laurel wreaths. In the **Pieta Chapel**: a life-size marble sculpture by *R.L. Boulton & Sons* of Cheltenham, unveiled 1913; dark green marble walls by *Leeds Marble Works*; cross by *Arthur Walker*, 1924. *Formilli*'s **baptistery** is a dull assemblage with Italian marble wall panels, 1926. Octagonal stone font supported by angels, probably mid C19, perhaps from 'Old St Anne'. Good wrought-iron gates (1963) by *Weightman & Bullen*: doves and droplets below a copper band representing flowing water.

Two Italian white marble statues in the s aisle: St Francis and St Anthony of Padua, presented in 1927. s chapel: **Shrine of the Diocesan Martyrs** (1988) dominated by a large iconographic painting by *Richard Lomas*. Against the s wall, the older Shrine of St Urban, by *Greenslade*: brown marble, metal casket with crowns and olive wreaths.

Stained Glass

E window, by *Eastwood*, 1912, with his sun-ray motif; his other designs were not completed. In the s transept faded figures depicting scenes from the life of Christ were bought privately by Canon Shine in 1920 and are of unknown provenance. Delicate patterned glass was installed by *Kayll & Reed*, 1931. It matches their work in the N transept: the Crucifixion (1927) and Resurrection (1929). Symbolic emblems in the Pietà Chapel and the baptistery, 1927.

Cathedral House (presbytery and offices), Great George Street, NE of the site, occupies almost a quarter of the total site. In the same attractive Free Style as the church but domestic, with stone changing to cream, sand-faced Suffolk brick with Ketton stone dressings. Three storeys and seven bays, with central deep porch and mullion-and-transom window frames, one in a canted bay.

Town Hall

Headrow

Built 1852–8 by *Cuthbert Brodrick*. 'The Town Hall of Leeds is one of the gorgeous structures of the class,' wrote the *Building News* in 1858. 'Profuse in its adornments, it represents an age in which wealth has passed beyond simple comfort to the enjoyment of luxury. It speaks of abundance and displays it. Its clustered columns, its profusion of lights, its ribbed vault, bespeak the wealth of its builders, and it is made to minister to their recreation and indulgence . . . The architect has undoubtedly achieved his aim, for he has given the people of Leeds a hall which tells of the luxury of kings.' Writing more succinctly a century later, Pevsner confirmed that 'Leeds can be proud of its town hall, one of the most convincing buildings of its date in the country, and of the classical buildings of its date no doubt the most successful'.

Leeds was not the first of the major industrial towns to express its increasing wealth and importance in terms of monumental masonry. Birmingham and Liverpool had led the way, but in 1851 a group of prominent citizens founded the Leeds Improvement Society in the belief that 'if a noble municipal palace that might fairly vie with some of the best [European] cities were to be erected in the middle of their hitherto squalid and unbeautiful town, it would become a practical admonition to the populace of the value of beauty and art, and in course of time men would learn to live up to it'.

It was a challenge, and in the same year as the Society was founded a site for a town hall was bought for £9,500 from John Blayds, a wealthy merchant and landowner. It was on the w side of the town adjacent to the grid pattern streets of Park Lane, bounded on the N by Great George Street, on the E by Calverley Street, and on the w by Oxford Place. In 1852 it was decided to hold an open architectural competition, of which the recently knighted Sir Charles Barry was appointed assessor. Of the sixteen designs submitted, that of *Cuthbert Brodrick*, a virtually unknown young man from Hull, was selected. He had been trained in the office of Henry Francis Lockwood and after completing his pupillage had travelled in Europe for two years making a serious study of historic and contemporary buildings. His three major buildings in Leeds especially draw on Parisian sources with which he evidently felt a strong affinity.

29. Town Hall, Headrow, by Cuthbert Brodrick, 1852–8

    Brodrick's success at Leeds seemed to have repeated the pattern of the competition for St George's Hall, Liverpool, which had been won by twenty-five-year-old Harvey Lonsdale Elmes in 1839. Both were young men when their designs were selected, and it was commented that 'previously quite unknown talent has suddenly burst into notice'. Indeed, some members of the Leeds Town Council wanted reassurance that their building was going to be in safe, albeit young, hands. Barry generously replied that although 'previous to the competition he was not aware that such an architect existed . . . he was fully satisfied that the Council might trust him with the most perfect safety'. Barry is said to have given further reassurance by predicting that 'the new Town-hall would be the most perfect architectural gem outside London', which was praise from the architect of the Houses of Parliament; but there were some differences between competition design and the finished building. What was the initial brief?

Drawn up under the guidance of the Town Clerk in July 1852, the *Instructions to Architects,* which was sent to all the contestants, revealed the innovatory nature of the proposed building. It was to contain under one roof a hall capable of holding 8,000 people standing and with an orchestra and balcony, refreshment rooms and kitchens, servants' hall, changing rooms for musicians, a mayoral suite, a Council Chamber, accommodation for the council officers, four courtrooms and accommodation for the police. In this it exceeded Birmingham Town Hall (J.A. Hansom, begun 1832), in which the auditorium *was* the Roman temple with little space in the podium for other accommodation and even Elmes' famous building contains only two courtrooms in addition to the great central hall and a small concert hall. By contrast, Leeds wanted a municipal palace.

The meagre sum provided, £35,000, particularly when related to the stipulated capacity in the main hall, was derided in the professional journals. Maybe that is why only sixteen entries were received, compared with Birmingham's seventy; but Brodrick took the requirement seriously and suggested a rational **plan** in which the basilican hall was central and each of the four corners was to be expressed as a projecting pavilion containing a courtroom and adjacent accommodation. With great ingenuity Brodrick placed the Council Chamber at the s end of the Hall above the entrance hall. It was to be semicircular in plan, maybe deriving from Jacques Gondoin's École de Chirurgie (1769–74), one of the most famous late c18 buildings in Paris, and 'capable of forming part of the Hall; by merely opening the folding doors, this will give additional space for at least 300 spectators sitting'. This relatively simple, straightforward arrangement was altered by the decision to provide more accommodation by doubling the number of rooms on the E and W sides; giving the building its more solid quadrangular appearance which almost fills the site, and the decision to build a tower (*see* below) which required replanning of the s rooms.

The *Instructions* required 'a neat and commodious exterior' but made no reference to the architectural style that was to be adopted. Probably it was not thought necessary. Comparable buildings, such as St George's Hall, Liverpool, the Fitzwilliam Museum, Cambridge (G. Basevi and C.R. Cockerell, begun 1836) and the Royal Exchange, London (Sir W. Tite 1842–4) had been built in a classical style from which there was no reason to depart. Nor was there any reference to the materials but once again it would have been expected that stone would be used, especially as the West Yorkshire towns were close to many quarries that could offer a variety of different types.

The main contract, in the sum of £41,835 was signed on 25th July 1853. It specifically excluded the construction of a tower recommended by Sir Charles Barry. Brodrick, however, had anticipated the decision to build upwards when in 1853 he published an engraved perspective of the building. This was similar to that executed, but included a tall colonnaded structure consisting of an octagonal base surmounted by an elongated rotunda and a classical spire. This was not an entirely happy composition and in 1854 Brodrick displayed a magnificent watercolour perspective (now in Leeds City Art Gallery) which incorporates the executed design. In 1855 the Council took a half step forward and instructed Brodrick to make provision in the foundations for the present **tower** – a decision that involved a considerable amount of abortive sub-structural work and revised designs for the main vestibule and the Council Chamber.* The long-awaited decision to provide the money, £5,500, for a tower was only made in 1856 as a consequence of a growing pride in the building as it progressed and a realization, as was claimed at the laying of the foundation stone, that it was going to be a display of 'the wealth and importance of the town'. At that time Leeds was actively campaigning to be appointed the West Riding Assize town in opposition to the claims of Sheffield and Wakefield. Neither could offer a building like Leeds Town Hall and the original stipulation that its costs should not exceed £35,000 was quickly forgotten. As work progressed there was a willingness to allow further embellishments, and these subtly changed the character of what had begun as a design in the French Neoclassical style to one in which, wrote Pevsner, 'the Baroque is nearer'.

Exterior

The monumental flight of steps leading to the s **front** is an impressive prelude to the great ten-column Corinthian colonnade [29]. This is reminiscent of French Neoclassical buildings, many of which Brodrick had probably seen on his European tour, such as the Paris Bourse (A.T. Brongniart, 1808–25), the Grand Theatre, Bordeaux (V. Louis, 1773), the theatre in Nantes (M. Crucy, 1784–8) and the Palais de Justice, Lyons (L.P. Baltard, 1835–47). There are pavilions to left and right with Corinthian columns between coupled pilasters and arched windows in two storeys. This pattern is repeated with variations on the e and w elevations. The central part of the n **façade**, with smooth ashlar and rounded corners, also displays a French Neoclassical character.

The entrance steps are flanked by the access to the former police station (left) and cells (right), an alteration by Brodrick in 1864–7 in an appropriate rusticated Newgate style and guarded by four Portland stone lions carved by *William Day Keyworth*. *John Thomas*' carved allegory around the s entrance, probably suggested by the richness of decoration on the New Louvre in Paris (M. Lefuel, 1852–80), illustrates Leeds 'in its commercial and industrial character, fostering and encouraging the Arts and Sciences'.

*The scale of these works can be seen in the former police station where the brick-built bases supporting the mass of the tower add a dramatic sculptural quality.

Above the s colonnade is the proud **tower**, 225 ft (68.6 metres) high, with a detached square colonnade of six columns to each side and a big, tall rather elongated square lead-covered dome with concave sides crowned by a cupola. Pevsner commented that 'The architect has not quite made up his mind whether he wanted a dome like those of the Greenwich Hospital or a tower'. If there was a precedent it was the tower of Thomas Archer's St Philip's Church, Birmingham (early c18). The tower was to be the dominating symbol not only of the place of Leeds in the hierarchy of great northern cities, but also of municipal government in general with derivatives in other towns (e.g. Bolton) and in the Empire, amongst others Parliament House, Melbourne and Durban Town Hall. Embellishments added as work progressed include the monumental vases on the balustraded parapets, like those at Chatsworth and Castle Howard, and the utilitarian ventilation shafts which were turned into elaborately carved ornaments reminiscent of Roman *stele*. Stylized rosettes were added to the sculpture on the tower – a detail that was almost a signature of Brodrick's work. 'The result', wrote Henry-Russell Hitchcock, 'recalls in its grandiose scale the English Baroque of Vanburgh . . . Wallot in Berlin in the eighties approached Brodrick's mode of design in the Reichstag but had little of his command of scale or his almost Romantic Classical control of mass'.

Interior

In the competition design the colonnade on the s front was intended to be matched internally by a three-bay wide vestibule and a staircase leading to an upper Council Chamber; but the work required in anticipation of the erection of a tower caused a major revision of part of the building which resulted in a higher, square and domed **vestibule** with apses on the E and W sides. The floor was laid with Minton encaustic tiles in an elaborate geometric pattern; this was relaid by the same firm in 2002 as part of the restoration undertaken by *John Thorp*, the Civic Architect. In the centre was placed an 8 ft 6 in. (2.6 metres) high Carrara marble statue of Queen Victoria carved by *Matthew Noble*, above which the four pendentives of the dome are painted with a tribute from the four corners of the world, prompting a claim that 'for a time, if only for a few hours, the borough became the seat of empire of the greatest monarchy of the earth'. After the Prince Consort's death in 1861 the Vestibule acquired the character of a mausoleum. The Queen was moved to the E apse and a statue of the Prince, also by *Noble*, was placed in the opposite apse in 1865. Both stand on polished granite pedestals and the same funereal material was used in 1874 by *Alfred Morant*, the Borough Engineer, to face the dado of the Vestibule. He also added the more colourful decorative tiles in the corridors and staircases.

The Vestibule leads directly into the **Victoria Hall** [30], praised by Pevsner as a 'splendid concert hall'. Directly influenced by Liverpool's St George's Hall and indirectly by the Baths of Caracalla, the basilican

30. Town Hall, Victoria Hall, 1852–8, view from the s end

form is expressed by coupled Corinthian columns and pilasters separating the bays. Probably the use of this architectural feature reflects Brodrick's visit to Genoa where he saw and drew the staircase in the Palazzo Balbi. The pinioned owls in the capitals appear to be a Brodrick invention. They are a reference to the arms of the Savile family and alternate with rams' heads that are symbolic of the source of the civic wealth that was being displayed in the new building. These tributes to the Golden Fleece reappear in the carvings by *John Thomas* in keystones over the lunette windows above the entablature. The windows were originally glazed with coloured glass made by *Edmundson & Son* of Manchester. Brodrick also designed ten cut-glass chandeliers that were made by *Osler* of Birmingham to hang from Thomas' keystones; three have survived and now hang in the Civic Hall (*see* p. 82). The present 'Odeon' light fittings were installed in the 1930s but Brodrick's hall is relatively unchanged. The **balcony** across the s end of the hall was added by *W.H. Thorp* in 1890 while the four **side boxes** were added by *John Thorp* in 2000. Their design is based on an unsigned drawing attributed to Brodrick.

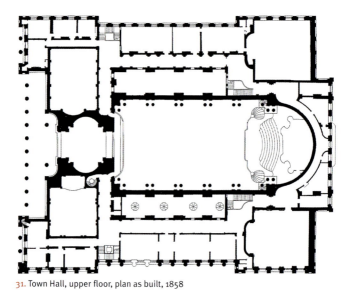

31. Town Hall, upper floor, plan as built, 1858

The richness of Victorian **decoration** is seen at its most opulent here, in which every possible surface and moulding is gilded or painted. *John Gregory Crace* was commissioned to decorate the two most important rooms, the Victoria Hall and the Vestibule;* although the present scheme (dating from 1978–9) is based on a proposal made in 1894 by his son, *John Dibblee Crace* and published in the latter's *The Art of Colour Decoration* (1912). The whole interior is an exercise in the simulation of paint, from the high dark green podium and the *rosso antico* columns and pilasters to the bronze-gilt capitals and the ornamented entablature, from which springs the blue and ivory panelled vault. One feature that is unusual, probably unique, is the Latin and English **mottoes** painted in the frieze around the Hall, amongst them HONESTY IS THE BEST POLICY; LABOR OMNIA VINCIT; WEAVE TRUTH WITH TRUST; IN UNION IS STRENGTH.

The visual climax to the sequence of spaces from the s colonnade to the N end of the Victoria Hall is the great **organ**. One of the largest in Europe, with four manuals and pedals, it had 6,500 pipes and the swell box was the largest yet built by an English firm. The organ was designed by *Henry Smart & William Spark*, the architectural case by Brodrick. At the summit against a deep blue apse powdered with golden stars he placed the civic arms, and slightly lower are flanking pairs of circular towers of pipes, on each of which stands a gilded angelic figure; lower still, at the original console level, four Baroque terms are sounding a celebratory trumpeting.

*Traces of *John Gregory Crace*'s original decorative scheme have been found during recent work. According to a contemporary description, the background colour was pale green 'bordered with a fret ornamental margin . . . standing upon a surbase inlaid with precious and rare specimens of marbles'.

The Roof of the Victoria Hall

Drawings show how Brodrick developed his ideas for spanning the large Victoria Hall, including wrought-iron ribs and cast-iron trusses, and even proposing flying buttresses to strengthen the walls. He probably consulted Sir Joseph Paxton, and certainly took advice from Sir Charles Barry. Finally he settled on incorporating semicircular laminated timber ribs formed of twelve 1½ in. (3.8 cm) planks 9 in. (22.9 cm) wide, nailed together and fastened with bolts and straps which, because of the absence of tie beams, 'allows the ceiling beams being brought nearer to the exterior . . . than is usually the case'. This was not an innovative method of construction in England; Charles Fowler, for example, had experimented with it on the Lower Market, Exeter (1834), but Brodrick was probably influenced in his choice by French examples, in particular through accounts of the innovatory timber dome of the Halle au Blé, Paris, erected by Jacques-Guillaume Legrand and Jacques Molinos in 1782 (destroyed 1802). This was achieved by bolting planks together with staggered joints to form a string of ribs connected by purlins and iron straps. Its iron replacement influenced the design of Brodrick's Corn Exchange (*see* p. 68).

The other rooms in the Town Hall have survived less well. Brodrick was also responsible for the decoration of the courtrooms and the Council Chamber, varying the character of the rooms according to their use. The **Civil Court** (NE corner; now subdivided) was lit by large side windows and had coupled Corinthian pilasters with an elegant serpentine-fronted cast-iron public gallery. Its character was almost c18, while the austere top-lit **Borough Court** (NW) with its grained, solid divisions and single Corinthian pilasters, represents the severity of the law and the solemnity of the justice meted out here. The **Criminal Court** (SW) was partly destroyed by fire in 1991 and has not been reinstated. The original **Council Chamber** (now the Albert Room, E of the Vestibule) still retains much of a richly-decorated palazzo-like room, top-lit through a pattern of little painted glass domes. Here the coupled pilasters are fluted and the capitals include an owl looking outwards on each side.

The Town Hall was opened by Queen Victoria on 7th September 1858. It had cost almost four times the original amount and it became a byword in the municipal world for lavish spending; but it had achieved its purpose and 'given the people of Leeds a hall which tells of the luxury of kings'.

Derek Linstrum

Corn Exchange

Call Lane

1860–2 by *Cuthbert Brodrick* [32]. A building of national, maybe international importance, described by Pevsner as 'remarkably independent and functional . . . Reserved for members originally and not in the least inviting', a deficiency partly countered by its conversion for a shopping centre in 1989–90 by *Alsop & Lyall*.

The traditional site for the display of samples of grain was at Cross Parish at the N end of Briggate, and when it was resolved to erect a purpose-designed Exchange in 1826 it was built on the same site. The architect was a local man, *Samuel Chapman*, and the modest Ionic building served its purpose for thirty years before local opinion came to think that 'a building sufficiently good to please the Leeds people ten years ago will not pass muster now'. Brodrick's Town Hall had set a new standard. In 1860 it was reported in *The Builder* that a new Exchange was to be built on a different site close to the White Cloth Hall and general market area.

The conditions attached to the competition caused some dissatisfaction. Not only were designs requested, but also complete working drawings, specifications and details 'sufficient to enable contractors to tender from' or, suspected some competitors, sufficient to build from without employing the winning architect. There was also a clause that 'if the cost of the selected plan, when contracted for, exceeds the architect's estimate, he will be held to have forfeited his claim to the premium'. One disgruntled writer feared 'the lucky author of the first prize will . . . have his hundred pounds handed over to him, and no further questions asked, as the custom is with fortunate finders of gentlemen's pocket-books or ladies' pet-dogs'. After the Borough Engineer had given an assurance that it was the Council's intention to instruct the chosen architect to carry out the design as well as to receive the premium, the entries were examined; Brodrick was announced the winner, *William Hill* of Leeds second, and *Lockwood & Mawson* of Bradford third.

Many regard Brodrick's design for the corn merchants as his finest work, possessing as it does an unusual unity of the various external and internal elements as well as a repertoire of his idiosyncratic details of

32. Corn Exchange, Call Lane, by Cuthbert Brodrick, 1860–2, view E towards Third White Cloth Hall, 1776–7

stonework. There were many precedents for an oval plan-form as a space within Baroque churches and palaces, but relatively few free-standing buildings of that shape. The obvious source was the Halle au Blé in Paris by Nicolas Le Camus de Mézières (1763–9): a free-standing structure with a 150 ft (45.7 metres) wide open courtyard surrounded by a vaulted arcade with access through open arches, and spanned by an innovative cast-iron dome erected by F.-J. Bélanger after 1803 – seen by Brodrick on his first visit to Paris in 1844. It has been said that one of Le Camus' principal aims was to form two markets in one, the open market-place surrounded by buildings and the covered market hall. Brodrick's large airy hall surrounded by two storeys of offices seems to be following the same pattern. Like its Parisian source it has been likened to those great buildings of antiquity, the Pantheon and the Colosseum.

The **exterior** of the Corn Exchange is faced completely with meticulously cut diamond-pointed rusticated local stone, probably Northern Italian in inspiration, out of which are punched two rows of identical semicircular-headed windows. At first-floor level there is a continuous *guilloche* band of what are probably little millstones, binding the building together, as does the upper frieze of garlands and ox skulls. The use of curves throughout is continued in two projecting ears, one being a semicircular hexastyle Tuscan portico and the other a partly enclosed matching bay containing a staircase leading to the upper floor of offices. The whole sits on a rusticated base and the subsidiary entrances are marked by massive scrolls that seem to have been hewn out of the living rock. At the upper level between each pair of windows Brodrick placed one of his characteristic rosettes or paterae which were becoming his lithic signature; they were also incorporated in the idiosyncratic pediment over a side door, and another version appears in metal ventilator gratings placed at regular intervals in the patterned masonry. Everything is precisely conceived and executed.

Brodrick's first thoughts about the **interior** are shown on his fine watercolour perspective (in the RIBA Drawings Collection) in which the light-coloured, probably plastered but possibly stone, wall is decorated on the top floor with a procession of pilasters. Instead, fair-faced coloured brickwork was used, whose background may have been buff or light red (suggested by old photographs) with darker bricks, possibly blue or black, used to emphasize the semicircular-headed frames to the doorways and to the heavy moulded entablature from which the ribs of the great dome spring. But all the brickwork has been painted several times and no records of the original colours appear to have survived. The York stone paving remains on the basement floor, but conversion in 1989–90 necessitated cutting a large circle out of the ground floor to open up the basement and to connect the three levels. Brodrick had originally devised these to separate the different activities of buying and selling, offices and storage. The new balustrades and staircases copy Brodrick's original designs.

33. Corn Exchange, interior, 1860–2, altered by Alsop & Lyall, 1989–90

The Halle au Blé, 150 ft (45.5 metres) in diameter, is exceeded by the dimensions of the Leeds Exchange which is 190 ft (58 metres) long, 136 ft (41.5 metres) wide and 86 ft (26 metres) high from the basement to the top of the dome. Bélanger employed cast-iron ribs tied with wrought-iron rings, which had the advantage of being light-weight and transparent. Brodrick employed a mixture of wrought iron, cast iron and timber to achieve similar objectives with a light-weight criss-cross pattern that presages C20 space frames. In the centre of the great dome is an elliptical oculus envisaged from the beginning; this natural lighting was increased by adding another glazed panel on the N side which is the only asymmetrical element in the building. At each end of the dome the longitudinal ribs are drawn together in this apotheosis of the curve behind a large cast-iron lunette; one bears the Leeds civic arms and the other symbols of the building's purpose. The cost of the ironwork was £8,050 (approximately two-thirds that of the masonry); it was fabricated locally by *Butler & Co.*, the successors to the long-established Kirkstall Forge.

Derek Linstrum

Leeds Institute

Cookridge Street

Formerly the Mechanics' Institute, 1865–8 by *Cuthbert Brodrick* [34], succeeding the first Mechanics' Institute established in Park Row in 1825. A competition was announced for the Institute in 1860, almost at the same time as Brodrick had won the contest for the Corn Exchange (*see* p. 68), but that did not deter him from entering. The accommodation required included a large lecture room; a library and reading room; a drawing from casts room; studios for painting, carving and modelling; engineering and plumbing workshops; classrooms; dining rooms and a large room for moral instruction. To all these Brodrick took the liberty of adding a dramatic entrance and staircase and a few of the columns for which he was noted.

Brodrick was declared the winner; *Perkin & Backhouse* were second, and *John Shaw* third, all local architects, as pointed out by a critic in *The Builder*, who favoured a Gothic design by *W.H. Crossland*. Notwithstanding the battle of words in *The Builder* there were good comments about Brodrick's design. 'The internal arrangements . . . appear, except in some slight particulars, all that could be desired', while its external appearance was of a 'grand and well-designed structure' except for the upper part of the building which, 'after its inevitable blackening by smoke, would be like a huge leaden coffin and excessively ugly'.

The **exterior** is indeed heavy and serious, another of Brodrick's essays on the character of local stone, which was confined to the s and w façades as the N and E were not exposed at the time it was built. This facing is treated as a repetitive pattern of a single window set within an arch filled with a shell tympanum and a roundel, in reality a small circular window, in each of the interstices. It was, perhaps, a memory of Alberti's church of San Francesco, Rimini (1450–61), although it also refers to the published designs of J.N.L. Durand (1760–1834). Placed dramatically in the centre of the w façade is a very Parisian concept of a frontispiece, partly outside and partly inside the high recessed doorway or loggia. The latter has giant-order pilasters, above which is a sculptured tympanum similar in style and execution to contemporary decoration of the Paris Opéra (1860–75) and the New Louvre (1862–75).

The plan is centred on a circular lecture room fitted into a rectangular shell which contains the workshops, studios etc. After ascending the generous great flight of steps and entering the loggia one passes into the

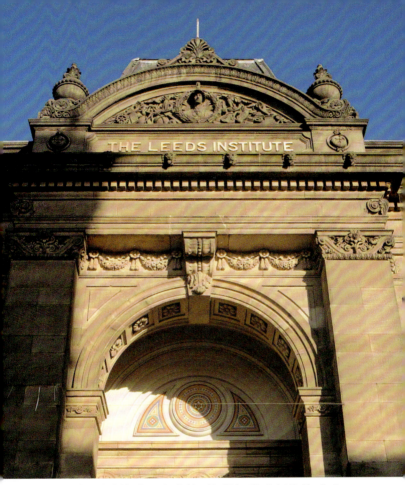

34. Leeds Institute, Cookridge Street, by Cuthbert Brodrick, 1865–8, detail of frontispiece

building at staircase-landing level with stairs up and down. Ahead is one of the entrances into the **lecture room** and here is another memory of Parisian architecture, this time of the Cirque d'Hiver in the Champs Elysées by J-I. Hittorff (1851–2), adapted by Brodrick with a balcony and cast-iron balustrade, above which is 'an iron roof of somewhat novel construction, with windows immediately below it'. The construction of the circular floor was also novel, its weight supported on a central cast-iron column below. There was little opportunity for the use of colour, except for the lecture room, library and reading room and for the staircase entrance, but these spaces did offer Brodrick the chance to insert a few Ionic columns. In 1949 the lecture room was remodelled as the Civic Theatre with the minimum of alterations; in 2005 it is proposed to adapt the entire building as the City Museum, perpetuating its use for educational purposes. Plans are by *Austin-Smith:Lord*.

Derek Linstrum

Municipal Buildings
(School Board Offices, Central Library and City Art Gallery)

Calverley Street and Victoria Square

Built 1878–84 by *George Corson,* one of Leeds' most prominent architects. The contractor for the work was *James Wood.* In 1876 the Corporation launched a competition for new buildings to house its gas, water and sanitary departments which were scattered across the rapidly expanding town. Room was also needed for the Public Library (then in the old Infirmary) and the new School Board. The eight final selections, assessed by *F.P. Cockerell,* all reflected the strong influence of the neighbouring Town Hall. Corson proposed a long Italianate palace façade, with roofs over the centre and end bays of a concave profile in the manner of Brodrick's tower. This was to extend the full length of

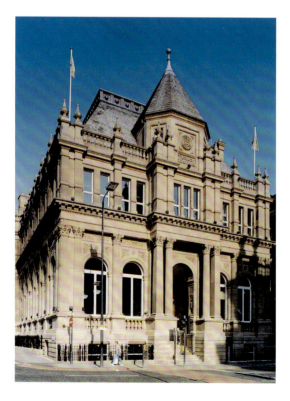

35. School Board Offices, Calverley Street, by George Corson, 1878–81

Calverley Street. *The Builder* was highly critical, considering it 'heavy and unoriginal', and suggested that the School Board offices be given a separate and distinctive character. Corson appears to have followed this advice with great success, placing the new buildings on either side of Alexander Street. The Municipal Offices were extended to house the City Art Gallery in 1886–8, by *W.H. Thorp*.

First, the former **School Board Offices** [35], completed 1881, one of Leeds' most impressive Victorian buildings, standing confidently at the corner of Calverley Street with Great George Street. They opened quietly amidst mixed local comment: criticism for 'wanton extravagance' against praise for 'one of the finest buildings in the country'. Tall, deeper than it is wide, with a five-bay frontage to the street and projecting centre rising to an octagonal attic pavilion with carved coat of arms and pointed roof. Solid rusticated basement of Burley stone (containing storerooms and a passage under the road to the Town Hall) with two tall upper storeys each of five bays in Pool Bank stone. The raised ground floor reads as a splendid *piano nobile* with round-arched windows divided by fluted Corinthian columns and enriched with balusters and carving in the spandrels. A heavy cornice separates this from the attic storey with pairs of narrow windows which once lit examination rooms. At the top, the design of the finials on the balustrade piers pays open homage to the Town Hall opposite. The outer entrance arch has richly ornamented reveals, with high niches from where figures of neatly (and very fashionably) dressed schoolchildren gaze down. Major refurbishment by *Carey Jones Architects* in 1994 restored the interior and preserved the decoration. The inner porch is lined with terracotta tiles, their flower motifs carried across new plate-glass inner doors. There is a central tunnel-vaulted corridor, its walls lined with fluted pilasters. At the rear of the building is a hidden treasure: a cantilevered double-helix **staircase** in a square top-lit well, rising Escher-like to the upper-floor examination rooms and doubtless intended to awe and inspire children and pupil teachers alike. Stout stone columns with stiff-leaf capitals are linked by scrolled, iron balustrades and the walls lined with glazed light-reflecting white tiles, some patterned in blue and brown. On the top floor, a vast central top-lit hall (since subdivided) had galleries for one hundred pupils.

The principal range to the s contained the **Municipal Offices** and **library** (now entirely in library use). Symmetrical, of five bays but of three storeys and on a grand scale with the central and outer bays breaking forward slightly, their paired corner pilasters carried up to chunky finials at the corners of tall pavilion roofs with attic dormers under ornate segmental pediments. Much of the detail is clearly derived from the Town Hall. High rusticated basement storey and heavily corniced ground floor of Pateley Bridge stone, the dressings in local stone from Harehills and Potternewton. Carving is minimal but solid, with coupled columns and pilasters in superimposed orders. The central

portico **entrance** is quite narrow, up a short flight of granite-faced steps; a separate (and now much more heavily used) side entrance to the library was inserted later, through one of the window bays on Victoria Square (then Centenary Street) to the s. Fine heavy iron gates by *Mr Jones* of Manchester, and railings with pairs of delightful crowned owl finials.

The plan of the **interior** is roughly square with N and S wings projecting a little to the E. Most of the building was devoted to municipal use, with the library contained in the s wing. The main entrance (used by rate payers, departmental officers and clerks) rises to a short **vestibule** now cluttered by ugly security barriers. On each side Doric columns of golden brown Devonshire marble support a vaulted, coffered ceiling. The elaborate carving on the alabaster screen to the inner hall is by *Farmer & Brindley*; the opening ceremony, in 1884, is commemorated in stones set oddly in the walling above. Beyond, the top-lit **inner hall** rises through the full height of the building. The overall effect is unexpectedly dramatic, richly Byzantine after the sobriety of the exterior, with walls of polished stone and bright stained glass screens patterned with flowers and leaves, including roses, thistles and shamrocks. The former **pay office**, now the Lending Library, opens off this hall, through another glazed screen described in *The British Architect* (February 1884) as 'carved into devices and patterns of great beauty' by *J.W. Appleyard*, who also carved the stone roundel above, depicting the tax-collector. Citizens in medieval dress queue to pay, overlooked by Leeds' protective owl. On either side a double-arched arcade divided by marble columns with elaborately figured capitals; the first arch passing over a broad staircase, the second spanning the main corridor. The N stair led to the offices, and the s to the library. Both have remarkable ensembles of animals and grotesques clinging to the handrails [37], carved in Hopton Wood stone and reminiscent of the exotic style of Cardiff Castle by William Burges (d.1881). On the Library stairs are additional handrails, of the early 1900s, beautified with faceted and twisted ironwork. The richness of decoration is astonishing, not only in these spaces but throughout the interior. Carved stone, coloured glass, Doulton's terracotta and mosaic are accompanied by a bewildering variety of tile designs to the walls, supplied by *Smith & Co.* of Coalville, *Minton, Hollins & Co.* and *Maw & Co.* Patterns are painstakingly matched in bands of blue and brown, flowered and plain.

The original Library rooms are in the s wing. On the ground floor is the former **News Room** [36]. A long hall, 80 ft (24.5 metres) long and 40 ft (12 metres) wide, with pairs of polished granite columns and capitals of Harehills stone carved into delicate foliage, all different. Between the columns, transverse iron girders support segmental vaults – a fire-proofing device also used in contemporary mills but here made

36. Library, former News Room, 1884, detail showing roof vaults

37. Municipal Buildings, 1884, detail of carving on staircase

38. 'Reclining Woman (elbow)', by Henry Moore, 1980

beautiful by gorgeous, glazed hexagonal bricks made by the *Farnley Iron Company* set in multi-coloured patterns. Decorative gold bosses conceal air vents. The tiled walls are enhanced by pale pink terracotta portrait medallions of great writers by *Benjamin Creswick* of London. Parquet floor of oak, ebony and walnut, a considerate choice at a time when many users wore clogs. The E end was remodelled in 1886 when the room was incorporated into the new Art Gallery, *see* below.

On the first floor, is the former **Lending Library** (now the Music Library), with vaults carried on arches clad in delicate pale terracotta tiles; its walnut bookcases were removed in the mid C20 when converted for the City Museum, which began in the smaller corner room at this level. Upstairs again to the **Reference Library** (now Business and Research) occupying the upper storey and attic. Long and narrow with a gallery on four sides and clerestory windows. At each level bookstacks are recessed within segmental, terracotta-lined openings. Pitched ceiled roof constructed of semicircular cast-iron ribs made in 1881 by *Dawson & Nunneley* (there are similar trusses in the N wing). The mirrored end walls are probably part of the 1901–10 refurbishment, when new shelving was put in by the City Engineer, *W.T. Lancaster*. Electric lighting was introduced as the building neared completion, a significantly early use – plans dated 1884 accompany the Electric Lighting Report by *Henry F. Joel* of London. Two twelve HP Crossley gas-powered dynamos were set up in a railed-off section of the basement engine room.

The decision to extend the building for the **City Art Gallery** was made in 1886 and actively promoted by Colonel T. Walter Harding of

Tower Works, who contributed to the collection. Corson's proposals were not accepted, and a more austere two-storey, seven-bay extension by *W.H. Thorp* built instead; completed 1888. The Library's News Room (*see* above) was cleverly incorporated as the entrance hall and sculpture gallery, opening at its E end into a large staircase hall. A new Public News Room was built in Alexander Street. Thorp's work is now obscured by the blank façade of the **Henry Moore Sculpture Gallery** of 1980–2 by *John Thorp* with *Neville Conder* of *Casson & Conder* as consultant architect. A clean and bold design in light Crosland Hill stone, reusing a C19 window as the entrance. *Henry Moore* took an active interest in the design of the building; his '*Reclining Woman (elbow)*' of 1980 [38], one of the last of his monumental works on this theme, rests patiently on the ramp-access retaining wall. Inside the spaces are constricted, with insufficient natural light on the ground floor. The 1888 gallery has an impressive Imperial staircase with giant columns of Hopton Wood stone. Beyond, the recently refurbished Queen's Room has paintings from the original collection. Opposite the staircase stands Leeds' earliest civic sculpture, a weathered white marble **statue** of Queen Anne, by *Andrew Carpenter*, 1712, taken from the 1710 Moot Hall in Briggate. The Latin inscription proclaimed that it was 'distinguished beyond the one at St Paul's, London . . . allowed by all to be by far the greater representation'. It was paid for by William Milner, a merchant and J.P. (For the Henry Moore Institute *see* p. 166.)

Civic Hall

Millennium Square

1931–3 by *E. Vincent Harris*, one of the most prolific architects of inter-war public buildings [2, 39]. Leeds' Civic Hall followed Harris' design for Sheffield's City Hall and continued his development of a free classical style, seen also in his designs for Manchester during the 1930s. The concept is broadly Palladian, of Portland stone under a roof of green Cumbrian slates, with a symmetrical front and pedimented Corinthian portico flanked by Wren-style towers. Pevsner's assessment was one of qualified approval: 'As ambitious as the Town Hall but not quite as self-confident . . . 1933 could no longer use the classical or Baroque idiom with anything like the robust conviction of the Victorians. England in its official architecture clung to the mood of grandeur, but the bottom had fallen out of it. Yet the towers by their very thinness and duplication impress from a distance, and the oddities of detail – oddities imitated from Lutyens – are at least more acceptable than the deadly correctness of others of the incorrigible classicists of 1930.'

39. Civic Hall, s front, by E. Vincent Harris, 1931–3

Exterior

The Civic Hall stands on a steep s-facing slope making it a forceful landmark on Millennium Square [77]. Its site is triangular, broadening as it climbs the hill so that the long rear wings are splayed as they stretch out from the principal block. The main s portico of four giant Corinthian columns under a heavy attic is impressive close to, with a carved coat of arms by *John Hodge* just contained by the pediment. Three pairs of elaborate wrought-iron gates by *Wippell* screen the entrance doors; pedimented Gibbs surrounds to the windows of the ground floor and enormous sash windows light the banqueting hall above. The controlled simplicity is undermined by the monumental flanking towers which are topped by niched, pedimented pavilions and tall, tapering spires like that of St Vedast, Cheapside, straightened and stiffened.* Perched at the top are comical gilded owl finials by *John Hodge*. At the base of the towers, over side entrances, are four busy cherubs by *Hermon Cawthra*, originally intended for a balustraded s terrace. Projecting stiffly at the sides are massive carved and gilded brackets in late C17 style, holding clocks.

The splayed E **and** W **wings** are of unequal length and the longer W wing is angled at the N end to enclose a spacious N courtyard. At the centre of each are staff entrances marked by tall piers with flat iron overthrows. There is an apparent scarcity of detail but above each entrance there is ornament including a Yorkshire rose and radiating flames. The first floor is treated as a *piano nobile* with rusticated and round-arched windows and, on alternate bays, ornate carved keystones display armorial symbols below, foliage and masks above, by *Frank Tory* of Sheffield. The rear of the principal block is built up so that the inner faces of the wings are only four storey. Within the courtyard, a pedimented porch is watched over by a large owl in a cheerful floral wreath, probably by *Hodge*. The Council Chamber rises behind, its parapet with ramped walls, between two service towers.

Interior

The public entrance is through the s portico. In contrast to the stark exterior, the interior is full of rich colour, dignified and sombre. Harris devised a continuous processional route starting from the 90 ft (27.5 metres) long low T-plan **Entrance Hall**, tunnel vaulted with walls lined with grey gritstone and twenty-six vivid green scagliola columns by *Bellman, Ivey & Carter*. Marble floors throughout; at the N end the grand **staircase** is lit by the atmospheric glow from four stained glass windows with Yorkist heraldry by *George Kruger Gray*, a frequent collaborator with Harris. On the first floor the **Reception Hall**, a

---

*The spire of St Vedast is accepted to be the work of Nicholas Hawksmoor; Harris' first design published in *The Builder*, 1931, proposed shorter towers, each with a dome reminiscent of the Town Hall.

ceremonial space with a ceiling of three saucer domes on deep pendentives separated by barrel vaults, a variation on the design for Sheffield and, as there, richly painted by *Gray*. The English coat of arms in the centre, flanked by those of the ecclesiastical province of York and the old West Riding. This space is lit by C19 chandeliers from the Town Hall, and dramatized by lighting concealed in slots round the base of the domes and in niches of the vaults. Double doors open into the 100 ft (30.5 metre) long **Assembly Hall** set across the width of the front. The room is lined with limed oak panelling, fluted Corinthian pilasters and Kent-style doorpieces. A gallery at each end. Three huge gilt wood candelabra complete the early Georgian effect. E and W are placed the **Lord Mayor's and Lady Mayoress' parlours**, also panelled, in English walnut, made by *John P. White & Sons*. Marble fireplaces and a rose-tinted mirror in the Lady Mayoress's room.

The **Councillors' entrance** from the N courtyard (at first-floor level), is to the **Anteroom** where modern materials combine with stone and wood carving in rich variety. 'Manu-marble' was used for the reception room floor and elsewhere for wall linings, imitating stone and black marbles. The amphitheatre-style **Council Chamber** is sunk in three tiers below entrance level and lit by a high clerestory. Galleries and wall linings of English walnut, the upper parts of the walls are faced in 'Maycoustic' artificial stone, hollow acoustic panels by the *May Acoustic Co.* The room was originally lit by ninety-nine bulbs hung from an elliptical fitting suspended from the ceiling, but these were found to be too hot and dazzling; the room is now, strangely, lit by reflected light from external arc lamps.

Leeds General Infirmary

Great George Street

By *George Gilbert Scott*, 1863–9, in domineering Gothic [41]. The Infirmary was not only one of the first hospitals in England to adopt the pavilion layout of ward blocks pioneered in France, but also, as Derek Linstrum has noted, 'marks a stylistic turning point in West Yorkshire public building', popularizing the style in Leeds for the rest of the C19. Extended 1891–2 by *George Corson* and with numerous additions in the C20.*

The original Infirmary (*see* topic box, p. 84) was founded in 1768–71 in smart Palladian buildings by *John Carr*; in spite of extension the building was inadequate for the rapidly expanding population of mid-C19 Leeds and in 1860 the Medical Faculty commissioned a report from *John Dobson* (the architect of Newcastle Infirmary's new wing, 1852–5), who recommended building on a new site. After much deliberation the Sunny Bank estate, a s-facing hill slope close to the new Town Hall, was purchased in 1862. A Baptist chapel on the corner of Great George Street was sold, the stones marked, and taken away to be rebuilt (with a belfry) as St Simon's Ventnor Street. Part of the adjoining Mount Pleasant estate was also bought, the site now occupied by the School of Medicine.

The selection of an architect was made by the Infirmary Building Committee which included the influential banker William Beckett. He wrote to three London architects: *G.E. Street*, *G.G. Scott* and *Benjamin Ferrey*, asking their advice; all recommended using a person already known and trusted, without the expense and delay of a competition. 'Go to an architect who has already erected a similar work which satis- fies you' wrote Street; 'select your architect at once' wrote Ferrey. But who would supervise the work if the architect was based in London? Scott regarded the employment of a local architect as a potential cause of trouble – reflecting perhaps his problems with William Beckett's elder brother Edmund, his 'friend and tormentor' with whom he worked on St James Doncaster in 1858, and his relations with Leeds architect William Perkin, his collaborator on William Beckett's new bank in Park Row, completed in 1867 (dem. 1965).

Dr Chadwick, the Infirmary's chief physician, thought 'Scott's work will hand him down to posterity . . . he will do it well'. Scott was given

*This account is indebted to S.T. Anning's two-volume *The General Infirmary at Leeds* 1966.

The Old Infirmary

Charitable giving by local merchants and fundraising, which included a public dissection, provided Leeds with its first Infirmary, built in 1768–71. It was designed by *John Carr*, assisted by *Mr Wilkinson* of Wakefield and latterly Carr's brother Robert. The building was placed in an area of rapid later C18 development (*see* p. 105). Originally two storeys, of brick and stone, symmetrical with a pedimented centre and Venetian windows under relieving arches to first floor. Wings added in 1782 and 1786 and an attic storey in 1792. Enlarged again in 1822, demolished 1893. The prison reformer John Howard praised its cleanliness, plan and substantial character in 1788, which included 'six circular apertures, or ventilators open into a passage 5 ft 6 in. wide'. A House of Recovery (to provide a quarantine for smallpox) was built in Vicar Lane in 1802–4; ear and eye infections were treated in St Peter's Square (where the West Yorkshire Playhouse now stands) from the 1820s and outpatients were treated at the Public Dispensary from 1824.

the job and agreed to appoint his own assistant to oversee the work when he was away. Together with Dr Chadwick, Scott visited hospitals in Brussels and Bruges and the Lariboisière Hospital in Paris, the model for Sir Douglas Galton's Royal Herbert Hospital at Woolwich, the first to be built on the pavilion plan in England. Florence Nightingale advised on the layout, encouraging a covered entrance portico, storage for wine and beer (brewed on the premises), an ice house, dispensary, chapel and hydraulic hoists. Wards were also on the Nightingale model, i.e. well ventilated by doors at each end and tall side windows, their ceilings at least 16 ft (4.9 metres) high.

Scott's design, published in *The Builder* on February 13th 1864, is still recognizable in spite of extensive additions. It closely follows the orthodox pavilion **plan** of Lariboisière: a central glazed courtyard and chapel range aligned E–W with N and S corridors serving three long parallel pavilion wings set at right angles on each side, each containing two floors of wards. Terminating the outer ends of each wing are splayed turrets containing water-closets. Open-ended courts lay between each wing (now infilled) and in the middle of each ward there was a fireplace with 'Pearce's descending flue'. Scott's design also marks an important stage in his application of Gothic, the choice of which he defended, stating 'some form of architecture founded on the medieval styles but freely treated would meet the requirements of such a building better than any other style'. The Infirmary also provided an opportunity for realizing aspects of Scott's unexecuted 1859 design for the Foreign Office and prefigures much of the good Italian detail and materials employed by him at the celebrated Midland Hotel, St Pancras (won in competition in 1865–6 while the Infirmary was under construction).

Although the main entrance was on Thoresby Place, Scott reserved decorative display for the impressive symmetrical s façade towards Great George Street. Corson's matching wing, right, was added later (*see* below). The lesser façades are plainer and reflect the building's function. The **main front** [41] is three storeys high, with lively roof-line of steep slopes and pinnacles. Highly decorated in red brick with Bramley Fall stone dressings, richly patterned Venetian Gothic windows and red granite pillars, an early use in Leeds and much copied thereafter. Scott took advantage of the sloping site on this side, placing the outer two-storey wards over offices, so that they are level with the wards at the rear, with arcaded single-storey links between the wings. A central three-bay porte cochère, similar to that designed for St Pancras, with corner pillars of Derbyshire limestone full of fossils. The two small sandstone draped urns flanking the entrance steps were brought from John Carr's Infirmary.

Inside, the entrance hall has a Baronial fireplace. To the left were private rooms for staff, food stores and kitchens around two open courts; to the right reception areas, consulting rooms, baths and bakehouse. A glazed corridor leads toward the main stair, its roof trusses supported on short attached columns, their capitals sprouting medicinal plants carved by *Brindley*. Colourful mosaic and polychrome tile floor laid in 1895. A Gothic arcade with a central round arch of three orders, crisply carved, is flanked by pointed openings. It screens the cantilevered stone stair with a cast-iron balustrade with fleur-de-lys finials. On the first floor on each side of the staircase landing great splashes of colour from tall three-light lancets with elaborate patterned glass by

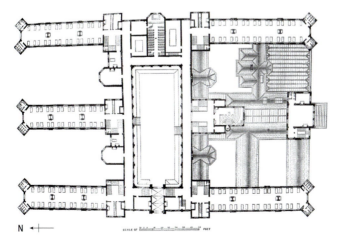

40. General Infirmary, Great George Street, plan of 1864, by George Gilbert Scott

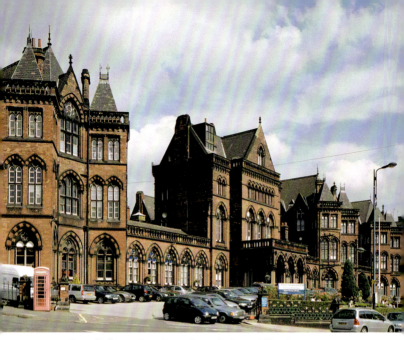

41. General Infirmary, Great George Street, by George Gilbert Scott, 1863–8

O'Connor of London, 1868. A three-bay N arcade with polished granite columns leads into the s corridor, lit from the central courtyard garden (its glazed roof was removed in 1911). s of the landing was the original lantern-roofed operating theatre. E of the courtyard garden is the small **chapel** of St Luke, opened 1869. Three-light canted E window, **stained glass** of 1868 and 1880 given by Sir Andrew and Lady Fairbairn and John Deakin Heaton, honorary physician 1850–80. w organ gallery and 'Lamb of God' rose window with angel figures playing instruments. Carved oak pulpit (dedicated to the memory of William Gott), 1863, moved from its original position, and panelled **reredos** of 1926–9 which incorporated small oak figures of Florence Nightingale and St Luke.

Enthusiasm for Gothic, though dissipated elsewhere in England by the end of the C19, was maintained in Leeds, indicated by the matching façade of the E **extension** by *George Corson*, 1891–2. A four-bay open colonnade (now with ugly blocking) linked to a new three-storey pavilion wing, a faithful copy of Scott's work (further replica wards were considered as late as 1910). Set back (concealed from the street by later extensions), is Corson's grand Outpatients' Building, continuing the E–w axis of Scott's plan. Central waiting hall with a clerestory and barrel-vaulted roof, with curved steel trusses springing from corbels. Romanesque arcaded 'aisles' led to consulting rooms on the E and s.

Later extensions E along Great George Street and Portland Street are entirely different and less mindful of Scott's building: first, the five-storey Wellcome Trust Block of 1961. Functional with horizontal window bands and a brick service tower; next the flat-roofed red brick **King Edward Memorial Wing** of 1913, by *Sidney Kitson*, classical with attached columns to the façade. On the corner with Calverley Street, laid out as the Infirmary's boundary in 1913, is the Portland stone **Brotherton Wing**, planned in 1926 but not opened until 1940. By *Kitson, Parish, Ledgard & Pyman* in collaboration with *Stanley Hall & Easton & Robertson*. Dignified, with a monotonous frontage towards Calverley Street, entirely in sympathy with Vincent Harris' Civic Hall nearby. Plainly modern with tiers of streamlined sun balconies at the s end. Dull outpatients department uphill. On the Infirmary's N side is a very plain range, on land bought in 1911: the **Sunny Bank** wing of 1937 by *Kitson* links his earlier King Edward Nurses' Home of 1915–17 (much altered) to *W.H. & R.W. Thorp*'s **Stables Nurses' Home**, dated 1897. Three storeys, domestic Tudor style in brick and stone.

w of Scott's Infirmary, in Thoresby Place, *W.H. Thorp*'s **Medical School** for eighty students of the Yorkshire College (*see* p. 175), opened October 1894. Leeds' first medical school was founded in 1831, occupied a house in East Parade by 1834, and purpose-built premises lower down Park Street, designed by George Corson in 1865. Tudor Gothic, of three storeys and attics, local brick with Mansfield stone dressings, all carving by *J.W. Appleyard*. On an awkward island site, a U-plan open on the w side, the main entrance towards the Infirmary crowned with a battlemented tower surmounted by a wooden domed lantern. Refurbished 1984–5 by *John Brunton Partnership*. The arched outer porch with traceried and carved spandrels, marble mosaic floor and panelled oak ceiling opens into a gorgeous and well-preserved **interior**. The hexagonal arcaded entrance hall is paved in lovely glowing pink mosaic with bands of flowers; the walls lined with Burmantofts' mellow green faience moulded into naturalistic patterns and coats of arms of the Royal Colleges of Physicians and Surgeons and the Victoria University. The Latin inscription is taken from Matthew 10, v 8, 'Heal the sick . . .' Vaulting shafts of faience support the ribs of the groined oak roof. Off the hall, a wide staircase with ornate iron balustrade. Separate departments, including museum and library in the s wing. The w side was closed by *John C. Procter*'s plain brick wing in 1930. Standing modestly to the w and a pleasing contrast, the three-storey **Algernon Firth Institute of Pathology**, is also by Procter, 1933. Reinforced concrete clad in sombre brown brick with a keyed Portland stone doorcase. Texture and interest provided by the stepped façade, full-height dentilled window recesses and herringbone panels.

A major 1960s scheme to develop the hospital and medical school as a single unit bridging the Ring Road N towards the University campus was only partly implemented in the next decade. The six-storey **Worsley Medical and Dental Schools** by *Building Design Partnership (Preston Group)*, 1979 has a double courtyard plan, the vertical window slots separated by full-height concrete-clad piers. Next to it, the hospi-

42. General Infirmary, Jubilee Wing, by Llewelyn Davies Weeks, 1993–9

tal's dramatic **Generating Station**: concrete and steel frames, up to four storeys; grey brick cladding; and paired tapering fluted concrete chimneys. The mundane **Clarendon Wing** stands over the Ring Road; the only part of the projected new hospital to be built. Four storeys of dark brick with three tiers of continuous grey slate canopies along the front. Deep plan around a courtyard.

Finally, a massive expansion of the 1990s; the **Jubilee Wing** by *Llewelyn Davies Weeks*, 1993–9 [42], designed to provide a link between the old and new parts of the hospital with a new curved glass entrance off Clarendon Way. L-plan, seven storeys, containing 250 beds. Smooth red brick and white metal cladding with louvred sun-shades. Barrel-vaulted roofs and a higher storey for the helicopter pad. Landscaping by *Tess Jaray*, to **Jubilee Square** – the sloping approach from Clarendon Way. It has a 5 metre-high screen wall to the road and sinuous lines of flower beds richly moulded in red brick, patterned with blue and white. Five spiky metal sculptures by *Tom Lomax*.

Central Leeds

The Old Town

Medieval Leeds grew up close to the N bank of the Aire between the parish church on the E and the castle, later manor house, on Mill Hill to the W, where several corn mills were also established. From the C13 building plots were laid out for burgesses on each side of the 'bridge gate', now Briggate, a wide street rising uphill from the river crossing. The inhabitants earned their living from trade or manufacturing, and built houses close to the highway. Leeds Bridge became the site of a woollen cloth market and by the late C17 Briggate was the centre of the West Riding's wool trade, with extensive trading links to Europe. By 1615 at the top of Briggate stood the prestigious Moot Hall and St John's church was built beyond it by 1632–4 (*see* p. 48). 'The Increase of the Cloathing Trade . . . now is the very Life of these parts' wrote Ralph Thoresby in his *Ducatus Leodensis* (1715) but, while the street plan remains, there are few traces of his market centre surviving and only one C17 house in recognizable form. Vast improvements in trade came in 1700 when the Aire was made navigable and from that date wharves and warehousing were built along the N bank of the river with quick access to merchants' cloth-finishing workshops and their Cloth Hall. But by the later C18 the old town had been deserted by the wealthier merchants and old properties began to fill with shabby housing and slums. Some were cleared for the Corn Exchange in 1860. The North Eastern Railway marched through the heart of the old town in 1869 and, slightly later, the great commercial rebuildings of the Victorian and Edwardian city gave the area much of its present character. The walks in this section are divided into two but can be followed sequentially if desired.

a) Leeds Bridge to Briggate

The walk begins on **Leeds Bridge** of 1870–3 by *T. Dyne Steel*, engineer (*W.H. Barlow*, consulting engineer) [44]. The medieval bridge was built, according to Thoresby, on the site of a ferry over the 'Broad Are'; there was a tradition that the large squared stones of its pillars and arches were quarried from the castle. The old bridge was widened 'to take double carriages' in 1730 and again in 1760 when the buildings crowding the approaches were cleared. Its replacement has rusticated ashlar abutments supporting a single graceful segmental arch of cast-iron ribs made by *John Butler* of Stanningley, embellished with flowing vine

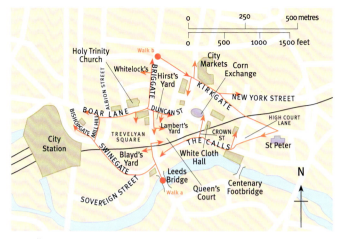

43. Walk 1

scrolls. Cast-iron balustrade, delicately effected in perforated and inter-
linked rings with embossed flower heads beneath a heavy rail. In the
central E panel the Corporation's arms, the civic pride in this enterprise
expressed in the names of the town's aldermen and councillors on the
opposite panel. In **Bridge End**, N flanking buildings are of contemporary date, **Windsor House**, left, is of red brick with sandstone dressings,
the first floor windows set behind iron columns with gilded capitals.
The ground floor has square piers, clumsily re-clad during refurbishment in 1994, and finely carved stiff-leaf capitals (good copies of the
originals) in Crosland Hill stone. Another warehouse opposite,
descending to the quayside; the corner building stands on the site of the
medieval chantry Chapel of St Mary.

　　Briggate lies straight ahead, laid out from 1207, it became the town's
main thoroughfare and later the centre of its cloth trade. The lower part
of Briggate is separated from the main part of the street uphill by the
railway **viaduct** of 1869 by *T.E. Harrison*, engineer for the North Eastern
Railway. On each side the narrow medieval burgage plots were bought
up in the early C18 for the building of larger houses, of which Nos. 3–5
(w side) is an important survival. Seven bays, the central three projecting with quoins and dentil cornice. Later subdivided, with shopfronts,
now poorly treated. Occupied in 1740 by T. Horncastle, apothecary, part
continued as a druggist's shop until the mid C19. C18 and early C19 warehouses and cottages lie behind in **Blayd's Yard**, with a long three-storey
workshop in **Heaton's Yard** (now Court), alongside the railway arches.
Another major early C18 survival lies opposite, beyond the viaduct –
Queen's Court, an elegant brick cloth merchant's house and business
premises. Eight bays between stone quoins, the central two bays breaking forward slightly, over a narrow-arched passage to the yard behind.
Three-storey wings in a U-plan to the rear housed cloth finishing and

44. Leeds Bridge, by J. Atkinson Grimshaw (1880). View down stream showing the Aire & Calder Navigation wharf (right) and Navigation warehouse (left)

packaging workshops and warehouses. By the mid C19 the yard was lined with 'blind-back' slum cottages and workshops. At the back of the yard a narrow alleyway leads to Call Lane, which follows the line of a medieval lane at the back of the original burgage plots. For the rest of Briggate, *see* p. 99.

The tour now proceeds w along **Swinegate**, the medieval route from the river to the manor house. The corner with lower Briggate is dominated by the **Golden Lion Hotel**, Italianate of 1879 by *Thomas Ambler*, for the clothing manufacturer John Barran, built on the site of his first ready-made clothing workshop (*see* topic box, p. 21). A couple of minor commercial buildings lie beyond (Nos. 14 and 16) – shops and offices for J.D. Heaton by *George Corson*, 1870, with a corner tower on corbel rounds, the other with a narrow Dutch gable and corner entrance. Swinegate's s side has the **Malmaison Hotel**, originally the headquarters of Leeds City Tramways. Dated 1915. Free Edwardian Baroque, very red, with lots of unorthodox mannerist details and fine carved coat of arms; dressed up on its conversion in 1999 with this hotel chain's trademark vaguely Art Nouveau ironwork and Horta-style canopies over the doorways. Until *c.* 1900 the curving line of Swinegate was shadowed to the s by a series of goits which were diverted from the Aire upstream at the High Dam (*see* p. 126) to power corn and fulling mills in this area. They have long gone; the streams were culverted in the early C20 and overlaid by Concordia and Sovereign Streets, which now have riverside offices and apartments to the s (*see* p. 139). A relic of the past is **Prospect House**, four-storey former offices and warehouse of Charles Walker, Mill Furnishers, with ornate pedimented gables, *c.* 1900. Between Sovereign Street and the railway, a large site remains undeveloped in 2004 (proposals by *Ian Simpson* envisage a pair of very tall, angular glass shards as part of a mixed development, Criterion Place; in the late 1990s the site was the subject of a similar scheme by *Foster & Partners*). Against the railway to the N, **QPark** by *Carey Jones Architects* 2004, a multi-storey car park over a restaurant, a successful functional design with glazed stair-tower, large louvred panels and small openings to the decks. Swinegate now runs beneath broad viaducts carrying the railway and New Station Street to City Station (*see* p. 125). Abutment walls faced with cream glazed bricks above stolid gritstone footings. Archways open into tunnel-vaulted storage areas below the track. Beyond, Swinegate divides and becomes Bishopgate Street (left) and Mill Hill (right), close to the site of the Norman castle and later of the moated manor house (*see* topic box, p. 6). A relic of this may survive within **The Scarbrough** pub and hotel in **Bishopgate Street** which was extended and refronted for Tetley's in the early C20 with brick and glazed terracotta tiles. Attached Ionic columns, moulded swags and a dentilled cornice with parapet bearing the name of the hotel and brewery in raised letters.

Uphill now along **Mill Hill**. First, tucked in close to the viaduct, the plain **Prince of Wales** pub with the Prince's badge in elaborate carved brick. Of greater interest Nos. 9–10, a three-storey merchant's house and workshop of the first half of the C18. Six-bay façade of dark brick with gauged brick headers, divided in the late C19 into two shops with chambers over. Inside slender knopped stair balusters, fielded panel shutters and kingpost roof trusses. Next door, Nos. 7–8 is a much larger early C19 workshop and warehouse, of four storeys with a top-lit attic, the taking-in doors reduced to windows with bracketed lintels in the later C19. Nos. 4–6 is a refronting *c.* 1870 of a mid-C18 merchant's house of three storeys with a central archway to the rear yard, flanked by two sets of paired windows.

Boar Lane was the medieval route between the manor house and Briggate; the name is thought to be a corruption of 'Borough'. Its s side was lined by houses in the early C18 but widened and redeveloped 1869–76 with commercial premises following the building of the new railway station. The designs are all attributed to *Thomas Ambler*, working for the mighty Alderman John Barran, tailor and outfitter (*see* topic box, p. 21). Ambler employed different styles and motifs to achieve a satisfying variety of tall façades topped by a delightful skyline of moulded parapets, dormers, statuary and spiky turrets. The sunny N side was mostly demolished after 1968 under the city's plans to build a series of linked shopping precincts and arcades with high-level pedestrian walkways crossing Boar Lane. A remnant of this ill-fated scheme is the unlovely **Leeds Shopping Plaza** by *John Brunton & Partners* of Bradford, 1974–8; refurbished 2004. E of Albion Street, however, are some 1870s survivors: Nos. 58–63 are Italianate four-storey warehouses with shops, completed 1875. The ashlar façades vary: No. 58 has paired round-arched windows, attached columns and dentilled eaves, but with an added dash of Art Deco restyling in the fenestration and carved first-floor plaques. No. 59 is palazzo-style with pedimented windows and a lunette dormer, a difference in style perhaps reflecting the taste of the client J.A. Doyle, who had his glass and china warehouse here. No. 60 matches No. 58; Nos. 61–63 (Peel Buildings) are also identical, their paired windows flanked by pilasters with carved capitals beneath decorative panels of scrolls and key patterns, and second-floor balconies. Less frivolous, the hefty former C&A store by its usual architects *North & Partners*, 1968, in dark brown brick, off-white ceramic and granite, thankfully limited to five storeys, but otherwise indifferent to its Victorian neighbours. Next to it Trinity Street rises sharply uphill N into the dreary **Trinity Arcade**, completed in 1974, which was originally intended to connect with a walkway over Boar Lane (due for redevelopment in 2005 as a series of covered precincts with striking, amorphous glass roofs, by *EMBT* and *Stanley Bragg Partnership*).

Set back on the N side, **Holy Trinity Church** is the sole C18 survivor, built in the classical style in 1722–7 by *William Etty* of York, for the fashionable merchant class in this area. Funds were raised by, among others, the merchant, diarist and historian Ralph Thoresby (*see* topic box, p. 4) with a substantial gift from Lady Elizabeth Hastings. Etty's tower had a balustraded (clock) stage and a timber spire, which blew down in 1839 and was replaced by *R.D. Chantrell's* graceful three-stage diminishing square tower rising to 180 ft (55 metres). The influence of Gibbs is obvious, presented in sombre grey coarse-grained Millstone Grit from the Meanwood Quarries. Massive blocks are used to great effect for the giant Doric pilasters supporting a triglyph frieze, cornice and blocking course surmounted by flaming urns. Seven bays to Boar Lane with Gibbs surrounds to doorways at each end (the E door is blocked). Five round-headed windows with alternating broken pediments, their keyed arches and aprons carved without fuss in response to the gritstone's character. Giant pilasters flank both the shallow apse with a massive Venetian E window and the elaborate w façade. Fleeces stamped onto the lead drainpipe fixings are a small reminder of the town's source of wealth. The **interior** is a delightful contrast [45], high and light, with elaborate detailing in plaster and carved wood. Giant Corinthian columns support a shallow tunnel-vault with narrow side aisles; N windows blocked by the Church Hall (*see* below). Thorough restoration in 1883–4 by *Thomas Winn* who removed the old box pews, galleries, choir stalls, flooring and interior fittings. Oak was reused for seating and the pedestals of the columns apparently lowered. Marble steps to the raised E end and red and black floor tiles laid at the w. – **Woodwork**: royal arms; panelling; pews carved with key and scroll patterns; pulpit on s side with inlaid side panels and tester with star inlay; reredos with swags and gilded pelican. In the Lady Chapel (N aisle) a **painting** of the Annunciation in Pre-Raphaelite style; the altar table has been raised, obscuring the lower panel. – **Stained glass**: E window by *William Wailes*, 1848; the Ascension with the Evangelists in the side windows. In the s aisle two windows by *Michael O'Connor*, 1866, lustrous

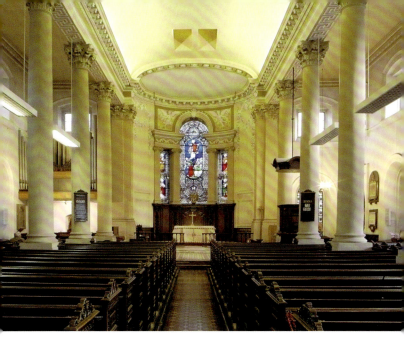

45. Holy Trinity, Boar Lane, by William Etty, 1722–7

roundels and the Resurrection. s clerestory, raising of Jairus's daughter, 1887, signed by *Powell Bros*; the Good Shepherd in the centre of the s aisle is of 1903. The side walls are lined with **memorials**; a few were removed from St Paul, Park Square when it was demolished in 1905. N aisle, w end, a fine Greek Revival memorial with urn and weeping willow, to Anne Sheepshanks 'of simple and domestic habits' d.1821. Also on the N wall, Henry Robinson, d.1736, an important local benefactor and founder of the church. Palladian marble aedicule supported by putti and garlands with Latin inscription. To its left, a plaque carved with drapery lists his acts of charity 'to procure the bounty of Q. Anne' for twenty-one vicarages, chapels and churches. The memorial was erected by his nephew, James Scott, first minister of Holy Trinity d.1782. He is commemorated in the doorway at the s aisle's E end, 'Regretted by the wife, and lamented by the good'. **Church Hall** on N side, 1982–3. Gritstone.

E of Holy Trinity to Briggate are more Italianate shops and offices by *Ambler*, pared down and rendered in the C20, but recently improved. The corner with Briggate is a facsimile of 1983.

Almost the entire Victorian s side of Boar Lane has been retained, at least in part the result of campaigning by conservationists after 1975, when, in spite of listing, permission was granted for its demolition and replacement with a shopping centre. The plans were fortunately discarded in favour of refurbishment. It begins at the w end with a pre-Ambler, business-like 1830s warehouse range in brick with stone dressings. Its neighbour is a late c20 facsimile; then the grand sweep of *Thomas Ambler*'s frontages begins. First the splendid Gothic **Griffin Hotel**, *c.* 1872 [46], of red brick with finely-carved stone details, cast-iron cresting, oriel windows, pinnacles and gargoyles. Its corner has a pavilion roof and clock (with letters rather than numerals) well-placed to encourage travellers to the station. On the opposite corner with Mill Hill, the former Saracen's Head, Italianate with elaborate corner pediment. Its panelled pilaster strips with carved capitals repeat across the classical frontages of **Victoria Buildings** (Nos. 24–28), which continues into New Station Street, a carriage road made in 1873 to the remodelled station. High up on the corner, a bust of Queen Victoria in a pedimented niche; the parapet was originally crowned with urns. On New Station Street's E side is a thin sliver of brick Neo-Jacobean with stone window surrounds, panelled gables, and clinging stone beasts. Next door the former Leeds Mercantile Bank is the only building to retain its original ground floor. Four storeys of substantial Italianate, in ashlar with moulded arches and fine carved panels of foliage and birds

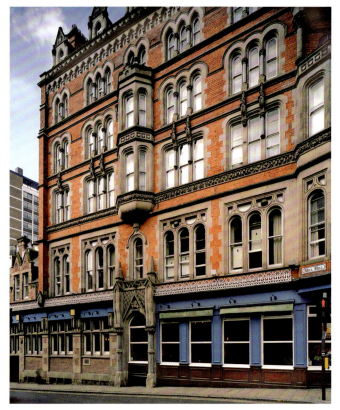

46. Griffin Hotel, Mill Hill, by Thomas Ambler, *c.* 1872

including the Leeds owl, rising to a deep, bracketed eaves cornice, made top-heavy by paired dormer windows under segmental arches. It turns the corner where it is cleverly integrated with the mirror-glazed front of **The Bourse** of 1993, by the *Sir Basil Spence Partnership*, which sits back from the building line, built across a former side street, reflecting the C19 façades. Then Nos. 19–21, a proper three-storey Italian palazzo in solidly sculpted gritstone ashlar, lightened by the oriel windows above the side entrance. Built as the Leeds Corporation Gas Offices but converted after 1884 by *C.S. Nelson* of Leeds into a hotel, restaurant and bodega (wine merchant) with a rear extension. Rustication and recessed plain panels to the renewed shop fronts, motifs carried through the restrained brick and stone corner block attached to the left.

Nos. 15 and 16 Boar Lane were built as five narrow properties, each treated differently but creating a symmetrical composition of eclectic style. Ornament is kept to the central three bays with Italianate round arches to the first and second floors beneath a pierced stone parapet but with quirky decorative fish-scale-slated tourelles above the splayed outer corners. Singer, whose sewing machines helped to make John Barran's fortune (*see* topic box, p. 21), had premises here. Rear rebuilt in 1992–3 by *Chapman Taylor & Partners*, who also planned **Trevelyan Square** on land to the rear, which had been cleared by developers before the decision was taken to keep Ambler's frontages. By the same firm is the six-storey building which encloses the s side of the Square. It successfully evokes the city's late Victorian architecture, with contrasting brick bands, tiered bays and vast gable windows. Closing the E side the dull Marriott Hotel. In the centre of the square are gardens and the popular **Talbot Fountain**, protected by hounds with fleur-de-lys ears, salvaged from a clothiers house near Halifax, demolished *c.* 1960.

Returning to **Boar Lane**, Ambler's sequence continues with two narrow ornate four-storey façades, both Gothic, the first of brick with stone detailing and gargoyles on the gabled finials, the second of stone with elaborate ogee tracery based on Ruskin's illustrations of the Ca' d'Oro in Venice. Finally, to the corner with Briggate, Ambler's *tour de force* for Barran, who reserved this prime site for his shop, with chambers and the Trevelyan Temperance Hotel above.* Of brick and stone, in Italianate Second Empire style with dormers and mansards peppering the roof-line of its thirteen-bay façade. Two tall entrances surmounted by carved pediments with cornucopia and carved heads (Milton and Shakespeare?).

The line of Boar Lane continues E of Briggate as **Duncan Street**, terminated by Brodrick's stout Corn Exchange (*see* p. 68). The N side was rebuilt *c.* 1900. Three elaborate Baroque Revival blocks with a touch of Art Nouveau decoration, and two narrow gabled brick frontages in a

---

*Probably named after Sir Walter C. Trevelyan (1797–1879), president of the United Kingdom Temperance Alliance.

more modest Jacobean. On the corner, shops and offices by *Percy Robinson* for Messrs Hepworth, gents' outfitters, *c.* 1904. Four storeys faced in the Leeds Fireclay Company's terracotta (*see* topic box, p. 225) modelled with high-relief ornament – swags, scrolls and female figures by *E. Caldwell Spruce*. Ornate gabled attic storey with corner turret. Nos. 5–9 also by *Robinson*: No. 7 has a pedimented gable with obelisk finial and square turrets to the outer bays, the parapets rebuilt in 1992. *H.A. Chapman & J.W. Thackray* designed **Duncan Chambers**, the paired shops and offices at the E end in 1905, their names impressed at each end of the building. In similar style but clad in faience with distinctive semicircular attic windows to the third floor and another domed corner tower.

The s side is quite different: first, *H. Wilson*'s Art Deco Burton's in white Marmo with black steel window frames and ornamented panels, but the rest is by *Ambler* again: a long classical seven-bay range of brick with ashlar dressings, built 1882 as offices and warehouse for William Tunstall. Symmetrical with a central carriage arch, pilastered shopfronts and a fine carving of the town's coat of arms under an arch. Access to the warehouse was at the rear, through the archway to **Hirst's Yard**, where there are still two-storey brick workshops complete with hoist, loading door and bollards, providing a good impression of its character in the early C19. The Neo-Tudor former Whip Inn is by *Ambler*.

Now back to **Briggate**. On the E side, close to the railway, is Queen's Court, already seen. Otherwise on this side later C19 and C20 refrontings conceal surprising late medieval remnants. A narrow opening leads to **Lambert's Yard**, where standing in a quiet corner is the city's earliest surviving building. A late C16 or early C17 timber-framed, three-storey house with jettied upper storeys beneath a gable. Possibly the cross-wing of a larger hall house. Then Nos. 160–161, Regent House, a 1980s fibreglass replica of the rusticated classical façade of the 1834 Royal Buildings and Hotel, itself a modernization of the New King's Arms of 1692. Only the royal arms above the entrance are original.

No. 158 is narrow, the width of a medieval croft but dressed up in Northern Renaissance style of red brick and terracotta, 1894. On the w side, the great attraction is the fascinating **Time Ball Buildings**, two C17 houses, barely identifiable behind the elaborate stucco decoration applied in 1876 by John Dyson, jeweller and watch maker. It takes its name from the elaborate time ball mechanism attached to the large clock above the entrance [47], which was linked to Greenwich and dropped at exactly 1 p.m. each day. It was installed in 1910 along with a second clock with a gilded figure of Father Time carved by *J.W. Appleyard*. The shopfront shutters were raised by a mechanism in the basement and a full-height display window was made under a dome. Interior converted, but retaining most of its ornate late Victorian fittings, including chandeliers bought at the 1890 Paris exhibition, galleries and rear workshop.

47. Time Ball Buildings, Briggate, refronted 1876, clock of *c.* 1910

N into the main part of **Briggate** the street's character changes with c20 commercial buildings dominating on both sides. On the E side bleakly functional blocks flank the ebullient former **Post Office Exchange**, 1907 by *Percy Robinson*: it repeats in brick and terracotta the Renaissance-style columns, wreaths and swags of his Duncan Street buildings. There was a grocery exchange on the first floor with a reading and writing room; the post and telegraph offices were above with telephone boxes and letter boxes. The less-ornate top storey was added by Woolworth's in the 1920s. Inside massive cylindrical columns with roll mouldings survive on the ground and upper floors. On the W side, N of Boar Lane: **Burton's** shop and arcade, steel frame and pre-cast concrete with white tile cladding of 1963 by *T.H. French*, crisp lines and a modern look of deeply-recessed window bays in the upper floor. Then a Leeds institution: **Marks & Spencer**, who began with a stall at

Kirkgate Market in 1884. The present building, begun in 1939 (completed Postwar) by *Norman Jones & Rigby* of Southport, was built to the modular system devised for M&S by their consultant architect, *Robert Lutyens*. The stripped classical black granite façade is unusual, the only example besides Lutyens' own store in London's Oxford Street: a measure of its importance. From black to white for Nos. 50–51, the premises of Thornton & Co., India Rubber Manufacturers. The left-hand section was built in 1918 by *Sidney Kitson* with classical fluted columns *in antis*, soon replicated for its extension. Steel frame and reinforced concrete clad in Burmantofts matt-faced 'Marmo' faience. A narrow passage N of this building leads to the cramped **Turk's Yard** and **Whitelock's** pub. There was an inn here in 1715, licensed as 'The Turk's Head' in 1784, the likely date for the present two-storey ranges of pub, brewhouse and five former cottages. The three cottages at the far end are of three storeys, a single room to each floor and sliding sash windows at the top. The pub was grandly renamed 'Whitelock's First City Luncheon Bar' by the landlord John Lupton Whitelock, who made alterations in 1886. Its richly-decorated interior of stained glass, marble counters, engraved mirrors, faience tiles and brasswork [48] was further enhanced for use by The Leeds Savage Club, an Edwardian art society.

The tour may end here or continue E along Kirkgate. The yards and rebuilding of the N end of Briggate are covered in Walk 5.

48. Whitelock's pub, interior, *c.* 1886

b) Kirkgate to the Calls

Kirkgate was the village street between the parish church and the open fields, established before Briggate was set out in 1207. The first Cloth Hall was built on the s side of Kirkgate in 1711 and became the focus of the town's expanding trading area. The street starts badly with the monotonous former **Littlewood's** (s corner) of 1971, giving the impression that Kirkgate is an uninteresting side street, belying its historical importance. Opposite – *Chorley, Gribbon & Foggitt*'s **Debenham's**, of 1936, has attractive zigzag bronze fenestration. Further on, beyond Fish Street, interest is confined to the upper floors, in particular the former **Golden Cock Inn**, an Art Deco refronting in white 'Marmo', with fluted half-columns, blue tiles and the inn sign set high up. The Leeds Library (*see* p. 121) was founded on this site in 1768. Opposite, **Central Buildings** by *Thomas W. Cutler*, 1901, shops and offices built on the site of the Central Market, Duncan Street, 1824–7 (*see* topic box, p. 119). Bold Queen Anne revival in brick with brown faience giant rusticated pilasters between the shopfronts surmounted by brackets with obelisk finials. Fine wrought-iron gates to the inner yard. From a level stretch at the top of Kirkgate, Chantrell's careful siting of the parish church tower (*see* p. 43) can be appreciated in the view downhill to the se, since 1869 bisected by the railway viaduct. Closer to, the eye is unavoidably drawn to the ornate **City Markets** of 1904 by *John & Joseph Leeming* [49] at the busy junction with Vicar Lane. It stands on the site of the early c18 Vicar's Croft, which was taken over by Briggate's fruit and vegetable traders in 1822.* A glass and iron market hall was erected there in 1857 and extended in 1875 for the butchers' rows, previously in Briggate. Only the latter survived when the earlier part was swept away for the present enormous building. It provides an extravagant display in Flemish style, with Art Nouveau detailing, from *Thewlis & Co.*'s draped well-fed putti supporting the entablature between shops on the ground floor, to the elaborate chimneys, balustrades, domes and steeple of the skyline. The street frontage comprised eighteen shops, a hotel, restaurant, billiard hall, coffee and club rooms. Refurbished 1992 by *Povall Worthington*. Inside the restored market hall the atmosphere is rich and airy. The massive steel and cast-iron structure by *J. Bagshaw & Sons*, engineers of Batley, has a total of twenty-eight clustered Corinthian columns supporting a glazed clerestory, lantern roofs and central octagon carried on lightweight trusses. Fierce dragons support the gallery, reached via spiral stone stairs at the corner entrances. These have moulded inner arches of Burmantofts faience and walls lined with glazed bricks. At the e end are brick rows added to the previous market in 1875 for grocery shops.

*The vicarage was purchased by the Commissioners under the terms of the town's 1824 Improvement Act and the vicar given a new home at No. 6 Park Place.

49. City Markets, Kirkgate, structure by J. Bagshaw & Sons, 1904

s of the Markets in **New Market Street**, Nos. 22–24, **Backawell House** of *c.* 1880 is attributed to *Smith & Tweedale*. Four-storeys, strongly characterful with two high moulded brick arches, infilled with tiers of canted bay windows. Continuing downhill along **Kirkgate**, on the sw side, the former **London & Midland Bank**, 1892 by *William Bakewell*. Tall, confident, two-storey Italianate stone front with paired Corinthian pilasters and deep-set Florentine tracery to the upper windows. Fine carving by J.W. Appleyard includes King Midas. The front looks rather comical, having been exposed on one side after the demolition of corner buildings. Kirkgate was widened *c.* 1870 and its NE side largely rebuilt. The substantial former **Yorkshire Penny Bank**, by *Smith & Tweedale*, 1899, squats on the corner with New York Street. Brick with terracotta to ground floor, banded upper floor, short columns and three lead domes.

On **New York Street**, Nos. 1–19, *c.* 1885 by *William Belton Perkin* for Charles Burrow, a shoe dealer. A cocoa house, bank and shops below, workshops and offices above, a modest Italianate development, enhanced by moulded string courses and some terracotta. Further E, a second temperance establishment; *Thomas Ambler*'s **St James' Hall and Westminster Buildings** of 1877, providing coffee, dining and reading rooms. Tall windows with traceried heads lit an upper-floor lecture room and club rooms, while plain sash windows lit dormitories for 'strangers and working men' on the third floor. Extended in 1884 by *Ambler* and *William Thorp* for William James Armitage, the owner of the Farnley Iron Company. Polychromatic Gothic with a neat crocketed gable above the entrance to Westminster Buildings.

The southern side of **Kirkgate** was untouched by road widening and still has plain brick shops and houses of the mid C19 with narrow frontages, the only reminder of the town's character round the old parish church. Behind the boarded-up frontage of Nos. 98–101 is an astonishing survival: the **First White Cloth Hall** of 1711 built to provide a covered trading area for undyed cloth, while dyed-cloth merchants continued trading in Briggate (*see* topic box, p. 104). Originally a U-plan open to the street, its yard was infilled with housing in the early C19 by *James Boyne*. Plans of 1997 for refurbishment by *John Lyall Architects* remain unrealized.

Beyond the railway viaduct lies the parish church of St Peter (*see* p. 43), crudely cut off from the town by the line, which ploughed through the N part of its extended churchyard. Gravestones litter the embankment. Tucked into the railway arches is a row of four large blue steel pods with hinged fronts, like giant handbags, for a bar and night-club by *Union North Architects*, 2001: a clever scheme, but the siting is unfortunate. The medieval churchyard was, as usual, s of the church, and there is now a hint of a quiet sw precinct here. Early C19 buildings on **High Court Lane** then, on the N side of High Court, **Wharf Street**, and the headquarters of Leeds Civic Trust in a pair of houses dating from *c.* 1865, workshops beyond.

On the corner with **The Calls**, the Old Brewery, polychrome brick, 1868. Nos. 40–44 stand on part of probably the oldest river wharf, between Leeds Bridge and the church. Much of the structure on the road side dates from 1866, part of the **Fletland Corn Mills** complex. Its industrial character has been well preserved in conversion to a smart hotel, 1991, with sensitive barge-boarded additions. Three gabled bays overlook the river, (*see* p. 143), outer bays *c.* 1800; stone blocks strengthen the brick walls. A silver ball-fountain commemorates the Leeds Development Corporation's regeneration work here, 1988–95. Beyond, Nos. 30–32, a large early C19 warehouse, six storeys to The Calls, seven to the river, straddling an ancient mill goit. Plain brick, grittily industrial, two tiers of loading doors. Converted to offices and flats by *Allen Tod Architects*, 1994–5. No. 28, three storeys with a canted façade, awaits conversion. Late C18 and in use as a grain store until converted by H.G. Atkinson, Builders' Merchants *c.* 1898; bold lettering and render covering an added storey and refenestration. From here to Leeds

The Cloth Halls

The **First White Cloth Hall**, Kirkgate (*see* p. 103), was initiated by Lord Irwin of Temple Newsam and built 1711. Ralph Thoresby was one of the sponsors and provides us with a contemporary description: 'a stately hall, built on pillars on arches in the form of an exchange, with a quad-rangular court within'. After 1756 it was succeeded by the much larger **Second White Cloth Hall**, Meadow Lane. This was of three storeys, 210 ft (64 metres) long and 30 ft (9 metres) wide, with a central pediment. The merchants met the cost of the **Third White Cloth Hall**, Crown Street (*see* below) completed in 1776–7, at a time when three-quarters of the cloth passing through Leeds was exported. Partly demolished by the North Eastern Railway who paid for the **Fourth White Cloth Hall**, King Street, in 1868. By this date the cloth halls were in decline, as pro-duction was industrialized and buyers dealt directly with mill owners who traded from elaborate warehouses. The King Street hall was demolished in 1895, its cupola retained for the roof of the nearby Hotel Metropole (*see* p. 110). Coloured cloth was sold on the market stalls of Briggate until the opening of the massive **Coloured** or **Mixed Cloth Hall** in 1757, by *John Moxson*, Surveyor of Highways. It was almost 400 ft (122 metres) long and 200 ft (61 metres) wide, with wings housing nearly 2,000 stalls and a rectangular courtyard capable of holding 20,000 people. Demolished 1890 for the construction of City Square. In 1793 the **Tom Paine** or **Irregulars' Hall** was opened on Albion Street, for the sale of cloth made by unapprenticed clothiers.

Bridge was Warehouse Hill, the river bank wharf next to the Aire and Calder Navigation's warehouse (*see* p. 141).

Crown Street was the direct route uphill from the river to the **Third White Cloth Hall** built in 1776–7, attributed to *William Johnson*. Partly demolished by the railway in 1864–9, beyond the viaduct's striding arches are the remains of the entrance range. Single storeyed with blank arcading and an entrance with a tunnel-vaulted passage behind. Round cupola on a square base; it housed the bell from the previous hall of 1756. Behind, single-storey wings originally enclosed a large courtyard, now partly infilled with a restaurant and offices by *John Lyall Architects*, 1991–2. The two-storey N wing, now separated by Assembly Street, has an arcaded lower storey and was originally designed with assembly rooms on the upper floor. Reception room and large ballroom with original plaster decoration and fine Palladian windows. Refurbished by *David Readman, c.* 1990. **Cloth Hall Street** has a five-storey block clad in a mosaic of glazing, coloured ceramic panels and brickwork by *Allford Hall Monaghan Morris*, 2003, its gentle arc reflecting the grand ellipse of the Corn Exchange opposite (*see* p. 68).

Walk 2.

Parades and Squares

There are two walks here: the first exploring City Square w to Park Square; the second Park Row and neighbourhood. They examine the effect of Leeds' expansion in the second half of the c18, from about 6,000 in 1700 (80 per cent probably wool and linen traders) to 16,380 by 1771. New building was largely contained within the old town and its congestion partly drove the release of the Wilson family's Park Estate to the w. The Coloured Cloth Hall was erected at the w end of Boar Lane in 1757 and from the 1770s a grid of streets was laid out on the s-facing slope overlooking the Aire valley. Houses in Park Row, Park Square, Park Place and South Parade were underway by the 1780s but Albion Street and Commercial Street, E of Park Row, were not fully developed until the mid C19. By that time the Park Estate was being vacated by its residents for the fresh air of Headingley, away from industry along the river. The area's residential character was further diminished following the arrival of the railways, which saw merchants' houses replaced by large warehouses and offices and the transformation of this neighbourhood into the town's financial and trading centre, a role that it preserves today.

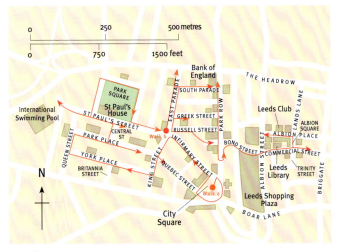

50. Walk 2

a) City Square to Park Square

City Square [51] provides the first impression of Leeds for visitors arriving at City Station. It was laid out in 1893–1903, and was intended to celebrate Leeds' elevation to City status. The square was the idea of the industrialist and Lord Mayor, T. Walter Harding, and was designed by *William Bakewell*, architect of Harding's Tower Works (*see* p. 128–9). Though severely reduced and altered in the 1960s, its dignity was restored in 2002 in a thoughtful reordering by *John Thorp*, Civic Architect, who introduced new lighting, animated water jets and planting to provide a screen from the hectic traffic. Harding intended the square as a bravura display of British art. He presented the statue of the Black Prince by *Thomas Brock*, a massive equestrian bronze showing the Prince in full armour. It took seven years to make and was brought from Belgium via Hull along the Aire & Calder Navigation. The figure stands in his stirrups and points E along Boar Lane towards the heart of the medieval town. The high granite pedestal has bronze plaques with the battles of Crecy and Poitiers in low relief, and an elaborate carved band with the names of great men of the C14. The Prince remains unmoved, but the marble balustrade, which originally encircled him, now forms a gentle arc around the square. Raised on pedestals are eight nymphs, 'Morn' and 'Even' by *Alfred Drury*, holding lamps aloft. On the square's W side are life-size statues representing local industrial, social, religious and scientific endeavour: James Watt (many wish it were Matthew Murray, *see* p. 15) and John Harrison by *H.C. Fehr*, Dean Hook by *F.W. Pomeroy* and Joseph Priestley by *Drury* (the last two donated by Harding). Priestley is set in line with the entrance to Mill Hill chapel (*see* below), as a reminder of his historic link with its predecessor.

Now the eclectic mix of buildings around the Square, beginning with the imposing **General Post Office** (now closed), which was built on the site of the Mixed Cloth Hall (*see* topic box, p. 104), in 1896 by *Sir Henry Tanner* in his usual Northern Renaissance style with a lively roof-line of gables, chimneys and central turret; good sculpture including four statues by *W.S. Frith* above the entrances representing forms of communication, and figures of Art and Science. Then, moving clockwise along the N side, **No. 1 City Square** of 1996–8 [21] by *Dominic Boyes* of *Abbey Hanson Rowe* for Norwich Union, whose early 1960s block on this site was rightly declared by Pevsner to do 'no good' to the square. Its successor is impressively Postmodern. Twelve-storeys with a solid black granite base blending into upper storeys of white limestone. Rounded S façade bisected by a marble-faced atrium with wall-climber lifts and a tensile sun shade. Striking bronze Egyptian-style detail to the windows.

Across Park Row, to the E, the more pedestrian **No. 1 Park Row** of 1996–7 by *Fletcher Joseph Architects* tries too hard to pay homage to the late C19 buildings in Park Row with bands of red granite and an octagonal corner dome. It replaced schools associated with the **Mill Hill Unitarian Chapel**, which is the only survival of before 1893. Built

City Square, as remodelled in 2002 by John Thorp, Civic Architect. View from the NE towards the General Post Office, by Henry Tanner, 1896

1847–8 by *Bowman & Crowther* [52], replacing an earlier chapel of 1674, where Joseph Priestley was minister in the late C18. Spiky Perp, marking as Pevsner noted 'the change from Georgian classical to Victorian Gothic allegiance among Nonconformist chapels'. Its design is indebted to Chantrell's parish church but there is, of course, no tower. Large window over the w entrance, bold lantern finials at the corners and slender buttresses, now sadly missing their pinnacles. Poor s porch of *c.* 1960, when this end of the nave was partitioned off for a hall. Inside, clustered columns support the arch-braced nave roof and angels carved in wood and stone hover above the tall elaborate Caen stone **pulpit**. Original numbered **pews** with ornate crocketed finials and doors. Shallow N chancel, elaborated from the later C19, when the small congregation was led by the eminent Sir James Kitson, later first Lord Airedale (d.1911). **Reredos** with mosaics (Christ and the Prophets) by *Salviati, c.* 1884; the raised green marble flooring is of 1924, with inset memorial to the influential minister Charles Hargrove (d.1918). **Stained glass**: E wall, obscured by the s gallery stairs, a fine *Morris & Co.* window, 1875, in memory of Ann Kitson, mayoress: pelican in her piety and figures of Ruth, Martha and Mary Magdalen designed by *Morris*; Dorcas by *Ford Madox Brown*. Martha and Mary again in the next, by *Powell Bros*, 1876, then two by *Clayton & Bell c.* 1880. Chancel: Lord Airedale memorial window by *A.K. Nicholson* of London, 1912, with figures of Ralph Thoresby, Joseph Priestley and Kitson himself. w side. Scenes from the life of Christ by *Warrington* of London, 1848.

52. Mill Hill Unitarian Chapel, by Bowman & Crowther, 1847–8, and Priestley Hall, a school, by George Corson, 1858–9 (dem. 1968). Photograph late C19

The **Park Plaza Hotel** is a 2003 re-cladding of *Kitson, Pyman & Partners*' Exchange House, an office tower of 1965. Pevsner admired it for the curve of the podium into Boar Lane, which is answered on the s side of the road by the copper-domed rotunda of the stolid granite **Yorkshire District Bank** (now a bar), by *W.W. Gwyther*, 1899. Ten giant Corinthian attached columns and parapet embellished with statues and urns. Panels carved by *J. Thewlis*.

Dominant on the square's s side, the rather dull, stripped classical façade of the **Queen's Hotel** of 1937 by *W.H. Hamlyn*, architect to the London Midland & Scottish Railway. Ten storeys faced in white Portland stone, with brown brick sides and rear. Pedimented attic pavilions and a porte cochère carried on massive drum columns with the companies' heraldic shields. The principal rooms, and even some of the bedrooms, retain their original stylish Art Deco fittings, e.g. veneered doors, light fittings and lift, the work of the consultant architect, *W. Curtis Green*, who fitted out London's Dorchester Hotel in the early 1930s. On the w side, in similar style, a separate smaller block with an angled front to Aire Street for the Company's offices. It contains the entrance to the contemporary station concourse (*see* p. 125) and originally included a cinema (now nightclub). Finally, between Wellington Street and Quebec Street, *Pascal J. Stienlet*'s exuberant former **Majestic Cinema** (now Majestyk nightclub) dated 1921, constructed of glazed 'Marmo' (*see* topic box, p. 225), once gleaming white, now weathered to grey. Moulded decorative swags and panels depict musical instruments. Inside, a Greek-style frieze and coffered dome within the former auditorium.

Behind the Post Office lies **Infirmary Street**, laid out after 1805 as 'West Street' and originally open on its N side as far as South Parade. The Infirmary (*see* topic box, p. 84) on its SW side was replaced in 1893–4 by *G.B. Bulmer*'s Yorkshire Penny Bank (now **Yorkshire Bank**). Exuberant Baronial Gothic with five arcaded windows to the banking hall and an emphatic corner staircase-tower topped with gargoyles and slated spire. Good carved decoration on both façades of winged lions, badges of the countries of Great Britain and date plaques. Elaborate wrought-iron gates and railings with foliage motifs, by *George Wragge* of Manchester; exquisitely detailed lamps over the entrances. Inside, original panelled rooms and marble fireplaces, stained glass windows by *Powell Bros* of Leeds; marble and mosaic work by *Pattison & Sons* of Manchester. Bulmer added an extra bay for offices and dining room in 1904.

Turning the corner with **King Street** is **Goodbard House** (Allied Irish Bank) built as the 'Hotel de Ville' hotel, restaurant and offices in 1905. Edwardian Baroque, Peterhead granite on the ground floor, fine-grained local sandstone for delicately carved Art Nouveau details above. Central oriel window; the attic storey is of the 1980s when the ground-floor windows were infilled. Across King Street, on the S corner of St Paul's Street, an imposing example of the new building methods and materials of 1910: **Atlas House** [53], five-storey insurance offices by *Perkin & Bulmer* in Renaissance style. Built using the Kahn system of concrete framing and faced in dazzling white 'Marmo'. Confidently composed display of Renaissance trim with wide curving pilastered corner and ornate sculpture by *Thewlis & Co.* including Atlas struggling beneath the weight of the globe. Next on this side, at the entrance to Park Place, the rather overbearing former **Bank of England**, 1969–71 by *K. Appleby* of the *Building Design Partnership* (Manchester). An inverted ziggurat, its form perhaps influenced by Kallman, McKinnell & Knowles' Boston City Hall (1962–8) with each floor projecting out over the one below and strongly vertical window sections. Grey Cornish granite and bronze cladding. The finesse of the design is sadly compromised by a shot-blasted concrete deck, designed to receive an anticipated (but unexecuted) elevated walkway. The expensively fin-ished entrance hall had a sculpted ceiling by *Alan Boyson* and etched glass by *Warwick Hutton*.

Off the E side of King Street, **Quebec Street** begins with the bulky but impressive **Cloth Hall Court** of 1980–3 by *T.P. Bennett & Son*. Stone-clad, with C18 sympathies: shallow cambered arches to the ground floor. Facing is the **Leeds & County Liberal Club** (now a hotel) in exuberant red Ruabon terracotta, by *Chorley & Connon*, 1890. Eccentric Free Renaissance with Art Nouveau motifs to the elaborate iron gates. Splendid interior, including a sweeping staircase with lions supporting wrought-iron lamps on the balustrade and a stair window with stained glass badges of Yorkshire towns by *Powell Bros*.

53. Atlas House, King Street, by Perkin & Bulmer, 1910, sculpture by Thewlis & Co.

Further down **King Street** is *Connon, Chorley & Connon*'s **Hotel Metropole**, 1897–9 [54], in undisciplined French Loire taste. Red Ruabon terracotta, with writhing sculptural detail to a three-storey bowed centre with columns and canted oriels on giant, elongated consoles. Buff coursing higher up, drawing the eye to the stone cupola, retained from the White Cloth Hall of 1868 (*see* topic box, p. 104). Inside, giant columns and a cantilevered, bronze-panelled staircase evoke the extravagance of late Victorian Leeds.

Now w along **York Place** (originally Cobourg Place), which began as an open path between King and Queen Streets, across the gardens in front of the houses on Park Place to the N. Development at the w end of the street *c*. 1834–50 provided houses for wool merchants but major warehouses and offices encroached soon on both sides. Most impressive is No. 1 (Aintree House), on the s side, by *Stephen Smith*, *c*. 1870 for G.R. Portway & Co., woollen manufacturers of Swinnow Mill, Stanningley.

54. Hotel Metropole, King Street, by Connon, Chorley & Connon, 1897–9

Pevsner described it as 'the best of the functional warehouses' in the area. It has arched ground-floor windows and three upper storeys all linked by slender giant arcading. Heavy rustication to the basement piers and deep, bracketed eaves cornice. Smith was articled to William Hill and both were strongly influenced by Cuthbert Brodrick's confident style. **York Place Buildings** (Nos. 6–8) is a refronting of 1902 with brick pilasters and moulded terracotta architraves. Then, on the corner with Britannia Street, Nos. 11 and 12, a matching pair of three-storey red brick houses over basements. Steps up to panelled entrance doors with deep scrolled brackets supporting an entablature and cornice. Occupied by a 'woad grower' and a 'gentleman' by 1870 but in use as woollen warehouses by 1886. No. 21 is a wide five-bay house of some distinction, the entrance having heavy pilasters, entablature and cornice; round-arched stair window to rear. On the N side, the former Hepper & Sons' Horse & Carriage Repository (now car park) with an attractive frontage. No. 30

55. Nos. 17–19 Park Place, by William Hargrave, late C18

and Nos. 37–41 are two Gothic Revival warehouses of *c.* 1870. The latter (**Devonshire House** and **Lion House**) by *George Corson* is ornamented with sculpted lion, griffin and gargoyles.

In **Queen Street** on the w side **Prince William House**, *c.* 1982, faces down Park Place and occupies the site of Queen Street Chapel (1823–5). 'Leeds Look' (*see* topic box, p. 36) with some quality but rather out of scale, the fierce red brick and arcading suggesting the style of *Stephen Smith* seen earlier in York Place.

Now into **Park Place** and a good view of the houses built on the Park Estate from the 1770s. Only the N side was then developed, preserving fine views s over the Aire Valley. Two almost-symmetrical groups (a central three-storey pedimented house flanked by slightly lower neighbours) flank Central Street, each of local red brick with stone detailing. Pedimented doorcases, twelve-pane sashes and some original area railings with acorn finials. Nos. 5, 6 and 7, by *William Lindley* of Doncaster, were begun in 1777 for the banker John Arthington, who lived at No. 6.[*] It has stone architraves to the centre windows and an oculus in the pediment, but lost its ground floor in the mid 1960s when plate glass was inserted. Nos. 5 and 7 were completed by Arthington's widow;[†] their top floors have also been rebuilt, breaking the line of the sill band. The rest of Park Place's N side was built 1788–1800 to designs by *William Hargrave*, master carpenter; by 1872 Thomas Ambler had his office at

[*]It became the parish vicarage after 1825.
[†]Lindley's correspondence mentions a design for a curved vestibule 'for widow Arthington', a repeat of a design for Denton Park, near Otley.

No. 9. At the w end Nos. 17–19 [55], a highly impressive Adamesque composition with a dignified pedimented centre and giant Ionic plasters dividing it into 3–5–3 bays. The arcaded ground floor and doorcases have been carefully restored. No. 16 strikes a different chord: its wide round-arched entrance and ground floor are entirely covered in relief-patterned tiles, apparently to a modest design by *F. Mosley*, listed in J.C. Edwards of Ruabon's catalogue of 1900. The c18 garden plots of Park Place's s side were infilled with commercial buildings from the mid c19; most notably Nos. 42–46, Gothic Revival offices and warehousing by *George Corson,* 1870, including an arched goods entrance to the rear yard of his warehouse in York Place (q.v.).

Now **St Paul's Street**, parallel to the N. At the eastern end two brick and stone warehouses: Moorish Nos. 5 and 7, **Gresham House** (s side), of *c.* 1870; Gothic Nos. 14–16 on the E corner to Park Square. The street's w end is dominated by *Thomas Ambler's* **St Paul's House** [56], a 164 ft (50 metre) long, emphatically Hispano-Moorish factory and warehouse for the pioneering clothing manufacturer John Barran, 1878. Red and pink brick and Doulton's terracotta. Owen Jones' measured drawings of the decoration of the Alhambra published in 1842–6 were probably an inspiration. Ground-floor and mezzanine windows tied together by a giant segment-headed arch, first- and second-floor windows tied together by a giant trabeated frame. Then a small third floor with Moorish arches. Only the façade survived conversion to offices by *Booth Shaw & Partners* in 1975–6.* The 'truly Mohammedan cresting', as Pevsner described it, with pretty pierced parapet and cinquefoil openings is a reinstatement of the original, along with the four corner minaretlets, copied in fibreglass. The original spectacular tiled SE

*Pevsner performed the opening ceremony in July 1976.

56. St Paul's House, elevation to Park Square, by Thomas Ambler, 1878

corner entrance with cusped arch and paired columns has been reduced to a window, with a new entrance on Park Square. Reduced to fit this are ornate wrought-iron gates with ribbon-like scrolls and flowers by *Francis Skidmore*. Beyond it, on the corner with Park Square, **Park House**, functional, red brick with giant lesenes. Further w, on Little Queen Street, the **International Pool**, 1966 by *John Poulson* and the City Architect, *E.W. Stanley*. A symbol of sixties civic pride with a strong geometric silhouette, sadly under threat of demolition.

Park Square was laid out in 1788, with houses regarded at the time as 'not the equal of Park Place'. The rapid change from private houses to warehouses and offices in the C19 (many for legal firms, still in evidence in 2005) was followed by further alterations in the mid C20 but an increasing appreciation of the square's handsome qualities has seen the houses conserved and in use once more as residences. In the centre of the square are gardens with a bronze **statue** of Circe by *Alfred Drury*, 1894, the malign goddess shown the moment after transforming Odysseus' sailors into hogs. Moved here from the Art Gallery and now bereft of her wand, goblet and drapery.

Begin on the **w side** of the Square with Nos. 24–31, a row of modest three-storey houses, altered in the late C19 and C20 especially at the N end. Built by *John Cordingley*, carpenter, *c.* 1793–1806, with a varied show of doorcases and area railings with leaf, bud and spearhead finials. The fine interior of No. 26 has panelling, a fireplace with fluted Ionic columns, knopped staircase balusters and Adam-style plasterwork. Tuscan three-quarter stone columns outside No. 27. Behind No. 30 (No. 9 Somers Street) is a unique survival of the workshops and warehouses built behind most cloth merchants' houses in the late C18, this one probably *c.* 1793. Three storeys and five windows long, the top row has side-sliding sashes typical of the date. Cloth bought at the Cloth Halls was brought to these workshops to be checked, pressed and packaged for despatch. The offices and workshops of Powell Brothers, stained glass artists and church decorators, were at No. 30 in 1888. Three of the builders of the N **side** of the square from 1793 are known: *Thomas Johnson* designed Nos. 39 and 40, a three-storey, three-bay mirror-pair; stone console brackets support the entrance entablatures and there is a first-floor sill band [57]. In 1793 *John Cordingley* built the prestigious pedimented No. 42, of two storeys with panelled door and fanlight under an open pediment supported by three-quarter Tuscan columns. His carpentry skills are shown in the knopped column-on-vase balusters of the staircase. He sold it in 1799 for £1500. *William Hargrave* built two houses (Nos. 43–45), probably after 1800, the changing styles indicated by plain stone door surrounds, tripartite sash windows and a staircase with column newels and plain rail. In the centre, No. 41 is the grandest house, five bays wide, with Tuscan columns at the entrance and a pediment with oval window. It was built for Thomas Bolland, attorney and clerk. Nos. 36–38, built after 1815, have fine stone detailing:

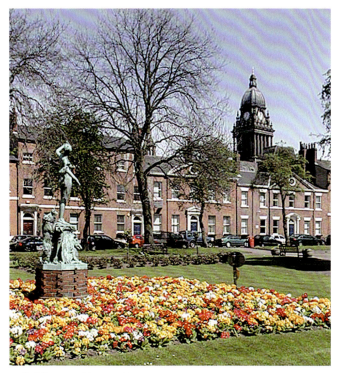

57. Park Square, N side, 1793–1815

stone parapet panels carved with festoons of drapery and flanking scrolls.

The E **side** of the square is the earliest, *c.* 1790. The most prominent house is No. 8, built by *William Hargrave* for William Wilson. Its centre projects very slightly and is pedimented, and the entrance has a carefully restored wooden doorcase with rusticated jambs and elaborate fluted columns supporting the open pediment. Pretty stucco ornamental festoon above the door. Vicarage Chambers (No. 9) was the vicarage to St Paul's, its terracotta façade added in 1908 following the demolition of the church.* The next three houses were built *c.* 1790 by *William Lawrance*, carpenter, joiner and architect. His lovely wood and plaster doorcases are particularly notable: fluted Corinthian columns at No. 10 and plaster lion and wreath at No. 11, the home of the engineer Peter Fairbairn in 1839.

*St Paul, which stood in the SE corner of the Square, was designed in 1791–3 by *William* or *Thomas Johnson*, and demolished 1905. Memorials were removed to Holy Trinity Boar Lane.

b) East Parade to Albion Street

The second walk explores the streets laid out closer to the town centre, where Victorian and Edwardian commercial pressures swept away the developments of the C18 and early C19. We begin at **East Parade**, laid out between 1779 and 1789 but now entirely of the C19 and C20. On NW corner with St Paul's Street, No. 1 **Zurich**, of 1992–4 by *William Gower & Partners*. Postmodern, but in the stripy C19 style of Waterhouse with small square windows and gables. Italianate offices at No. 9, for the County Fire and Provident Life Association, *c.* 1870, with a statue of Britannia and lion above the heavy modillion cornice. Next door **East Parade Chambers**, Free Renaissance-style offices for accountants, lawyers and assurance companies, 1899, in yellow faience with a shaped gable, slim buttresses and projecting timber oriels to the first floor. Beyond, is a 1980s rebuilding in facsimile of late C18 'wealthy Georgian brick houses' noted by Pevsner. They were the last of their kind here, although the wall and window sills of an C18 house are preserved in the basement of **Hepper House** (No. 17a) [58], rebuilt 1863 by *George Corson* as auction rooms for John Hepper. Venetian Gothic, an early example of the style in Leeds, in sandstone and Peterhead granite; Moorish terracotta tiles in the entrance lobby. The ground-floor windows were enlarged in 1911 by *William Bakewell* when his Pearl Assurance Buildings opposite (*see* p. 167) was found to have taken light. Two salerooms, both with coved ceilings and plain fire surrounds, are supported below on paired cast-iron columns. In the first-floor front office a marble fireplace.

58. Hepper House, East Parade, by George Corson, 1863. From *The Builder* (June 1863)

Now E to explore the parallel streets between East Parade and Park Row. In **South Parade**, E of Pearl Buildings, the former Legal and General Assurance Office, *c.* 1930–1 stripped classical by *Braithwaite & Jackman*, three storeys of Portland stone above a black granite base. (At the E end is the Branch Bank of England, *see* below). On the s side, No. 12, of *c.* 1900, substantial offices in ashlar with banded rustication. Columns support a segmental broken pediment above the entrance, and a wide hollow-chamfered window has a female mask on the keystone. Later upper storey. To the left the postwar **Friends Provident Building**, five storeys of clean white Portland stone, with an impressive entrance portal of columns *in antis* in a massive moulded surround with a carved plaque; stripped classical above.

Greek Street, s, was being developed in 1817 by Joseph Green of Bradford. The sole survivor is No. 7, a five-bay house, now restaurant and offices. Rendered brickwork and quoins with a central doorway with Ionic half-columns supporting a deep frieze and pediment. Between here and **Russell Street** is an innovative car park (an 'Auto-Silopark system') by *Maurice Sanders Associates*, 1968–70, for Leeds Corporation. Thirteen floors and two basements, of pre-cast concrete with vertical aluminium fins on each façade. Cars are left at the entrance to be elevated and 'pigeon-holed', making excellent use of space, a method first used in Japan. At the entrance to Russell Street, **Capitol House** of 1962–3 by *Kitson, Parish, Ledgard & Pyman* ('nothing special' said Pevsner), was the city's first tower block to be re-clad. Tucked behind, the pedestrianized **Bond Court** has a cheerful bronze group of 'Boules Players' by *Roger Burnett*, 2000. On Bond Court's s side a surprising survival, a prestigious early C19 house (Nos. 11–14), cement-rendered and lined to imitate ashlar, with continuous sill bands. Later C19 upper floor, the ground floor restored to look like a pair.

Park Row, the medieval N–S route between Park Lane (now The Headrow, *see* p. 166) and the manor house, was developed as the main thoroughfare of the C18 development. *Thomas Taylor*'s much admired Court House of 1811–13 stood at the s end but of this and the elegant Georgian houses erected in the 1770s there is no trace. These were replaced by the Victorian banks and offices celebrated by Atkinson Grimshaw in 1882 (*see* topic box, p. 23). In 1896 *The Builder* described it as 'the Pall-Mall of Leeds' and such is the street's continued commercial importance that all the buildings in Grimshaw's painting have been replaced and several others noted by Pevsner in 1959 have also gone. Notwithstanding, one may still experience the full flavour of commercial Leeds in Park Row alone.

Begin at the N end at The Headrow. On the w side is the former **Branch Bank of England** (Sovereign House) by *P.C.Hardwick*, 1862–4 [59]. Fine-grained Halifax sandstone on a base of massive Millstone Grit blocks. The entrance on South Parade has reveals of Peterhead granite, one of the first examples in the town. Symmetrical façades on three sides of three storeys beneath a balustraded parapet with urns.

59. Former Bank of England, Park Row, by P.C. Hardwick, 1862–4

Pedimented and segmental windows between channelled pilasters. Continuing on Park Row's w side the corners of the junctions with smaller streets invite dramatic display. First, the former Scottish Union & National Insurance Co. offices (**Royal Bank of Scotland**) of 1909 by *Perkin & Bulmer* in a lavish Baroque style. Four storeys and an attic with emphatic cornice and corner dome. The structure is a reinforced concrete frame, probably the earliest in the city, but clad in glazed 'Marmo' blocks (*see* topic box, p. 225). Excellent sculpture by *Thewlis & Co.* including allegorical figures and crouching females carrying the balconies. Next the former Bank of Liverpool & Martin's Bank of 1922–3 (now a pub). Portland Stone, rusticated and carved; plinth of rock-finished pale grey granite. Quoins extend the full height of the building, with vermiculated rustication. Then **Greek Street Chambers** of 1898 by *Alfred Waterhouse* for Williams, Brown & Company's Bank. Pink and grey granite ground floor, an odd match with red brick and Burmantofts buff faience above. Peterhead granite columns at the entrance. On the Bond Court corner **HSBC**, 1966–9 by *Whinney, Son & Austen Hall*, a box faced with granite and concrete, black igneous rock in the window bases. The site of the Philosophical Hall (*see* topic box, p. 119).

Returning to the N end E side, first Peacock's Buildings (*see* p. 167–8), next **St Andrews Chambers**, 1869 by *George Corson* for the Scottish Widows' Fund. Porch supported by four monolithic Peterhead granite pillars resting on blue-grey Aberdeen granite; Yorkshire sandstones carved with Scottish emblems on the first floor, revealed after recent

The *Leeds Intelligencer* reported in 1824: 'Scarcely a week elapses that we have not the pleasure to announce some project for improving and adorning the town'. Little, alas, of this period has survived the rebuildings of the C19 and C20. The following is a list of the major losses.

Court House and Prison, Park Row. 1811–13, by *Thomas Taylor*, his first important commission in Leeds after training in the office of James Wyatt. Nine-bay façade with dramatic prostyle Corinthian portico, and single-storey wings ornamented with carved stone plaques. Altered by *R.D. Chantrell* in 1834–5, demolished 1901.

Philosophical Hall, Park Row. 1819–22, by *R.D. Chantrell*, pupil of Sir John Soane. A modest classical building for members of the newly established Philosophical and Literary Society. Two storeys with façades to Park Row and Bond Street. Rusticated ground floor, paired and single pilasters on the upper floor.

South Market, Hunslet Lane. 1823–4, also by *Chantrell*. Its innovative design included a circular Doric 'temple' over the Butter Cross. Demolished after 1906.

Central Market, Duncan Street. 1824–7 by *Francis Goodwin*, who was then working on Manchester Town Hall (completed 1825). Handsome Neo-Grecian façade with Ionic columns *in antis* and blocking course surmounted by a small pediment. Inside was a covered market modelled on similar buildings in Liverpool and Manchester, with a large hall with rows of shops on three sides, mainly for butchers and fishmongers; fruit and vegetable stalls in the centre. Demolished after a fire in 1893.

Commercial Buildings, corner of Park Row and Boar Lane. 1826–9 won in competition by *John Clark* of Edinburgh; this was his first work in Leeds of a 'New Athenian' character. Giant Ionic columns *in antis* dominated its façade, topped by a deep cornice and blocking course with a crown-like cresting to a corner rotunda, beneath which was a circular vestibule where merchants met between 12 p.m. and 1 p.m. on business days to discuss commercial affairs. The building also contained a hotel, the Commercial News Room, refreshment and meeting rooms, offices for solicitors, brokers and the West Riding Insurance Company. Demolished 1872.

cleaning. Then *Alfred Waterhouse*'s striking Northern Renaissance former **Prudential Assurance Building** of 1890–4. Granite below, stripes of red brick and Burmantofts buff terracotta above, not popular with his clients who preferred their usual red. In the mid 1960s the roof was stripped above eaves level, including its gable dormers and corner spire, restored in 1989–90 by *Abbey Hanson Rowe*, who retained the façade for new offices, with good fresh terracotta work by *Shaw* of Darwen. Next, the small four-storey Free Baroque former **West Riding Union Bank** (No. 18), 1900 by *Oliver & Dodgshun* who had their offices here. A visual treat using a variety of stones and boasting some of the city's best sculpture. Ground floor of rich red Swedish granite carved with strapwork, and above this a full-width sculpted sandstone frieze signed by *Joseph Thewlis*, representing the bank's international trading interests. Minerva sits on an Art Nouveau throne flanked by figures representing shipping interests in Africa and American railroad investment. Over the entrances 'trade' and 'commerce' are personified by male and female figures (representing peace and justice, purity and plenty). They support coats of arms, and there are badges in cartouches between the first-floor windows. Fluted Corinthian pilasters rise to a heavy cornice. On the site of Corson's Sun Fire Offices is **Nos. 15–16 Park Row** of 1995, by *Carey Jones Architects*, a seven-storey planar glass frontage set between granite flanks – a rare and refreshing appearance of the High-Tech school in Leeds. The **National Westminster Bank** takes the corner with Bond Street, an unworthy successor to *George Gilbert Scott*'s renowned Beckett's Bank built in 1863–7 and demolished 1965 [11]. Nine storeys, stripped classical, of grey granite with dressings of ebony diorite. The two-storey entrance on Bond Street, with its giant pilasters and high pediment with the bank's badge, looks strangely detached.

s of Bond Street, on the E side, **Lloyds Bank**, 1972–7 by *Abbey Hanson Rowe*, is an impressive ten-storey block over shops and car park, clad in brown Finnish granite. The high-level entrance on the podium was part of the infamous late 1960s scheme for elevated walkways. On the base a sculpture in steel rods by *Peter Tysoe*, emblematic of the black horse rearing and apparently breaking free of its traces – a powerful symbol. Across the road, No. 35, on the corner with Bond Court, the palazzo-style former **York City & County Bank**, by *Smith & Tweedale*, 1892. Pedimented corner entrance with monolithic Peterhead granite columns; vermiculated rustication to ground floor, arcaded windows in the upper floor between attached pairs of Corinthian columns. The carved detail is by *J.W. Appleyard*. Finally, the smart Neo-Georgian Telephone Exchange by the *Office of Works*, 1939.

Now E along **Bond Street**, and on the s corner with Albion Street **Boots**, part of the major redevelopment in the 1970s for the Bond Street Shopping Centre (now Leeds Shopping Plaza, *see* p. 93). Vast reflecting panels and local Yorkshire sandstone cladding. **Albion Street**, a steep road linking Boar Lane and The Headrow, was developed in the 1790s by *Thomas Johnson*. Plots were offered for sale in 1792, intended for superior residences, not shops. Towering above is the overpowering landmark of **West Riding House**, 1970, by *Trevor Spence & Partners*, a sixteen-storey slab-on-a-podium with horizontal bands of glazing.

Commercial Street has early–mid C19 survivals at the w end, but E towards Briggate rebuilding was rapid from 1900. First, on the N corner, a glorious Venetian palazzo of 1852–5 by *W. Bruce Gingell* of Bristol, for the **Leeds & Yorkshire Fire Assurance Co.** This was one of the first purpose-built offices in the town, leading the way for the grand architecture seen in Park Row. Heavily vermiculated plinth with paired giant Corinthian three-quarter columns and entablature decorated with festoons and masks, all sumptuously carved. Next, Nos. 21–23, a mid-C19 shop and offices, ashlar, three storeys and classical, with wide three-light windows. The only major Georgian public building in the city centre is the refined Neo-Grecian **Leeds Library**. Founded in Kirkgate in 1768, now the oldest 'proprietary' subscription library in Britain and a remarkable survival, having expanded throughout the C19 without losing all its charm. The part facing the street is of 1808 by *Thomas Johnson*, of five bays and two and a half storeys with a rusticated ground floor containing shops under wide segment-headed arches; giant unfluted pilasters above. The original entrance in the left bay was moved to the centre in 1880–81 by *Thomas Ambler*, who created the present tiled hall and staircase. Johnson's first-floor reading room is at the front: E gallery with slender spiral staircase of 1821 (ironwork by *T. Nelson*); N and W galleries of 1836 by *R.D. Chantrell;* the W staircase a replica [60]. Parallel at the rear, Ambler's 'New Room' of 1881, with steel gallery of 1900 by *H.F. Chorley* with *George Corson*; scrolled ironwork by *James Allan & Son*. The early C19 scale continues opposite, where the corner building (Etam) appears to be *Thomas Taylor*'s **Union Bank** of 1812–13. Three storeys and five bays, with later parapet and urns.

Further E No. 31, on a narrow plot, rendered, four storeys with giant Doric corner pilasters; a furniture warehouse by 1831. Then plaster and stone refacings of *c.* 1925: the **Halifax Bank** with a shallow pediment and, on the corner, the elaborately swagged **Trinity House**. Opposite, a contrasting small three-storey shop (No. 14) of 1868 by *George Corson*, in his eclectic Gothic style with stepped gables. The ground floor originally had showy arched windows. Then eccentric striped red and white terracotta for the Leeds Goldsmiths' Company on the corner to Lands Lane, by *Thomas Winn*, 1901. Three storeys and attic, alive with dormers, pinnacles and a bold cylindrical turret. Inside is an elaborate balustered staircase lit by stained glass with abstract flower motifs. The E end of Commercial Street was extended to Briggate *c.* 1900. Of that date the corner buildings with Lands Lane (N) and Trinity Street (S), including 'Record Chambers' (S side) built for the Irish Linen Co. with curved plate-glass display windows on the upper floor. But this junction ('Central Square') has been the centre of too much attention, with improvements of 1991–2 by *FaulknerBrowns* introducing a mess of street furniture, including lamps and steel poles and wires.

Albion Place, parallel to the N, was extended to Briggate in 1903 and now provides one of the most attractive views in Leeds, eastwards across Briggate towards the City Markets. On the N side, No. 1, the **Leeds Law Society Offices** (since 1878) at the W end, was originally a house and consulting rooms built in 1795 by *Thomas Johnson* for the

surgeon William Hey who owned most of the land on Commercial and Bond Streets. Nine bays with five-bay pediment. Buff sandstone plinth and warm red brick above. Stone steps rise to an impressive entrance with Tuscan columns *in antis* and keyed arch over the fanlight. The **Leeds Club** was built in 1863 for the town's flourishing professional classes. Italianate and very grand. *Brodrick* was a member from 1853, was he the architect? Three storeys and seven windows wide, with moulded round arches to the ground floor. Porch with paired Ionic columns. Equally grand inside – original fine classical plaster decoration, big marble fireplaces, panelled doors, fluted Composite columns. On the ground floor a reception lounge and dining room; a wide staircase with ornate cast-iron balusters rises to the splendid meeting room lined with composite pilasters, ornate frieze and coved ceiling. Billiard room with raised seating. In the basement a much-admired later C19 cloakroom (marble sinks and stall dividers, mahogany doors, original fittings). Later C19 Italianate office block next door, No. 4, brick, Doric columns support a grand balustraded balcony over the porch. At the corner with Lands Lane is the former **Church Institute**. Polychrome gabled Gothic, in the style of *c.* 1300 but of 1866–8 by *Adams & Kelly*. It contained a lecture hall for 800, a library with 10,000 volumes and walls painted with frescoes of the saints. Converted to shops and offices by *Hadfield Cawkwell Davidson & Partners* in 1980 and given projecting Gothic display windows.

On the s side Nos. 19–23, returning westwards, were built as shops and offices in 1904. Three storeys and five bays, Free Style in brick and terracotta. No. 26 is one bay wide, early C20 terracotta again, probably an entrance bay to Joseph Longley's emporium at No. 6 Lands Lane. He was a bedding manufacturer and flock and feather merchant; his name is proudly displayed on the parapet. Across Lands Lane, the former **County and High Courts** of 1870, by the County Court Surveyor *T.C. Sorby*, built in two sections, of red brick with stone dressings. First, the two-storey, five-bay former County Court with Doric columns supporting an entablature to the entrances, on its right is the High Court of three storeys and three bays with a rusticated ashlar ground floor and heavy cornices. Heavy square-section area railings with strapwork panels to front. Finally, the **YMCA** by *W.H. Thorp* on the sw corner with Albion Street, 1900. Grand Baroque with swagged urns over the segmental-pedimented porch and a Venetian stair window to first floor.

60. Leeds Library, Commercial Street, by Thomas Johnson, 1808; reading room w staircase, by R.D.Chantrell, 1836, reinstated in replica 1990.

Walk 3.

Transport and Industry

The linked walks in this section explore the buildings on or near the banks of the Aire, and the evidence for Leeds' rapid development as a centre of machine manufacture, and textile and clothing production. Work to make the Aire and Calder rivers navigable (*see* topic box, p. 142) was completed in 1704 and the Town Warehouse E of Leeds Bridge was opened for goods from Hull, London, and the Continent. In 1770 a waterway link westwards 127 miles long, the Leeds–Liverpool Canal, was begun (*see* topic box, p. 128). Before its completion in 1816, the surrounding area had been transformed by diverse industrial enterprises, not only for innovative flax and woollen mills but also increasingly for associated engineering works necessary to develop the machines and steam engines to power the expanding textile industry. The small settlement around the Hol Beck on the s side of the canal was almost entirely built up with works by the mid C19. The railways arrived in the town centre in the 1840s: the Leeds & Bradford (later Midland) Railway's Wellington Station in 1846; and a second terminus to its w, Leeds Central Station, built by the Leeds & Thirsk Railway in 1849. Purpose-built warehouses and offices, of ever increasing bravura, now began to appear in the streets N of the stations.

The general affluence of late Victorian and Edwardian Leeds masked a decline in the older textile industries and waterborne trades but the more serious decline of the industrial riverside followed in the mid C20. By the 1980s, manufacturing along the riverside was redundant and the area in need of regeneration. The Leeds Development Corporation (1988–95) was given power over the riverside areas with the aim of integrating them into the city centre. Its principal preoccupation was the encouragement of development for business and residential use by relaxing planning restrictions in this zone. The intention was also expressed to promote more adventurous architecture, although the results are decidedly mixed. Access to the riverside was another intended improvement, not always successfully realized, and since 1995 increasingly compromised by developments for luxury flats. Only in the late 1990s did conservation of the important industrial enclave at Holbeck begin as part of a wider plan for the creation of Holbeck Urban Village. In 2005 work continues to create a new commercial and residential quarter on former industrial lands at Whitehall Quays.

61. City Station, concourse interior, by W.H. Hamlyn, 1938

Each of the walks can begin at **Leeds City Station**, outwardly a dreary 1967 rebuilding of New Station of 1869 by *Thomas Prosser*, architect to the North Eastern Railway. This had been opened as a through station on the line linking the NER with the London & North Western Railway and stood alongside the Midland Railway's Wellington Station. The two remained separate until 1938 when they were linked by a **concourse** at the rear of the London, Midland & Scottish Railway's* hotel and offices on City Square (*see* p. 108). This stylish Art Deco hall by *W.H. Hamlyn* is a worthy introduction to the visitor, coolly spacious with concrete arch crossframes dividing it vertically into bays with broad windows in the alternate bays of the upper parts of the s side and a top-lit coffered ceiling with pendant lights [61]. Original shopfronts, beautifully restored as part of refurbishment since 1999 by *Carey Jones Architects*. The roofs over the platforms were extensively rebuilt in 2001–3, by *Mackellar Architecture* to a scheme by *EGS Design Architects* of Manchester: High Tech, with monopitch roofs carried on tree-like trusses with clerestory lighting to the platforms. Platforms 1–3 are set lower than the rest, representing the level of the old Wellington Station.

a) The Leeds–Liverpool Canal and Holbeck

The E entrance to City Station was rebuilt in 1967 and lies below the contemporary thirteen-storey **City House**, a banal office slab with curtain walling and panels of brick infill by *John Poulson*. It bestrides both the station and Neville Street which is reached down steps within a rotunda. **Neville Street** was created as a route to the river in 1829; it

*The LMS absorbed the LNWR in 1923.

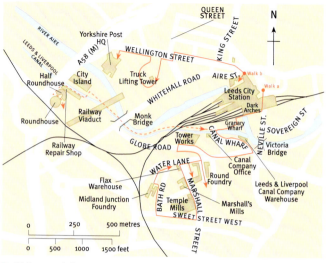

62. Walks 3a and 3b

passes under viaducts carrying New Station Street and the 1869 link to the North Eastern Railway's station at Marsh Lane. On the right a segmental arch with rusticated voussoirs forms the entrance to the well-named '**Dark Arches**' [8, 63], a line of mighty red brick groined vaults covering an access tunnel built beneath the railway and forming the sub-structure to New Station. *T.E. Harrison* was the Consulting Engineer, its construction supervised by *Robert Hodgson*. The richly atmospheric gloom is animated by the sounds and smells of the Aire which crosses the tunnel's w end and is spanned by a cast-iron bridge of *c.* 1900. From the bridge are sublime views upstream through tall arches faced with giant blocks of rock-faced gritstone; those lining the river bed are visible when the water is low. The river's turbulence is caused by a sharp turn s at the ancient weir or 'High Dam' (visible from Princes Square, *see* p. 134) where, in the medieval period, water was diverted E as a stream powering the manorial corn mill. The gritstone voussoirs of the 1846 viaduct for Wellington Station are just visible in the distance. Several of the vaults were rebuilt with blue engineering brick, *c.* 1900–4, replacing a temporary bridging following a fire in 1892 in the 16,000 tons of soap products stored here. w of the river, the vaults have been imaginatively refurbished as shop units.

s of the Dark Arches we emerge into daylight and onto the Leeds–Liverpool Canal Co.'s wharf, begun 1770, now known as **Granary Wharf**. On the canal's s side, close to the River Lock where it enters the Aire is the Canal Company's former **warehouse** (first used as a grain store), *c.* 1776, engineer *Robert Owen*, converted to offices in 1994–5 by

63. 'Dark Arches', view N along the Aire

Leeds–Liverpool Canal

While the Aire & Calder Navigation (*see* topic box, p. 142) provided trading links eastwards to Europe for Leeds merchants, by the later c18 a similar connection was sought with the expanding port of Liverpool, for access to the transatlantic market, and the cloth-producing areas of the West Riding. The Halifax engineer *John Longbotham* suggested the canal's route and became clerk of works and its chief engineer. An Act of Parliament in 1770 allowed the canal's promoters to sell £100 shares. In 1777 Leeds was linked to Gargrave by a 33 mile stretch following the Aire Valley, with a branch to Bradford. Nearly 25,000 people celebrated the opening of the Leeds terminus in that year. At the w end a stretch linked Liverpool to Wigan. Difficulties over the mountainous terrain (the canal climbs 411 ft (125.5 metres), and has 1¼ miles of tunnel) caused costly delays to building work, but construction was resumed in 1791 and it was completed in 1816, the longest single canal in Britain at 127 ½ miles. From the beginning the canal was used to carry limestone, iron ore and coal, providing raw materials for building, soil improvement and industrial processes. Leeds' expansion as an inland port resulted in its early c19 building boom. The Canal Company's Leeds warehouse became a vast grain store, providing basic food for the mill towns along the canal's route. The proprietors could not have foreseen the importance of the canal to the development of the cloth industry, as steam-powered mills were built along its course in the mid c19.

BDP. Four storeys, gritstone, truly Pennine vernacular – massive walls, a stone roof, small windows with flat-faced mullions and tiers of loading doors. Inside later c19 fire-proof construction of cast-iron columns and brick arches, contemporary with a low extension built over a dock. The basin was enlarged 1818–20 and the wide Canal Dock extended to the river in 1845 (when the railway was under construction). Boats were then able to reach Bean Ing and other mills further up river. The Canal Dock is now cut short and new brickwork blocks the arches (its lock is buried beneath the railway). The walk continues w to a **bridge** across the canal (here a detour can be made following the towpath on the N side, *see* p. 133). Its parapet is continuous with the modest **Canal Office**, dating from the alterations to the canal basin of 1846. Single storey over a deep basement, wide panelled entrance, sash windows with margin lights and a slate hipped roof; a panelled boardroom inside. Brick lock-keeper's house added after 1847.

The view sw takes in the memorable skyline of **Tower Works** [65] on **Globe Road**, which is reached via Water Lane. Founded by T.R. Harding to manufacture steel pins for carding and combing machines for the

64. Tower Works, Globe Road, engine house, portrait medallions by Alfred Drury, 1899

textile industry; the family's interest in bringing art and fine architecture to the workplace is manifested in this remarkable Italianate group. First the thirteen-bay **Entrance Range** by *Thomas Shaw*, built 1864–6. Polychrome brickwork and fine ashlar entrance with paired pilasters and a giant keystone. The panelled gates are ornamented with monogrammed ironwork. Slender ornate brick chimney, with a belfry stage, deep cornice and tall octagonal crown, inspired by the (much taller) c13 Lamberti bell tower in Verona. Harding's son, T.W. Harding, was Lord Mayor of Leeds in 1899 when he commissioned *William Bakewell* to design an extension to the works including the splendid **Engine House**. The gabled engine house exterior is unremarkable (apart from a weathered foundation stone), but the brown and cream tiled interior is a rare survival. Arcaded walls are decorated with ten plaster portrait medallions designed by *Alfred Drury* [64]. They celebrate inventors of textile machinery including Arkwright (spinning), Cartwright (combing) and Lister (owner of Manningham Mills, Bradford), as well as the Hardings, father and son. There is a remnant of mosaic floor. Its four-stage 'Big

Tower', incorporating a filter system to retrieve steel dust, is clearly inspired by Giotto's campanile for the Duomo in Florence. Polychrome brick and moulded terracotta embellished with gilded Burmantofts tiles on the 'belfry' stage and a cast-iron crown and pinnacle. The third tower, a chimney dating from the 1920s when the works was extensively rebuilt, is squat and plain Italianate in the manner of the defensive C13 towers of San Gimignano but with brick panels below the parapet. The business closed in 1979 and redevelopment of the site is planned in 2005.

Return to **Water Lane** (named after the Hol Beck which is visible in a deep cut running parallel with the street's N side). On the s side between David and Marshall streets is the **Round Foundry Media Centre**, which was the first major initiative in the revival of this area as Holbeck Urban Village. This is a refurbishment and conversion by *Building Design Partnership* in 2001–4 (masterplan by *Regan Miller Associates*) of late C18 to mid C19 domestic and industrial buildings associated with Matthew Murray's Round Foundry. Murray, a mechanic born in Newcastle upon Tyne, developed a flax-spinning machine for John Marshall (at Scotland Mill, Adel) in the 1780s, and went on to make his fortune here developing one of the first integrated engineering works, making structural ironwork, machines, tools and steam engines. From David Street w, first No. 97, a foundry of the 1850s with seven bays of tall round-arched windows like a chapel. A bronze plaque erected in 1929 records Murray's achievements. Next, the wide three-storey gable-end of Murray's **Greensand Foundry** of *c.* 1796. The windows are later insertions, as secrecy from competitors was important to his innovative mould-making process. Next to it a row of early C19 two-storey offices and storerooms with built-up entry far right, abutting the taller original **Dry Sand Foundry** (where casting was done), on the corner with Foundry Street. Natural light was evidently important here. One tall narrow arched window to the street (a two-storey addition conceals other features) and more to Foundry Street, where a wide archway allowed easy access. Inside a high and airy open space, thin brick walls on slight stone foundations buttressed internally. On the E side to the yard, an entrance of some pretension – attached stone Tuscan columns support a round brick arch flanked by blind arcades. On its s side, the now rendered three-storey **Fitting-up Shop** of 1795–1802 has loading doors and an inserted cart-way.

On the w side of **Foundry Street** a white-painted single-storey Italianate corner office built 1870 for Jonas Brown & Sons, joiners, their monogram over the corner entrance. Behind are joiners' workshops and storage rooms of 1797 and later, extensively rebuilt 1860–77 and again in 2001–2. Behind, in **Saw Mill Yard**, the N and s ranges of joiners' workshops have been successfully converted; an arcaded ground floor and, on one wall, the groove left by a steam-engine flywheel. New flats, steel-framed, with glazed and aluminium panels and cedar

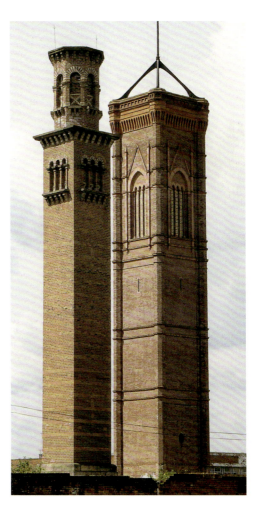

boards, blend well with the important survivals but apartment blocks between Saw Mill Yard and Marshall Street are bulky and poorly finished. At the s end of the site, conversion of the **Victoria Foundry** of 1863–82 has replicated its distinctive three-gabled NE façade and retained the steel structural frame. The famous Round Foundry burnt down in 1873; its site is marked by a circular inscription cast in steel enclosing a pavement of tumbled stone setts.

In **Marshall Street** to the w are the remains of **John Marshall's Mills**. He founded flax mills N of Hol Beck close to the canal in 1791, which were served by large reservoirs to the w. The C18 buildings have gone but a flax warehouse of 1806–8 survives at the N end of Marshall Street, now refurbished as offices. Plain local red bricks, with segmental-arched openings and a slate roof, stone window sills and blocks to strengthen the walling and support the floors. There is an original stone stair inside, part of fire-proofing measures which included cruciform cast-iron columns (made at Murray's foundry), iron floor beams and brick arches. Marshall's mills expanded s along his roadway and three wings of his massive U-plan brick **flax mill** remain. Five-storey N wing of 1817 distinguished by oculi and lunette windows and integral chimney in the road-side gable. Parallel s range built in 1827 and the linking 1830 block to the road, with distinctive inverted header arches below the lower windows and stone sill bands, both by *John Clark*.

Most remarkable of all are Marshall's Egyptian Revival **Temple Mills** [7], 1838–43, designed by *Joseph Bonomi Jun.*,* an Egyptologist and second curator of the Soane Museum; the painter David Roberts who travelled in Egypt and Syria in 1838–9 has sometimes been credited with influencing the design. The local engineer *James Combe* prepared the plans. Set back facing the street is the two-storey **office block** of 1840–3, its design based on the Temple of Antaeopolis recorded by Napoleon's Commission des Monuments d'Egypte, and the Temple of Horus at Edfu. Six beautiful lotus columns, and tall upper-floor sash windows comfortably recessed behind. The coarse gritstone is well suited to the battered walls and bold carving of snake motifs, hieroglyphs and winged solar discs. To the left, entered through a plain opening up a few steps is the vast **weaving shed** of 1838–40, top-lit and single-storey block over a basement, about two acres in extent; engine house on the N side. The inspiration for this form appears to have come from Paisley, where a Mr Smith had erected a similar building – until this date mills

*The oft-repeated attribution to Bonomi's brother Ignatius is erroneous.

66. Temple Mills, interior. Engraving from *The Penny Magazine*, 1843

were narrow and multi-storey, lit from side windows. The exterior is derived from the 'Typhonium' at Dendera, Egypt. Attached lotus columns along the battered walls and, on the flat roof, sixty-five conical glazed skylights – the roof was insulated with turf which was reputedly cropped by sheep. Inside, hollow cast-iron columns (acting as drain-pipes for the roof) imitate bundled lotus stalks. They support shallow groined brick vaults 21 ft (6.4 metres) high, pierced by circular openings through which light appears in shafts – an ingenious design in the spirit of Soane. The stone floor is carried on a brick vaulted basement, which originally contained the power transmission and ventilation systems for the complex flax-working process; a reversal of the usual overhead arrangement. There is also a tiny pylon-form gate lodge, but sadly the obelisk-chimney referred to by Pevsner has gone. Close by, a rare sur-vival, the two-storey former **Mill School** of *c*. 1830, rendered brick with a hipped roof, can be glimpsed from Union Place.

Returning to Water Lane, westwards lies the **L&NWR's viaduct** (1869), which was built over the Marshall Mills reservoirs and cut across **Silver Street** to the s, demolishing back-to-back houses. Here is another early industrial complex, the workshops of Joshua Wordsworth's **Midland Junction Foundry**, established 1793. Three-storey workshops and a small beam engine house of brick (with char-acteristic early stone strengtheners and round privy windows) flank a narrow cobbled yard, and there is a bridging range with cast-iron open-sided walkway and loading deck. Machines were made here for the linen textile industry. The foundry stood on the w edge of Marshall's vast reservoirs.

The walk returns to the far E end of Water Lane. For the riverside E, *see* p. 139.

Outliers

w of Granary Wharf along the canal towpath are several important survivors. Passing under the railway one emerges into a curve as the tow-path closely follows the s bank of the Aire, with views across to Whitehall Riverside (*see* p. 134). **Monk Bridge** by *Thomas Hewson*, engineer, 1886, carries Whitehall Road over river and canal. It replaced an unusual sus-pension bridge of 1827 by *George Leather Jun.* The main span is 108 ft (33 metres), of lattice girder construction with massive gritstone abutments. Further on, a 984 ft (300 metre) fragment of the impressive **railway viaduct** of 1846, serving the Leeds & Thirsk Railway's Central Station and Goods Depot (*see* p. 137), by the Scottish engineer *Thomas Grainger*. Massive gritstone ashlar blocks with chamfered rustication to voussoirs and keystones, one segmental arch over the Aire, another over canal and towpath, and about thirty more branching to the s. Parapet with vase-shaped balusters. In progress in 2004 **City Island**, between canal and river, by *Brewster Bye Architects* on the site of acres of railway sidings and coal depots. Two curved blocks with stepped rooflines.

The St Ann Ings canal lock makes it possible to cross s to explore three important railway survivals of the late 1840s by *Grainger* with *John Bourne*, resident engineer for the L&TR. Firstly, parallel to the canal, the **Railway Repair Shop**, an impressively long single-storey range of brick with stone dressings and tall round-arched windows separated by brick pilasters rising to an eaves band. Behind, the **Half Roundhouse**, transformed into commercial premises by *Jaques Associates*, 1998. A former heavy engineering repair shed, with pilasters outside and brick piers to support a travelling crane inside. Most impressive, and standing close to Grainger's viaduct, is the **Roundhouse**, designed for up to twenty locomotives. Single storey and really a polygon, a prestigious building of pressed brick with local stone dressings, and slate roof with a ridge louvre, open in the centre. The main entrance is on the E side, a tall elliptical arch with incised radiating voussoirs and a pediment above the cornice. Engines moved onto the turntable in the centre and were positioned onto radiating 'stabling roads' with pits below. Here the detour must return along the towpath to Granary Wharf.

b) North of the railway along Wellington Street

We begin outside the 1930s station concourse (*see* p. 125) in **Princes Square** which stands above the medieval High Dam. It has as its backdrop **Princes Exchange**, a highly successful design by *Carey Jones Architects*, 1999, on a triangular site [67]. Sharp, prow-like front with repetitive horizontal fins and glazed envelope extending over an open ground floor. Dramatically lit at night, a scheme by *Jonathan Wilson* of *Lighting Design Consultancy*. On the s side of the building, a view opens up along the N bank of the Aire. Lining the bank are developments associated with the creation of **Whitehall Riverside**, on former industrial land between the river and Whitehall Road. First to be completed was No. 1, Whitehall Road, offices by *Abbey Hanson Rowe* for Yorkshire Electricity, 1997, five storeys, clinical in white and green. The more recent phases are residential, including stylish riverside apartments completed 2004, by *Aedeas AHR*; up to fifteen storeys, brick cladding, aluminium and glass, with porthole windows and stepped roof-line. Further s more developments including Whitehall Quays by *Carey Jones Architects*, begun in 2004.

Wellington Street [68], N of Princes Square, is reached via Aire Street. The E end was built as Eye Bright Place, laid out *c.* 1809; represented on the N side by a small row of former houses. No. 38 was the West Riding Hotel by 1870, but its domestic Georgian proportions are just evident. No. 34, Queen's House was built *c.* 1870 for Mr Berry, a woollen merchant. Taller, of four storeys, with classical detailing and round-arched openings. Writhing Art Nouveau front railings, like seaweed. Opposite are Victorian warehouses, built close to the (demolished)

67. Princes Exchange, by Carey Jones Architects, 1999

68. Nos. 52–58 Wellington Street, warehouses of 1861–70

railway goods stations. Nos. 17 and 19 are by *George Corson*, 1859. The first (Churchill House) was built for Thomas Pawson, a woollen manufacturer who owned Stonebridge Mill, Wortley and the second has John Sykes and Son's initials over the door. Rusticated basement storeys and Moorish detailing to prominent central entrances; they originally extended further E. Then Nos. 21 and 23, an impressive six-storey brick-clad clothing factory and warehouse with full-height glazing to each floor, a rebuild of 1900 for R.B. Brown & Sons, wholesale clothiers. Built 'in the American system' i.e. steel-framed with open floors, fire-proof walls, and a water tank on the roof which fed a sprinkler system. It escaped the 'Great Fire of Leeds' in 1906, not so the much altered **Great Northern Hotel**, W of Thirsk Row, built in 1869 by the Sheffield architect *Matthew Ellison Hadfield* for the Great Northern Railway, close to Central Station. Its top three floors were destroyed in the fire. Now apartments. Opposite, at the King Street corner, **King's House** was one of *Corson*'s first warehouses, built for William Ledgard in 1861. Italian Gothic, the ground floor of rusticated ashlar masonry, and fine red brick with bands of blue, with a tower to King Street. Ornate extension of 1870 (Blemann House). Then No. 56, Gothic Revival of 1873 by *Henry Walker*: four bays of ashlar, the porch to the right carried up as a canted bay with turret and gargoyles. Gable filled with plate tracery and more stone beasts. It was built for the hide and leather manufacturer George Morrell whose tannery was in Armley. He specialized in kip butts (young animal hides trimmed square). Rooms for clerks and offices on the first floor, with basement and upper-floor stores for leather. *Edward*

Birchall lavished the most extravagant decoration on the façade of **Waterloo House** (No. 58, 1868), its seven bays and five storeys ornamented with stone banding and eccentric Gothic mouldings; pink granite columns support a heavy entrance porch and polychrome brickwork is used with abandon. Interior destroyed by fire in 1977. The owner was Walter Stead, a cloth manufacturer based at No. 60, one of a short row of plain mid-C19 shops and houses with tiny attic windows, which extends as far as the impressive and bulky *c*. 1840 woollen warehouse at No. 72. U-plan with wide central goods entrance on the side to Britannia Street. Heavy ashlar surround and shallow pediment, giant arcading. A good, though late, example of the 'Leeds Look' (*see* topic box, p. 36) at No. 76, **Springfield House**, 1998, six storeys in brick and stone. Strongly vertical. Also on the N side, on the corner to Queen Street, **Apsley House**, Crowe & Company's drapery and haberdashery warehouse, dated 1903, by *George Corson* and *W. Evan Jones* with *Perkin & Bulmer,* associate architects. Traditional warehouse composition with the usual elements of an ornate entrance, raised ground floor and elaborate railings. Steel-frame construction, clad in pink terracotta and red brick. Arched office windows and three storeys of large upper-floor windows, but here with slightly canted bays with ornamented panels between. Pilasters define the outer bays and are carried up to flat-topped Free Style finials. A final flowering of the city's great warehouses, and one of Corson's last projects (he died in 1910).

The S side of Wellington Street, W of Thirsk Row, was extensively redeveloped after 1970 following clearance of Central Station and twenty acres of former railway goods yards, warehouses and industrial buildings. Earliest was the former **Royal Mail Sorting Office**, on the site of the station, a Brutalist colossus, reinvented in 2004–5 by *Carey Jones Architects* for retail and leisure facilities and apartments, the tower of the old building transformed with terracotta and aluminium cladding and a glazed access shaft. To its SW, beyond Northern Street, is the **Aireside Centre** of 1983 by *D.Y. Davies Associates*. Single-storey steel-clad with brightly coloured trim. In its midst is a **Truck Lifting Tower** of 1846. Originally one of a pair built to move goods between the railway viaduct and the Leeds & Thirsk Railway's depot. Probably by *Thomas Grainger* who built the viaduct over the canal and river to the S (*see* p. 133). Snecked dressed gritstone with rusticated ashlar dressings, ornamented with string course and cornice, about 10 metres (32 ft) high overall, the lower stage arched, with the scars of the demolished viaduct on the S side.

Wellington Street's W end is dominated by several examples of the 'Leeds Look' with every effort made to give fine brickwork, slate roofs, deep eaves and pediments a modern look in the 1990s. An exception is the **Westgate Centre** (N side) by *Thompson Spencer Partnership* for British Telecom, 1985. Strongly massed separate office and car park in red brick blocks up to thirteen storeys high with chamfered corners and deep concrete bands at second-floor and roof level. At ground floor

Gott's Bean Ing Mills

In 1791 Benjamin Gott employed *John Sutcliffe* of Halifax (a millwright specializing in setting up industrial buildings and machinery), for seven weeks to draw up the plans for a new type of woollen mill. The site was to be isolated, on the N side of the river below the new Park Estate, in fields known as 'Bean Ing'. Gott called it Park Mills. All the production processes were to be completed by hired hands within its confines – the earliest proper factory in Leeds. In 1792–3 the first brick section with timber floors, for steam-powered wool scribbling, carding and fulling, was completed by the surveyor *John Moxson Jun.* Other buildings were for hand spinning, weaving, dyewood grinding and cloth finishing. By 1794 the long entrance range, four storeys high and 300 ft (91.5 metres) long, was built facing onto a trackway. This was later laid out as Wellington Street in 1817, with a bridge crossing the Aire designed by *John Rennie.* A fire in 1799 resulted in some rebuilding 1801–2, with experiments in fire-proof construction. By 1806 weaving shops, dye-houses and storage and finishing buildings were grouped around the main steam-powered multi-storeyed mill. *Boulton & Watt* provided designs for innovative gas lighting installations in 1806 and 1810, supplied by a gas-holder. The heated cloth dryhouse of 1814 was probably the first in Yorkshire. The engineer *William Fairbairn* designed ranges framed in cast iron in 1824–9, with entrance arch and bell cupola. By 1830 the site housed powered spinning and weaving, offices and a large warehouse. The mills were demolished in the early 1960s.

octagonal pillars rise through two storeys. At the far end of the street, against the elevated Inner Ring Road and a good neighbour for it, is the headquarters of the **Yorkshire Post Newspapers**. Built on the site of the great Bean Ing Mills and an impressive industrial structure in its own right. 1968–70 by the *John Madin Design Group*, designers of the Birmingham Post and Mail building of 1965. There, as here, the functional requirements for fully integrated newspaper production resulted in a composition of elements of different size and form, but availability of space permitted a horizontal layout. Mostly built in reinforced concrete with exposed Dorset shingle aggregate finish. The public entrance is a polygonal double-height transparent space with top-lit library in the storey above. Opening from the entrance foyer is the advertising hall; once a streamlined, airy space now compromised by alteration to floor and ceiling heights. Rising above this section a tall slab for offices, overlooking a roof garden. Finally, at the rear the Press Hall, 108 ft (33 metres) long and 34 ft (10.4 metres) high, of steel-frame construction designed for later expansion. A thrillingly busy interior, ably adapted to modern technology.

c) Victoria Bridge to Clarence Dock

s of City Station, Neville Street crosses the Aire at **Victoria Bridge**, built 1837–9 by *George Leather Jun.*, replacing an earlier footbridge with a graceful rusticated elliptical arch with Greek motifs. E of the bridge is a path along the river's s bank lined by the tedious, long low three-storey brick range of the **Asda Headquarters**, 1988 by *John Brunton Partnership:* one of the first commercial developments in this run-down area. Quasi-traditional, with an unnerving variety of window forms including canted oriels rising to gablets and a clerestory under deep eaves.

On the opposite bank, set above C18 and C19 stone retaining walls are a well-balanced group of late C20 offices, passably in a warehouse style, with their frontages to Sovereign Street. The most prominent building however is the gabled **Victoria Mills** [70], towering five storeys over the water with its 1836 datestone flanked by smart scrolled kneelers. New developments E towards Leeds Bridge include **Sovereign House**, luxury offices of the late 1990s by *Carey Jones Architects*. A confidently modern style. Sheer curtain walling and structural steel for the central glazed atrium but warehouse-style paired brick gables in brick with heavy stone detailing. Nearer Leeds Bridge **The Quays**, nine-storey apartments by the same architect, 2004–5. A rigid C21 design with brick cladding and stacked corner balconies, the canted façade unsympathetic to the river's gentle curve.

Water Lane E of Asda has a rare patch of undeveloped ground with a solitary stone warehouse entrance arch, contemporary with the converted early C19 four-storey warehouse at No. 2. Ashlar below and brick above, with tiers of loading doors. On the right the **Old Red Lion** retains its early C19 character – a corner block with symmetrical façade, leaded glass and blind windows and a relaxed stone lion above the entrance. Shops with chambers over follow on the left; 1870s in *Thomas Ambler*'s Italianate style. We are now at 'Bridge End', an area sadly blighted by traffic as five routes converge, creating a series of triangular

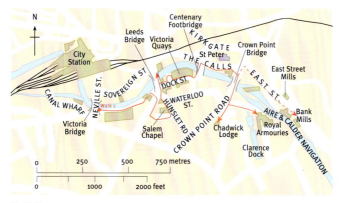

69. Walk 3c

70. Victoria Mills, 1836, and late C20 warehouse-style infill

sites. On the old **Hunslet Road** (s) stands **Bridge House**, *c.* 1875, a five-storey flat-iron-shaped landmark ornamented with Corinthian pilasters at the entrances, moulded brickwork and ashlar detailing. Behind, the former **Salem Congregational Chapel** opened in 1791. Squared gritstone, the original round-headed windows visible on the N and s sides. Its pediment was taken down in 1901 and the chapel extended with an elliptical entrance front and parapet with carved wreath. The chapel was supported in the C19 by an influential congregation of business and professional families. On both sides of Hunslet Lane to the s is the extensive **Tetley's Brewery**, founded in 1822. Major new buildings on this site of 1864–72 by *George Corson*, now replaced. Tetley's became a limited company in 1897, the date of the flagship **Adelphi** pub at the s corner of Dock Street; flamboyant Jacobethan by *Thomas Winn*. Three storeys with an attic behind the parapet. Polished granite for the ground floor, red brick and ashlar detailing above; palatial interior with tiled floors, mahogany and etched glass doors, tiling, overmantels and original furnishings. To its right is a three-storey brick and moulded terracotta Italianate commercial building of the 1860s exhibiting a fantastic variety of keystones with heads – twenty-two in all.

Return to the river now, passing Nos. 17 and 19 **Bridge End** which escaped the bridge's rebuilding in 1870–3. A substantial early C18 house

71. Dock Street, N side, early C19

and warehouse, brick with stone quoins, three storeys to the road, five to the river.* Leeds Bridge (*see* p. 90) marked the w end of the Aire & Calder Navigation, opened in 1700 (*see* topic box, p. 142). Visible downstream on the N bank are the massive rusticated tall arches of the **Navigation Warehouse** of 1827, shown in Atkinson Grimshaw's painting of 1880 [44]. The upper storeys are a rebuild following a fire in the mid 1960s, and echo the original two-gabled form. Its predecessor, shown on Cossins' map of *c.* 1726, gave its name to **Warehouse Hill** to the E, originally a narrow stretch of moorings cut off by an ancient mill race on its N side. It was packed with buildings by 1725 and part was known as 'Low Holland', a reference to Dutch trade. Set back are C19 warehouses on The Calls (*see* p. 103).

Now back to **Dock Street**. The N side of this most interesting street was occupied by the Navigation's early C19 wharf, now absorbed within housing developments. First on the N corner are the prestigious but uninspired **Navigation Offices** of 1906. Stone, free classical; refurbished as part of an extensive scheme of 2003–4 by *Carey Jones Architects*, who also converted a group of early C19 warehouses facing the river. Flats (No. 1 Dock Street) with exposed steel beams and ashlar cladding with

---

*Louis Le Prince made some of the world's earliest moving pictures when he filmed traffic on Leeds Bridge from its upper window in 1888.

Aire & Calder Navigation

Leeds became an inland port with completion in 1704 of the Aire & Calder Navigation, financed mainly by Leeds and Wakefield merchants. Previously unnavigable sections of the two rivers were cut or bypassed to allow large boats to reach Leeds directly from Hull (the first terminus was at Rawcliffe). Wool and corn were brought in, much of it from Lincolnshire and East Anglia; coal, flax and hemp were imported later. In 1744 the E terminus was moved to Airmyn, nearer the junction of the Aire and Ouse, and between 1712 and 1771 traffic increased seven-fold. In 1778–85 major improvements were made on the Aire for a canal to take large craft between Bank Dole and Selby, which now became the principal eastern terminus. The engineer was *William Jessop*, acting under the direction of *John Smeaton*. Wharfs and a dock basin were built at Leeds in the early C19 following the opening of the Leeds–Liverpool Canal, which provided a link upstream of Leeds Bridge as far the west coast. The increase in traffic was further enhanced by the cutting of a new canal between Knottingley and the Navigation's major new docks at Goole (completed 1826), designed by *George Leather Jun.*, who made improvements at Leeds including the Clarence Dock in 1840–3.

corner balconies on a rusticated stone plinth of undersized blocks. Navigation Walk leads into **Victoria Quays**. 1985–88 by *Downes Illingworth & Partners* for Barratts Urban Renewal Ltd, completed as the LDC (1987–95) took over development controls. Its centrepiece is the narrow preserved **basin** of 1818 by *Thomas Wood*, engineer and on its N side, the stately red brick **Flyboat Warehouse** of *c.* 1825 which extended over the edge of the dock with a large arched opening at water level. Two and three storey new build to the N, also brick. A vast timber shed originally spanned the W end of the basin but was lost in the redevelopment. Two of its roof trusses were salvaged and now bridge the water.

On the S side of **Dock Street** some fragments survive from the early years of the Navigation, including a row of small three-storey mid-C18 merchant houses and warehouses. At the E end No. 16, rendered brick with long and short stone quoins defining the entrance bay, stone plinth and key blocks, the right bay rebuilt. Much altered but a remarkable survival, now solicitors' offices. Further down, excellent warehouse conversions and impressive infill at No. 24 by *Carey Jones Architects*, of 1999. A showroom on the ground floor, steel and glass projecting angled front, balconies above. Then **Dock Street Workshops** [71], a row

*Louis Le Prince made possibly the world's first moving pictures when he filmed traffic on Leeds Bridge from its upper window in 1888.

of early C19 brick houses (Nos. 30–38) with round-arched doorways and entries, and small-pane sashes. Restored in 1986. Opposite, looming over the street, the front wall of the Navigation's mid-C19 former warehouse with four deep gables [71]. Massive stone detailing, quoins, brackets, loading platforms and two arched entries.

Tetley's Brewery Wharf at Dock Street's E end is a major residential development by *DLA Architecture.* It incorporates a three-storey glazed rotunda, designed as the brewery's exhibition centre in 1993 by *Carey Jones Architects* – now a restaurant. The **Centenary Footbridge**, a cable-stayed design of 1992–3 by *Ove Arup & Partners* for the Leeds Development Corporation, crosses the river and gives an excellent view along the N bank upstream. For these buildings *see* p. 103. Overlooking the river is the **Design Innovation Centre** (No. 46 The Calls), conversion of a grain and flour warehouse by *Allen Tod Architects*, 1988, with striking projecting gabled sections of timber, steel and glass above the river, in the style of loading bays.

Continuing across the bridge to **The Calls**, a narrow road which, like Dock Street, reflects the character of the C18 and C19 riverside (*see* p. 103 for its W end). From Kirk Ings Yard is a fine view of the Parish Church (*see* p. 43), and at the E end, **Chandler's Court**, housing of 1987 by *Denison Peters Ltd* which includes the conversion of William Turton's horse feed premises and stables of 1876. Four storeys, Italianate, with a round arch to the corner pedestrian entrance and a keystone with a horse's head above the wide yard entrance. A slender tower in the yard overlooks the river, a useful vantage point. Turton's business was founded in 1844, when horses were used to pull barges, and flourished as they continued to transport goods between the river and the railway termini.

Now to **Crown Point Bridge** built 1840–2 to designs by the Bradford engineer *George Leather Jun.* A Gothic-style cast-iron single-span arch with lattice steelwork in the spandrels, made at the Park Iron Works in Sheffield. There are quatrefoil panels in the stone abutments, and an ornate herringbone motif to the railed parapet. Widened and reconstructed 1994. Just below the bridge is **Leeds Dam**, a weir first documented in 1636, the tail race creating Fearn's Island on the N bank. Cross the bridge to the Navigation's **cut and locks**; first made in 1699–1700 to bypass the weir. The weir and cut were rebuilt *c.* 1835 by *Leather* who had completed the canal between the Aire at Knottingley and the new docks at Goole. The increase in traffic and the threat of competition from the railways must have driven the decision to build the large 'New' or **Clarence Dock** in 1840–3 which opens onto the river from the S bank through a lock. A rectangular basin (about 100 by 50 metres) with stone quay walls; extended in the later C19. The LDC hoped to encourage redevelopment of the dock's environs by launching a competition for a masterplan (won by *Browne Smith Baker*) and securing **The Royal Armouries** as a tourist attraction. 1995–6 by *Derek Walker Associates* [72], designed to house the collections previously displayed at the

72. The Royal Armouries, by Derek Walker Associates, 1995–6; Clarence Dock, by George Leather Jun., 1840–3

Tower of London. Fortress-like, of four windowless storeys of banded gunmetal-coloured brick, and a tall glazed octagonal staircase-tower hung with an exciting display of weaponry inside. Entrance on the s side, leading into a central top-lit street with double-height galleries on each side opening to exhibition spaces. The dock remained awkwardly inaccessible from the city centre for the non-motorist and early development was characterized by the village of early 1990s yellow and red brick student residences by *Carey Jones Architects*; since 2002 these have been followed by the same firm's luxury mixed-use development, for Crosby Homes.

A little further along **Crown Point Road**, at its junction with Black Bull Street, is **Chadwick Lodge**, built between 1779 and 1790 in open fields by John Chadwick whose dyeworks were on the river bank. Neat Millstone Grit façade, almost square in plan, five bays wide to the s with a moulded pediment over the central three, now cramped on a busy corner. The tour can now return to Leeds Bridge via Bowman Lane and Tetley's Brewery.

73. Bank Mills, 1824–88; w range (left) by John Clark, 1831–2; e range 1856

Outliers

The following buildings can form an extra walk beyond Crown Point Bridge on the N bank. **East Street Mills**: an L-plan flax (later woollen) mill of *c.* 1825 for Moses Atkinson, flax spinner, extended in the mid C19 to enclose a central yard. An excellent and now rare example of an unadorned brick mill complex. Even the chimney survives. The earliest block, to the right of the entrance and with five windows to the street, has cruciform iron columns inside. **Bank Mills** [73] were built further E on the N bank of the river by Hives and Atkinson, to process flax. Part was converted to offices, **Rose Wharf**, by *Carey Jones Architects* in 1997. The group is best seen from Clarence Dock on the s side. Four massive blocks of unusual height, up to six storeys. Three were designed by *John Clark* between 1824 and 1833. The part to the w is of 21 bays with a taller semicircular stair-tower. A four-storey, nine-window extension with rounded corners and dentilled eaves was built over the Lady Beck mill race in 1856. Roberts Mart & Co. bought the site for papermaking and printing in 1882 and added another five-storey wing in 1888. A new foot-bridge is planned in 2005 to link with Clarence Dock.

Walk 4.

The Civic Quarter

By the mid C19 the area N of Park Lane was still largely undeveloped except for isolated C18 villas and later terraces in the area of Little Woodhouse (*see* p. 188), served from 1838 by the church of St George. The decision to erect the Town Hall (*see* p. 60) transformed the area's identity and fostered the beginnings of a civic centre for the municipality which has been enhanced ever since. Major public and civic building proceeded with *Brodrick*'s Mechanics' Institute in Cookridge Street, followed in the 1870s by new Municipal Buildings, Library and offices for the School Board (*see* p. 74). Cookridge Street was extended N to Woodhouse Lane in 1861; Great George Street and Oxford Row were entirely built up by 1866 and by the early 1900s the area behind the Mechanics' Institution, between Cookridge Street and Woodhouse Lane, was occupied by other major educational establishments. Between 1899 and 1904 the R.C. church of St Anne on Park Lane was demolished for the widening of Cookridge Street and rebuilt on the corner of Great George Street (*see* p. 54). Part of the N side of Great George Street was cleared in 1932 to provide a large public space between the Town Hall and the new Civic Hall for the Mayor and City

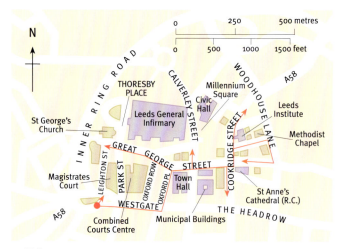

74. Walk 4

Council. The most recent additions have been new Court buildings along Westgate close to Park Square, the historic haunt of Leeds' lawyers. The close proximity of these major buildings has created a distinctive quarter, evocative of the dignified public realm of the C19 and C20; now greatly enhanced by the redevelopment of Millennium Square as an arena for public spectacle.

The walk begins in **Westgate**, w of the Town Hall, originally Park Lane, widened in the 1930s as part of the scheme for The Headrow (*see* p. 168). The backs of C18 houses in Park Square (*see* p. 114), line part of the s side, but the rest was extensively redeveloped in the later C20. Terminating the view w, **Westgate Point** typifies the 'Leeds Look' (*see* topic box, p. 36) of the 1980s. By *David Lyons & Associates*, 1987 [20], six and eight storeys in red and yellow brick with a cranked plan, deep eaves and stepped stair windows but weak for its landmark site. Visible across the submerged Ring Road is No. 1 **Park Lane**, a slick, glass office block, completed 2003 by *Carey Jones Architects*; and, to the n of Westgate Point, on **Leighton Street**, the eight-storey **Nuffield Hospital**, also by *Carey Jones* of 2002, with discreet brick cladding to the main road. Back along the n side of **Westgate**, three parallel streets link n to Great George Street – each begins with a strong corner building. First, at the corner with Park Street, the Postmodern **Leeds Magistrates' Court** by *R. Cornfield* & *J. Lindley* of the *Leeds Design Consultancy*, 1994. Curved front, highly coloured in pale buff brick with long flanks in red and blue. Central entrance with squat pedimented porch, columns *in antis*, coat of arms. At the flanks, projecting gabled pavilions step up and back. Successful interior with a dramatic curved cantilevered staircase. High up are *Coade* stone plaques from *Thomas Taylor*'s Park Row Court House of 1811–13 (dem. 1901). Luminous, narrow central atrium with plain columns, the terrazzo flooring carried up to form the bases, and sparkling gold-flecked walls. Similarly well-lit separate circulation areas for magistrates, prisoners and the public. Five floors of courtrooms, furnished in a different wood at each level, progressively lighter in tone from ground floor to top. Amusing owl motifs carved throughout.

Between Park Street and Oxford Row stands the **Combined Courts Centre** by *S. Spielrein* of the *Property Services Agency*, 1977–80, espousing an earlier, different approach to court design and clearly intended to defer to its C19 neighbours; it is kept low, just two storeys high with a defiant battered plinth and sheer walls of hard red brick with restrained diaper decoration and vertical openings. Concentrically planned with a top-lit public hall surrounded by courtrooms and an outer ring of offices. The Oxford Row entrance was remodelled in 2000 when a giant stone cube carved with the royal arms was re-set on a high plinth and an access ramp installed.

Between here and the Town Hall is the **Oxford Place Methodist Church**. The simple Oxford Row façade with round-headed windows

75. Oxford Place Methodist Church, by G.F. Danby & W.H. Thorp, 1896–1903

is *James Simpson*'s original chapel of 1835, which was remodelled to face the Town Hall in 1896–1903 by *G.F. Danby & W.H. Thorp* [75] in what Pevsner called 'Baroque taste with gusto'. Local red pressed brick with stripy Morley Moor sandstone dressings, a symmetrical two-storey façade with Ionic columns and obelisk finials. Gabled and pedimented centre with domed cupolas over the outer bays. Linking this to the contemporary, and matching, **Oxford Chambers** is a mighty tower, with a balustraded top stage and tall, stone cupola.

Further up **Oxford Place** is **Britannia Buildings**, probably contemporary with the development of this area after 1866. Three-storey brick offices in delightful Gothic Revival style with ornate stone arched entrance, slender columns with foliate capitals and quatrefoils. Probably designed by *Charles Fowler*, architect, surveyor and mapmaker who was practising here in 1867. Elaborate Gothic Revival shops of the 1870s (Nos. 35–41) and offices of similar date follow in a steady rhythm up to a turreted corner in Great George Street. The style strongly suggests *Ambler*'s hand.

The N side of **Great George Street** is dominated by *Scott*'s **General Infirmary** and its associated buildings (*see* p. 83), including the Old Medical School set uphill to the w. To its NW lay the Mount Pleasant estate of Christopher Beckett who provided land for the building of **St George's Church**. Austere Gothic by *John Clark*, 1836–8, on an impressive terraced site bounded by high railings. Tall lancet windows and a squat w tower, originally crowned with two tiers of crocketed pinnacles and a tall spire (removed 1962; reinstated 2006). E apse and vestry by *Henry Walker* added 1898–1900. The Long Room was added to the N side in 1974. The nave is very wide, aisleless, originally with galleries on three sides. Queenpost roof supported on deep brackets and moulded corbels. Reordering in 1962 included glazed screening for a narthex below the w gallery. The N and s galleries were removed in 1989–91 when the pews were discarded and fussy tiered seating installed by *James Thorp & Partners*. At the E end Henry Walker's chancel arch, shallow apse and vestry. Altarpiece **painting** of 1841 by *C. W. Cope*, commissioned by the mill owner John Atkinson for the original sanctuary, illustrating the text from St Paul's letter to the Hebrews: '. . . He ever liveth to make intercession for them'. At the foot of the cross suffering figures are directed to the ascended Christ by the raised eyes of Mary and St Paul's pointing finger. **Stained glass**. In the chancel apse two groups: SS Matthew, George and Mark, and SS Luke, Philip and John, by *William Pape*, for the centenary in 1938. In the nave N wall the upper part of 'Suffer Little Children' by *Powell Bros*, and on the E wall either side of the chancel, two with medallions of the Crucifixion and Resurrection, 1861. These echo the s nave window, the Baptism of Christ and The Sower, a memorial to Christopher Beckett (d.1855). A cleverly integrated central panel (inserted when the gallery was removed) depicts new growth. At the base of the tower a glazed panel with St Francis and a beggar commemorates the Rev. Don Robins (1900–48), who cleared and converted the crypt as a shelter for the unemployed. The crypt was designed by Clark for 700 bodies (only 300 places had been used when it was closed in 1855).* A major refurbishment in 1999, by *Mark Tabert* provided new stairs and bedrooms, both welcoming and functional. Near the w entrance, the mellow **Crypt Chapel** completed in 2003 – bare stone walls with a glowing brick vault above and, like icons on patches of old plaster, portraits of staff and clients by *Steve Simpson* on the theme of the Last Supper. NW additions for a church centre with housing of 2005, a careful scheme with stepped profile by *AXIS Architecture*.

On the s side of Great George Street, the bulky former **Centaur Clothing Factory**, 1889, by *E.J. Dodgshun* for R. Eastwood. Six storeys of red brick, eclectic in style, with a rounded corner crowned by a conoid roof and Dutch gables to the attic. An elaborate corner entrance with fluted columns and wrought ironwork. E of this, the s side is lined with modest houses, shops and offices of the mid C19. On the N side facing the back of the Town Hall, Nos. 24–28, an eclectic group of 1865 beginning with the **Victoria Hotel**, built to serve those attending the Assize Courts. Seven bays, symmetrical, Italianate Gothic marble columns with foliate capitals to the first floor and entrance [76]; the interior panelling, tiles and etched glass, probably dating from Tetley's purchase in 1916, are much admired but not all original. Next to it No. 26, by *George Corson* for Edmund and Joseph Wormald, photographers. Only one bay wide but designed to be noticed: its limited brick frontage elaborated with an arcaded entrance with cusped heads, moulded stone

*He also designed the General Cemetery, 1835, *see* p. 183.

76. Victoria Hotel, Great George Street; No. 26 (right), by George Corson, 1865

cornices and sill bands and canted first-floor oriel. Italianate brick cor-
belling and a truncated pyramid roof with gabled dormer and fleur-
de-lys finials. Small light well on the w side and considerable roof glazing. Next the two-storey ashlar former **Masonic Hall** by *Perkin & Sons*
(now a pub). An odd assemblage of Gothic motifs: gabled entrance to
the right and cusped arches with pilaster shafts to the first floor;
masonic emblems are carved in quatrefoil panels between the windows.
Corbelled cornice with trefoil openings in the parapet and a wide
stepped gable decorated with the six-pointed star and crocketed finials.
Inside, vaulted first-floor hall.

Great George Street's N side now opens to **Millennium Square** [77].
Created in 1999–2000 by the Civic Architect, *John Thorp* from the dull
wedge-shaped gardens laid out in 1933 as a setting for the Civic Hall (*see*

p. 80) and by closing Portland Crescent to extend the square E to Cookridge Street with a view to the Leeds Institute (*see* p. 72). The s part is **Mandela Gardens**, created in 2001 with formal planting, a busy pool and '*Both Hands*', a bronze by *Kenneth Armitage* evoking the spirit of reconciliation. Uphill, outside the hall, perched on Portland stone obelisks are sprightly Art Deco-style gilded owls [2], modelled on those which top the Hall's towers. The new square was levelled out for public performances with services and facilities mostly concealed underground, except in the NE corner where the lighting and sound control tower is incorporated into a striking grenade-shaped structure, 'Off-kilter', by the artist *Richard Wilson,* 2000 [77]. This abuts the long and extensively glazed frontage of a five-storey bar and apartment complex by *West & Machell*, 2000–1.

Completed in 2005, on the s side of the square, a major redevelopment for the **Carriageworks Theatre** by *Panter Hudspith Architects*, an adaptation of the West Riding Carriage Works of 1848 by *J.F. Clark*. The owner's house and offices were part of the handsome seven-bay arcaded frontage to **Great George Street** of rusticated ashlar and brick. In the centre is an entrance opening into the courtyard behind; overlooked by former workshops with tiers of loading doors. The development also includes the Italianate corner warehouse of Roodhouse & Sons, cabinet manufacturers (No. 39 Cookridge Street). Probably *c.* 1866, brick and stone with large segmental and round-arched windows and a fancy corner entrance, with Doric columns *in antis* and rich carved stonework framing elaborate wrought-iron gates. Among the husks and scrolls are the initials of Chorley & Pickersgill, who extended the building for their printworks *c.* 1900, now known as the Electric Press Building from the white tiled lettering on the rear chimneystack. Immediately across Cookridge Street, the **Leonardo Building** (No. 4), contained the printworks' offices. Red brick, in an eclectic Italianate style with dramatic rear extension by *John Thorp*, Civic Architect, 2000. Four storeys with a higher, splayed corner tower displaying a rich mix of motifs.

Facing **Cookridge Street** is St Anne's Cathedral (R.C.) (*see* p. 54). Opposite Nos. 19 and 21, offices and warehouses built 1840–7 for William Smith, woollen cloth merchant of Allerton Hall, Gledhow, possibly by *James Simpson*. Three and four storeys; corner block with a bowed and recessed entrance. Wide cart entrance and courtyard plan, well proportioned pilastered façade, ashlar basement and red brick above. Continued as Nos. 11–17, now the Henry Moore Institute (*see* p. 166). Shopfronts of 1899 by *Thomas Ambler*. Sensitive restoration by *Michael Devenish* of *CoDA Conservation*, 1994. N along Cookridge Street is *Brodrick*'s mighty Leeds Institute of 1865–8 (*see* p. 72). It now looks onto Millennium Square but originally faced *Brodrick*'s Moorish Oriental Baths of 1866 (refronted in the ubiquitous Gothic style in 1882 and demolished 1969). Still surviving uphill,

77. Millennium Square: Civic Hall, apartments, by West & Machell, 2000–1; lighting tower, and 'Off-kilter' by Richard Wilson, 2000

49–51, a pair of shops with original fronts of 1864 by *Brodrick*. In a strange angular Gothic style: arcaded first-floor windows with low cusped wrought-iron balconies; paired sashes on the second floor set into blind Gothic arches and twin straight gables with triangular lights. Restored 1988. Dwarfing these the church-like spiky Gothic façade of the **Coliseum Theatre** by *William Bakewell*, 1885 (now a club). Tripartite façade of pale Morley sandstone, with gabled outer bays and a central portal beneath a rose window and round-headed plate-traceried windows on either side. Atop the central gable is a figure of Britannia. Functional brick flanks. Much altered interior, which once seated 3,000 for circuses and other spectacles. Converted into a cinema (the city's first) in 1905.

w of Cookridge Street are several educational establishments associated with the Mechanics' Institution. First, behind the Institute facing **Vernon Street**, the **Leeds College of Art and Design** by *Bedford & Kitson*, 1903. Five storeys, clad in red brick banded in Ancaster stone. The projecting entrance bay in a Gibbs surround on the w side is set below a large mosaic panel: two relaxed muses, 'Art' and 'Design' and

78. Leeds College of Art and Design, Vernon Street, mosaic by Gerald Moira, 1903

three laurel wreaths set against a brilliant gold background [78]. Designed by *Gerald Moira*, professor of painting and mural design, made by *Rust & Co.* in their 'new vitreous mosaic'. The Vernon Street façade is rigidly symmetrical, with finely detailed exposed steel lintels over tall windows. Inside, the basement and first-floor studios have a novel arrangement for maximizing light by setting the floor structure back from the wall to allow for taller windows. Glazed hipped roof. The sculptor E. Caldwell Spruce, whose work enhanced so many Leeds buildings, was a pupil and taught here in the 1890s. Henry Moore and the painter, Jacob Kramer were also students.

The College of Art was built on the playground of the **Leeds Boys' Modern School** of 1888 which faces **Rossington Street**. Probably by the School Board's Clerk of Works *William Landless*. Nine bays, two storeys with basement and attics, brick with stone classical detailing and distinctive terracotta panels including the date in the entrance pediment. On the N corner with Woodhouse Lane, the pedimented **Methodist New Connexion Chapel** by *William Hill*, built 1857–8 in brick with richly carved stonework. Schoolrooms and an institute in the basement, all substantially funded by the popular Alderman Henry Marsden, whose statue stands on Woodhouse Moor (*see* p. 198). Now a pub.

s of Rossington Street on a large site is the former **Leeds Higher Grade School**, 1889 by *Birchall & Kelly* [79]; a notable effort to provide more than elementary education. Its principal façade is to Woodhouse Lane, but is best seen from the open playground at the rear. Domineering classical, brick with giant stone Ionic pilasters, the coarse Millstone Grit boldly carved, supporting an entablature and a weighty attic added *c.* 1890 by *William Landless* to increase accommodation to 2,500 pupils. In two tiers, the upper part encloses a roof playground. Rooms were provided for blind, deaf and dumb children, and there was a caretaker's flat and gym in the deep basement. Converted to council offices in 1994–5 by *Leeds Design Consultancy*. To its w, facing **Great George Street**, the impressive **Pupil Teachers' College** for the Leeds School Board, 1900 by *W.S. Braithwaite* (now offices). In an eclectic

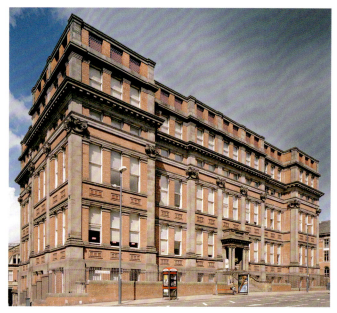

79. Leeds Higher Grade School, Woodhouse Lane, by Birchall & Kelly, 1889; extended *c*. 1890

Queen Anne style, four storeys, the principal façade facing E, with square open turrets, Diocletian windows and oval plaques. Inside, a beautiful balconied central hall, tiled and top-lit, surrounded by over thirty teaching rooms for 600 students. Facing across the street a former **Masonic Hall** by *J.M. Bottomley*, over-restored in 1991 as offices for the adjoining R.C. Cathedral (*see* p. 54). Red and yellow brick with a broad front under a pedimented gable, topped by a bell turret.

Walk 5.

The Arcades and The Headrow

This section explores the contrasting styles of the northern part of the city centre: from flamboyant Victorian and Edwardian commercial buildings to restrained interwar and postwar development. Much of this area was first developed in the medieval period around Briggate, laid out in 1207. At its N end it joined a route along the headland or field boundary, until the early C17 when John Harrison (*see* topic box, p. 10) extended Briggate further N, built the new church of St John (*see* p. 48) and began the development of a small residential enclave, including almshouses (dem.). Giles' map of 1815 shows the junction with Briggate dividing the road into the Upper Head Row (w to Park Lane via a short stretch called Butts Hill) and Lower Head Row (E to Vicar Lane). The new Town Hall was built in 1852–8 just outside this congested district, by then packed with tenements and markets. From the 1870s speculative rebuilding around Briggate, encouraged by the Corporation, provided ever more opulent shopping arcades and theatres for the city's increasingly wealthy middle class. But dense slums persisted into the C20, especially E of the city centre on Quarry Hill. However from 1924, the Corporation ensured the future monumentality of inner Leeds by insisting on a unified frontage all along the N side of the Headrow. This was an initiative unique outside London. A recent precedent was the

80. Walk 5

remodelling of The Quadrant, Regent Street, whose architect, *Sir Reginald Blomfield*, was engaged by Leeds to devise grand ranges of offices, shops and department stores extending E–W along a new boulevard 80 ft (24.4 metres) wide. W of the Town Hall the widened Park Lane was renamed Westgate, and at the E end a new road, Eastgate, was made by demolishing several streets of cramped housing and relegating the old E route (Lady Lane) to a back lane. To close the scheme at the E end the Corporation planned for the ambitious redevelopment of the Quarry Hill slums with a major scheme of flats (since dem.; *see* topic box, p. 171). Work on The Headrow proceeded from 1927–32 but was delayed by the depression and the Second World War. Work continued after 1945, at first largely in the approved Blomfield style, an architectural tradition rejected by the Modernist blocks of the next decade. By the late 1980s, interest in the Victorian and Edwardian legacy had revived, and refurbishment of the older arcades began, now accompanied by large shopping centres confirming the area as the principal shopping district.

a) The Arcades

A walk around the best buildings of the late Victorian and Edwardian shopping district. We begin on **The Headrow** at the corner with Lands Lane. The first building to note is **Thornton's Buildings** of 1873, a development of shops, offices and top-lit workshops for Charles Thornton, a local entrepreneur. Italianate, brick with sandstone details. Three storeys and a deep cornice, paired and triple-arched windows with pilasters. Large carved stone gables over the corner and entrance to its chambers on the nine-bay Headrow frontage. To its left is a narrow entrance to the upper balconies of the City Varieties theatre (*see* below) and the **Horse and Trumpet** hotel, probably 1870s, sandstone and brick, the stone carved all over with grapes, rosettes, foliage and a charming horse and trumpet. Down Lands Lane a turning left takes us into **Swan Street.** Here is the plain façade of the **City Varieties Music Hall**, which grew from the White Swan Inn. The music hall was built for Charles Thornton in 1865 by *George Smith* and its long, narrow auditorium is a remarkable and atmospheric survival; one of only three including London's Wilton's Music Hall and Hoxton Hall. Cast-iron columns with foliage capitals support two tiers of bow-fronted balconies (the upper tier slightly modified in the 1880s) with plaster enrichments of swags, medallions and female busts. The shallow stage projects under a three-centred proscenium arch surmounted by the royal arms.

Now into **Briggate**, the principal market street of the medieval town and still the thriving shopping area for the city. The medieval pattern of long, narrow plots with yards behind the frontages was easily adapted for a dazzling series of covered shopping arcades from the 1870s onwards. First, downhill on the right is **Thornton's Arcade** of 1877–8,

81. Thornton's Arcade, Briggate, by George Smith, 1877–8

also by *George Smith*. Mixed Gothic Renaissance façade of brick and painted stone, with a high arch and pavilion roof. This was built over the Old Talbot Inn Yard. Restored in 1990–2, the interior is long and narrow (242 ft by 15 ft; 74 by 4.5 metres) [81], with a glazed roof carried on cast-iron pierced Gothic cross-arches rising from slender shafts with foliate capitals. Brackets where angels might have flown are occupied by dragons. The shopfronts, with rooms above, are designed as a tripartite Gothic composition of arcade, triforium and clerestory. At the w end is a **clock** with its bell struck by a charming animated group of cast-iron figures from Walter Scott's *Ivanhoe*: Robin Hood, Friar Tuck, Richard Coeur de Lion, and Gurth the Swineherd. Designed by *J.W. Appleyard* and made by *Potts & Sons* of Leeds (*see* topic box, p. 158).

Downhill and parallel to Thornton's Arcade is the **Queen's Arcade** of 1889 by *Edward Clark* of London, built on the site of the Rose-and-Crown Yard behind three- and four-storey older frontages of the C18 and C19 and altered in 1896 when two shops s of the entrance were rebuilt and the arcade entrance widened. It is announced by another fine clock, this time on a bracket over the street (the main front faces

William Potts & Sons, clockmakers

Several of Leeds' buildings are distinguished by the novel series of clocks made by the firm of *William Potts & Sons*. William Potts (1809–87), son of a Darlington clockmaker, learned his trade from the age of twelve. He set up business in Pudsey in 1833, and *c.* 1840 began to make large clocks for mills and churches. His work for the parish church at Ilkley brought him into contact with the architect and horologist, *Edmund Beckett Denison*, through whom Potts later secured work as clockmaker to the Great Northern Railway (Edmund Beckett Sen. was chairman of the company). In 1860 Potts took over responsibility from *Frederick Dent* of London for the clock at Leeds Town Hall and moved to the city in 1862. Potts was in partnership with his sons from the late 1860s, heralding a period of expansion and the introduction of larger, more novel clocks with chimes, including several along the newly rebuilt Boar Lane in 1877, one of which survives at the Griffin Hotel (*see* p. 96). Charles Thornton's innovative shopping arcade off Briggate of 1877–8 is enhanced by a tableau of mechanical figures from *Ivanhoe* appearing to strike the hours. The figures were made by the sculptor *John Wormald Appleyard* whose studio in Cookridge Street was near the Potts workshops. A similar clock in the Grand Arcade, Vicar Lane, of 1897 (*see* p. 162) has medieval knights guarding a castle and revolving figures. Numerous clocks were also made for the town's Board Schools and at their peak between 1880–1910 the firm supplied clocks worldwide from its workshops in Guildford Street (now The Headrow) and 19 Cookridge Street (*see* p. 151).

Lands Lane to the w – a classical stucco façade of four storeys). The interior, restored 1991–2, is rather garishly painted. Pilasters with ornate capitals separate the ground-floor shops; white glazed bricks line the walls above, reflecting light from the glass roof, which is supported by cast-iron trusses. Unlike Thornton's this has a novel two-storey galleried arrangement. On the upper floor of the N side was the Queen's Arcade Hotel, with office, bar, two billiard rooms and a smoke room. The upper floor on the s side was designed as a separate 'street' of small shops opening off the gallery, each with a kitchen and bedroom above the level of the arcade roof. The gallery is no longer accessible although the top of a spiral stair is visible at the Briggate end.

The walk now continues along **Briggate**. Between the two arcades, No. 76 (now Zodiac) was Marks & Spencer's new shop by 1909; extended into Queen's Arcade in 1926 and given a curious rendered Art Deco façade. Other points of interest on this side are **Angel Inn Yard** where the late C18 **Angel Inn** overlooks a small square. Walls of handmade red-brown bricks strengthened by stone blocks at second and third floor. Three storeys high with attics. Altered by *Thomas Winn*, 1904. Further down at the corner with Albion Place is a five-storey Edwardian Baroque shop by *Percy Robinson*, 1903, for Eveleigh Bishop, 'stationer, printer, fancy goods importer, jeweller and silversmith'. Clad in Burmantofts faience, and ornamented with green stone columns, pedimented dormers and obelisk finials above the ramped parapet. Across Albion Place a much-altered corner shop for Charles Kirkness by *Thomas Ambler & Son*, 1902. The **Pack Horse Inn** is in the yard of that name just below. Known as the Slipin when Jefferys' map was made in 1770, this alley was then the route between Briggate and the s end of Lands Lane. Its brick gabled end bay has part of a c16 or early c17 timber frame inside, preserved in a refurbishment in 1987.

The highlight of this walk is the spectacular development on Briggate's E side, now the **Victoria Quarter**. This was undertaken for the Leeds Estates Company who swept away the notorious slum area around the old meat market ('Shambles'), between here and Vicar Lane to the E. The work was carried out in 1898–1904 by *Frank Matcham* who designed three blocks, divided across two new streets: Queen Victoria Street and King Edward Street. The whole architecture is one and the same design. Each part is of three storeys and an attic, unified by flamboyant façades of warm pink and buff terracotta elaborated in a free Baroque style with swags, strapwork and scrolls, Dutch gables, domes and corner turrets. The N block cleverly incorporates the narrow entrance to the existing Bay Horse Yard under an ornate pedimented name plaque, but the main attraction of this building is the **County Arcade** within; one of the most beautiful interiors in the city [82]. T-plan, 394 ft (120 metres) long, and glowing with exuberant decoration in marble, mosaic and Burmantofts faience, all symbols of the city's wealth and confidence. Separating the mahogany shopfronts, with their curved glass display cases, are columns and pilasters of Siena marble which carry balustraded balconies and stone ball finials. Above, the arched cast-iron roof has, at intervals, three glazed domes raised on pendentives of richly coloured and gilded mosaics. The central dome, over the crossing, depicts figures representing Leeds' industries. Below is a fine circular mosaic floor by *J. Veevers*, part of the highly successful restoration by *Derek Latham & Co.* in 1988–90. This rescued the arcade from decline, restored the shopfronts (only six of the original fifty were intact) and glazed over Queen Victoria Street to unite the arcade with the block to the s which contains the **Cross Arcade**. The roof over Queen Victoria Street, carried above eaves level on a free-standing steel frame, has bright stained glass abstractly patterned like woven fabric – blue, yellow, red and green – by *Brian Clarke* and projects out over the Briggate entrance with no attempt to integrate. This is in poor contrast to the new work in the centre of the second block which originally contained Matcham's Empire Theatre, but was thoughtlessly destroyed in 1961 to make way for another arcade. Amends for this disgrace have

been made in the sensitive handling of its successor, the **Harvey Nichols** store of 1997 by *Brooker Flynn Architects* (interior design by *Hosker Moore & Kent*), who daringly inserted a glazed curtain between new moulded brickwork. It makes a worthy inheritor to the Leeds commercial tradition. The third block of the original scheme lies along **King Edward Street**, with the former County Café and King Edward Restaurant (now shops). The latter, on the corner with Fish Street, can be identified by gold mosaic plaques high up, representing fish, game and wine.

The Victoria Quarter presents an equally impressive façade to **Vicar Lane** (reached via King Edward Street). The E side is contemporary (for the City Markets to the s, *see* p. 101), with grand four-storey commercial buildings of *c.* 1900 in a variety of materials and styles. First, Nos. 50–56, on the corner with Harewood Street and Ludgate Hill, by *G.F. Bowman,* with an elaborate terracotta façade restored after a fire in 1993. Paired columns flank the former corner entrance to the Bradford Bank. Turret with lead dome and finial flanked by dormers with stepped gables at the top. Three-light segmental-arched furniture showroom windows to first floor. Next, Nos. 58–62, a non-matching pair of shops, offices and Temperance Hotel by *W.H. Thorp.* Brick, stone dressings and terracotta panels, modest Renaissance style with pediments and pinnacles on the skyline. **Wray's Buildings** extend along Sidney Street. Jacobean style, its original entrance and paired round-headed windows in moulded arches with a name plaque and relief of figures with flowers. Ornate Dutch gables and four massive clustered chimneys of moulded brick. Then **Coronation Buildings**, by *D. Dodgson,* 1902, clad in red terracotta, distinctive hexagonal banded pilasters rising to plinths above the cornice. Finally Nos. 76–88 on the corner to Eastgate by *G.F. Bowman.* Distinctive red brick with thin bands of buff terracotta, first-floor display-window with voussoirs and deep second-floor band; canted corner bay to Eastgate surmounted by a rather small turret and dome.

The walk now crosses The Headrow to continue N along **Vicar Lane**. Off to the right, downhill is **Lady Lane**, the old main route NE out of town before the creation of Eastgate. A sole relic of the mid C19 is **Templar House**, a former **Methodist Chapel**, 1840 by *James Simpson.* (It stands on the site of St Mary's, the first Roman Catholic chapel of 1793). Classical, two storeys, in red brick with stone detailing and paired entrances in architraves. Round-arched windows. Much abused and neglected after it was converted into a warehouse. The chapel stands at the edge of the **Leylands** district, which is now largely cut off by the inner Ring Road. It was a working-class industrial suburb, its largely Jewish population engaged in the clothing industry. Two landmark buildings on **North Street** are visible across the Ring Road. **Crispin House**, the former

82. County Arcade, Briggate, by Frank Matcham, 1898–1904

Heatons' Clothing Factory, was built 1914–16. Five storeys and seventeen bays of steel-framed fire-proof construction clad in red brick with white 'Marmo' detailing, distinctive corner dome. Heatons was founded by 1903, making clothes for the mass market; their vast new factory was delayed by the outbreak of the First World War but by 1918 they were making thousands of military uniforms. Conversion to apartments is in progress, with a roof-top extension. Prominent new build to the w for **Caspar Apartments**, social housing, by *Levitt Bernstein*, 2000, using prefabricated units. Also visible at this end of North Street is **Centenary House** by *Bedford & Kitson*, 1904, built as a public dispensary for the Leeds Society for Deaf and Blind People. Neo-Wren with Gibbs detailing. Five storeys, a bowed corner, brick with rusticated stone ground floor and basement ornamented with high-quality carving. Large putti support an oriel window above the round-arched main entrance. A woman holding a large book is carved in the tympanum above the entrance to the outpatients' department on the s side.

At the N end of New Briggate *William Hill*'s Italianate Chest Clinic, 1865. Now back to the main theme of our walk, and the **Grand Arcade** by *Smith & Tweedale*, 1897, in an eccentric Renaissance style with plenty of balusters and finials, using Burmantofts faience and blue and yellow tiles at the entrances. Two parallel arcades run between Vicar Lane and New Briggate, with a cross-passage opening onto Merrion Street. The plain brick façade has a round arch under a gable and three paired shopfronts with odd inverted consoles as mullions to the upper-floor windows. Inside, what little attention has been given to the interior in the later C20 has not brought out its charms. Glazed roof supported by timber arches and rows of shops with some original Ionic pilasters. There is no gallery here, only small bay windows, canted bays or deeply recessed with more curious mullions. At the E end another bizarre animated **clock** by *Potts* of Leeds (*see* topic box, p. 158): armoured knights guard castle doors which open to release exotic costumed figures.

Immediately s is the **Grand Theatre** of 1877–8. It is well named and, in scale and splendour, without equal outside London. The cost was £62,000. The design, in his eclectic style, is by *George Corson*, ably assisted by *J.R. Watson*, who provided detailed theatre knowledge. 162 ft (49.4 metre) long brick and stone façade in a hybrid of Romanesque and Gothic, including round arches to the main entrance with rose window above and gable tourelles. Six bays to the right for shops, originally set into Gothic arches but now with 1930s sunburst glazing. At the s end is an entrance to the separate Assembly Room under a squat tower with pyramid roof. The theatre interior is little altered: original ticket offices, steep main staircase and a labyrinth of passages leading to the magnificently decorated auditorium [83]. This has opulent red and green painted *carton-pierre* decoration glowing with gilding. Clustered Gothic shafts and boxes, flanked by draped figures, frame the proscenium; the saucer-domed richly encrusted ceiling is carried on

83. Grand Theatre, New Briggate, by J.R. Watson, 1877–8

four pendentives of fan vault form. Three tiers of balconies, their plaster fronts deeply undercut into elaborate foliated scrolls and bosses. The 1920s classical decoration of the Assembly Room (converted for a cinema in 1907), includes a serpentine fronted balcony. After serious decline the theatre was bought by the City Council in 1970 and restored by its Director of Architecture, *E.W. Stanley*. The home of Opera North since 1978, a major restoration programme is proposed in 2005.

84. St John's Place, Nash's Fish Restaurant, early c18 (right) and St John's House, by G.W. Atkinson, 1930 (left)

w of New Briggate is a small enclave around St John's Church (*see* p. 48). N of the church in a short *cul-de-sac* (formerly St John's Place) is an unexpected survival (now Nash's Fish Restaurant) [84]. It was built in 1720 for the merchant Matthew Wilson and the only one remaining of those shown on Cossin's *c.* 1726 map. The proportions survive, with a central entrance, sash windows and end stacks, but the red brick walls were given a heavy render imitating rock-faced ashlar after 1860. It later served as a clergy house and was occupied by Kemplay's Academy by 1817. (For the buildings to the left, *see* below.)

Merrion Street to the N, laid out in 1830, was widened at the same time as The Headrow, *c.* 1930. At the corner is a four-storey brick and Portland stone block of shops and offices with a canted corner, in the Blomfield style. Continuing w, immediately on the left are shops and **St John's House**, 1930, now a pub, by *G.W. Atkinson* who acted as Architect of the Receiver of Wades Charity (founded 1530), whose buildings had been cleared for The Headrow. Timber framing and brick, two storeys with attics, five irregular bays with external chimneystacks, and striking s front of jettied gables overlooking St John's churchyard. This early c17 vernacular revival is astonishingly convincing; the design approved by no less an authority than *W.D. Caröe* on behalf of the Charity Commissioners. The Charity's boardroom and offices were on the ground floor, on the first floor was a drawing office for Atkinson. More careful timber framing for the gatehouse to the Garden of Rest on the N side of the churchyard.

85. The Light, Albion Street, by DLG Architects, 2002

The rest of Merrion Street is less memorable, dominated by banal office blocks of the 1970s. Hard to ignore, however, is the massive **Merrion Shopping Centre**, occupying the entire site between Wade and Woodhouse Lanes, of 1962–4 by *Gillinson, Barnett & Allen.* This was a novel scheme for its date, integrating a nightclub, dance hall and cinema with a pedestrian shopping precinct. This was originally open (but soon enclosed) with shops on two levels connected by stairs and 'a moving pavement'. Fourteen-storey slab of offices and multi-storey car park, clad in dreary grey and white mosaic tiles. Challenging it at the corner of **Albion Street** and Great George Street is **K2 The Cube**, *Abbey Holford Rowe*'s sleek 2002 conversion and re-cladding of Dudley House (1972) into twenty storeys of apartments, offices and retail. Refurbishment (and new six-storey supporting blocks clad in glass and terracotta panels) won out over demolition here; sleek corner balconies and distinctive fin-like roof-line make a positive contribution.

Finally down Albion Street to *DLG Architects*' **The Light** [85], the last arcade of the walk. This commercial development on two levels is covered by a high glazed roof over Upper Fountaine Street, and incorporates Permanent House and the Headrow Buildings [87].* It includes shops and restaurants, those facilities which first so attracted the Victorian middle classes to Thornton's Arcade in the 1870s. The new-build includes a multi-screen cinema, reached from the bright and airy raised 'promenade' level by an escalator, and above the restaurants and shops there are those essential benefits of modern city living – a health club and nightclub.

b) The Headrow to Quarry Hill

Begin on the steps of the **Town Hall** (*see* p. 60), an excellent point from which to view The Headrow rising uphill to the E. Brodrick set his building at the N end of its site, leaving a wide, open space facing what was then Park Lane. *George Frampton*'s statue of Queen Victoria (now on Woodhouse Moor, *see* p. 197–8) was set up here in 1903. In 1936–7 *J.C. Procter* re-designed **Victoria Square** and levelled up the forecourt, allowing the widened Headrow to pass below. The square was extended E across Calverley Street alongside the **Municipal Buildings and Library** (*see* p. 75) by demolishing a row of houses in Centenary Street (the line of which is suggested by the sunken path on the square's N side). The focus of this unified civic space and Garden of Rest is *H.C. Fehr*'s **War Memorial** of 1922, previously in City Square. White Carrara marble plinth flanked by beautiful bronze statues of St George and the Dragon and Peace, a hooded woman releasing a dove. Fehr's figure of Victory was removed in 1967 and a winged figure with bowed head, by *Ian Judd* and *Andy Elton*, set up in 1992. Linked to the Art Gallery by a bridge over Alexander Street is the **Henry Moore Institute** of 1993 [86], by *Jeremy Dixon & Edward Jones,* with *BDP*, who converted warehouses on Cookridge Street (*see* p. 151) and dramatically refaced the gable end to Victoria Square in highly polished green igneous rock with a crenellated parapet and fissure-like entrance passage.

The range opposite Victoria Square begins at the corner of Park Cross Street with the flamboyant former **Jubilee Hotel and Chambers** of 1904 by *Thomas Winn*, with a corner tower and scrolled pediments in bright red brick and terracotta. In contrast, on the corner to East

*The centre is named after the staff newspaper issued by the Leeds Permanent Building Society (the first occupants of Headrow Buildings).

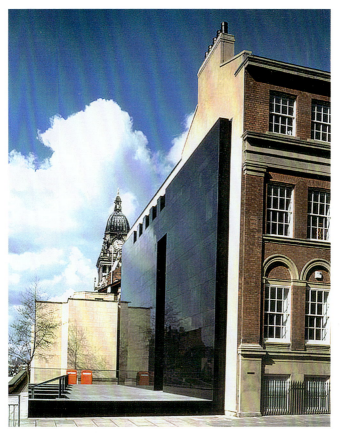

86. Henry Moore Institute, Victoria Square, by Jeremy Dixon & Edward Jones, 1993

Parade, the premises of the **Pearl Life Assurance Company** in gleaming Portland stone, one of the first uses in the city. Dated 1911 by the prolific *William Bakewell*, near the end of his career, in a free Gothic style and with a small statue of the company's founder in 1864, Patrick James Foley, gazing proudly out from the parapet between threatening griffins. Also by *Bakewell*, but in a more restrained Tudor Gothic style of *c.* 1890, is the four-storey **Athenaeum House** with tall robed figures in canopied niches, representing the Arts. The dignified five-bay frontage of **Victoria House** by *Fletcher Ross & Hickling*, 1979, reused stone from the original office façade. Now flats with added balconies. An eight-storey concrete and glass box at **Eagle Star House**, 1967, by *Charlton & Crowther*. Then, to the corner with Park Row, the finely carved rear façade of the late classical former Bank of England (*see* p. 117). On the opposite corner with Park Row, **St Andrew House**, by *Gillinson Barnet & Partners*, a rebuild of 1977, which retained the Park Row façade of *E.J. Dodgshun*'s elaborate Flemish style premises of 1894

87. Headrow Buildings, s elevation, by Sir Reginald Blomfield, 1929–31

for Peacock & Son, warehousemen, and the Bradford Old Bank. In spite of an attempt at horizontal continuity the Headrow frontage fails to connect visually to the retained Park Row façade. Uphill on this side, **The Guildford**, built *c*. 1900 as the Green Dragon Hotel on the corner of the yard of that name. Red brick with finely carved buff sandstone dressings, including muscular terms.

Leaving C19 opulence behind we come to the great rebuilding of the N side of **The Headrow**, begun in the 1920s. This begins E of Cookridge Street with *Sir Reginald Blomfield*'s **Permanent House** and **Headrow Buildings** of 1929–31 [87], a long classical range of brick and Portland stone stepping up the steep slope in five stages. 'Tame and dull' said Pevsner, 'but the scale is an asset'. In the centre is a tall arch surmounted by columns *in antis* striding over the junction with Cross Fountaine Street (now the entrance to The Light, *see* p. 166), a feature derived directly from Blomfield's contemporary rebuilding of the Quadrant, Regent Street. The Doric pilasters, balustrading and urns, the latter echoing the Town Hall, are also familiar Blomfield motifs (e.g. Goldsmith's College, London, 1907 and Moundsmere Manor, Hampshire, 1908). Nicely detailed corner entrances and delicate carved work. Seamless N extension along Cookridge Street by *G. W. Atkinson*, 1955.

Facing, on the s side at the corner with Albion Street, are five-storey offices for the **Leeds & Holbeck Building Society**, 1930, by *Chorley, Gribbon & Foggitt*. Classical orders in sand-faced brick and Portland stone, harmonizing handsomely with the Blomfield buildings but without the flamboyance. Extended down Albion Street in 1950. Inside the **Burley Bar Stone** still marks the 1725 town boundary. Across Albion Street, on the crown of the rise, is **Cavendish House** of 1967, a slab-and-podium in concrete and glass by *J.F. Rusted* of *Tripe & Wakeham*, firmly rejecting the Blomfield tradition, reconstruction in progress.

The Headrow now slopes gradually down to Eastgate and the city's shopping centre. E of Albion Street on the N side is **Headrow House**, planned for by Blomfield and following his style but built 1951–5 by *Arthur S. Ash* of London as a ten-storey block on a reduced site. It overlooks **Dortmund Square**, laid out in 1980 to celebrate the tenth anniversary of the twinning of the two industrial cities. In the centre stands the cheerful **Dortmund Drayman** (one wishes he could put his barrel down), a bronze by *Artur Schulze-Engels*. Behind him, the **St John's Centre** shopping mall by *Gillinson Partnership*, 1985, a bland design of red brick cladding and bronze panels; roof-top car park. Closing the E side of the Square **Allders**, originally Lewis's Department Store ('general drapers, tailors, bootmakers, hatters, hosiers, outfitters, silk mercers and bankers'), in a continuous range to New Briggate. Designed in 1931 by *Blomfield* as a seven-storey range, only the double-height ground floor and first floor, with heavily channelled stone plinth beneath a dentilled cornice and massive display windows, were completed when it opened in 1932. Even so, it was the largest department store outside London. A temporary furniture store was built in Nissen huts on the roof in 1949, the upper storeys being finally completed in the 1950s by *Atkinson & Shaw*, who omitted much of the original classical detail. Inside the original staircases have brass handrails, Egyptian motifs and marble walls.

Continuing on the N side of The Headrow, E of New Briggate, a large block executed to Blomfield's design by *George H. Shipley* and *G.W. Atkinson* 1929–30. It contained the former Paramount Cinema, with an interior designed by the cinema and theatre specialist *Frank T. Verity* (now destroyed). At the corner with Vicar Lane, **Lloyds Bank**, 1930–2 by *Blomfield*, giant Doric pilasters, badge, and fine classical detailing. It is matched on the opposite corners of this crossing by later designs for **Martin's** (NE) and **Barclays** (SW) of 1938.

At the same time as the grand rebuilding of the N side of The Headrow, surviving older frontages along the s side were refronted and improved. At the corner with Briggate is a remarkable survival of Late Georgian shops, shown in an 1828 engraving. Three storeys and eight bays. The shallow rusticated arches of the ground floor have gone (although shop divisions remain) but the fenestration, roof-line and chimneys survive. Cement stucco rustication and pedimented N gable added 1928–30 by *William Whitehead & Percy Robinson*. Inside, stone-lined cellars, original staircases and attic fireplaces survive. Next, Nos. 15–41, early C19 houses and shops refaced in stucco with pediments, pilasters and urns, by *William Whitehead*, 1929. Then the exceptional **Three Legs** pub, of *c.* 1900 with a treacle-brown glazed faience and buff terracotta for Tetley's brewery. The entrance to **Rockley Hall Yard** is a refronting of 1929 by *William Pearson*, classical with a shallow pedimented blocking course. Rockley Hall and its estate belonged to John Harrison (*see* topic box, p. 10) in the early C17; some of the hall's roof timbers are thought to survive in a C19 brick rear wing.

From Vicar Lane, **Eastgate** continues The Headrow scheme downhill, the buildings mostly executed postwar but following Blomfield's design. **Shell BP House** (N side) is of 1953 by *Cotton, Ballard & Blow* of Birmingham. Rusticated Portland stone ground floor, curved corner entrance, elaborate tall stair window in an aedicule at the w end. Then a plainer range by *G.W. Atkinson*, of four storeys stepping downhill, poorly imitated on the s side of Eastgate. The street frontages on each side are terminated by a pair of w-facing blocks: on the N side are the former premises of the Kingston Unity Friendly Society by *Kirk & Tomlinson*, 1930, on the s a similar design for the Yorkshire Hussar. Picturesquely sited at the end of Eastgate is a former **petrol station** by *Blomfield*, 1932, set on a traffic island. Tiny arcaded hexagon with tent-like copper roof and torch finial: a reminder of the days when the motor car was a more decorative feature of the city. It was given a new role as the centrepiece of the Millennium fountain by *John Thorp*, the Civic Architect in 2000. On the s side is a **statue** of the Leeds airman Arthur Aaron V.C. (d.1943), by *Graham Ibbeson*, 2001. A sentimental figure-group shows Aaron with the future generation.

Directly ahead lies **Quarry Hill**, where the Quarry Hill Flats (*see* topic box, p. 171) made a striking counterpoint to the formal boulevard of The Headrow until their demolition in 1978. Equally dominant on the skyline today is the forbidding bulk of **Quarry House**, a 'design and build' scheme of 1993 by *Building Design Partnership* for Norwest Holst. Intended for the Departments of Health and Social Security and others, it proved (surprisingly) too small. Overbearing façades in red brick and sandstone on a granite plinth, with a dark glazed curtain wall lighting the central galleried atrium, flanked by wings behind portcullis-like grids of glazing. On the E side, away from the city, a central drum-like tower with finial disguising a chimney flue. Inside, offices arranged around two courtyards, finely landscaped by *Susan Tebby*, using blue and green Lake District slate. Quarry House followed in the wake of an unrealized masterplan for Quarry Hill by *Terry Farrell* of 1990, which promised the creation of a formal axial group of buildings serving as a new cultural quarter. It would have incorporated the **West Yorkshire Playhouse** of 1985–90 by the *Appleton Partnership* which stands on **St Peter's Street**. Buff and brown banded brickwork, blue window frames,

The Quarry Hill Flats

88. Quarry Hill Flats, by R.A.H. Livett; E. Mopin & Co., consulting engineers, 1935–41. Photograph *c.* 1959, view from NW

Quarry Hill has been the site of a prehistoric camp, a Roman fort and an isolation settlement for plague victims. By the C19 it was a squalid slum; home to 9,000 people and many more rats. Plans for its clearance began in 1934, when the charismatic chairman of the council's housing committee, the Rev. Charles Jenkinson, and *R.A.H. Livett*, director of the new Housing Department, began to devise a visionary scheme as the culmination of the redevelopment of Headrow and Eastgate (then under construction). They visited *avant-garde* municipal housing in Europe and two schemes proved particularly influential: the Karl Marx Hof, Vienna (*Karl Ehn*, begun 1926) with flats and communal facilities for over 1,000 people, and La Muette, Drancy (begun 1932), which employed an early form of system building using steel frames and pre-cast concrete cladding. Its engineers, *E. Mopin & Co.*, were employed as consulting engineers at Quarry Hill, slightly modifying their system with steel stanchions and floor beams welded into complete sections and lifted into position by cranes. Floors were of poured concrete, the walls of concrete panels. Begun in 1935, the first phase was opened in 1938 and completed in 1941, when it was the largest municipal housing estate in England, with 938 flats for 3,280 people. The layout was also innovative for England, with flats mostly contained within an encircling outer block described by Pevsner as 'semicircular towards Eastgate and straight to the N and S, quite sheer, with horizontal windows, somewhat forbidding, though undeniably impressive'. Dramatic parabolic or round-arched entrances penetrated this outer range, leading to lower blocks behind, which were surrounded by playgrounds and formal gardens. Communal laundries and drying rooms, kindergartens and a row of shops were directly inspired by the Viennese example. Inside, flats were arranged in pairs, separated by staircases, and served by the innovative French 'Garchey' waste disposal system which carried domestic refuse and sink waste direct to central incinerators. The flats were demolished in 1978.

89. BBC Building, St Peter's Street, by DLA Architecture, 2002–4

long low slate roof and distinctive diaper-patterned flytower display the awkwardness of the 'Leeds Look'. The entrance faces N, not a welcoming arrangement but one which could still be made to work by erecting corresponding buildings on this line. The interior is more successful and ambitious, containing the amphitheatre-style 750-seat Quarry Theatre and the more intimate 350-seat gallery-style Courtyard Theatre. Exposed structural girders and services have been screened by a tent-like canopy in the restaurant – a raised area with fine views over the Eastgate approach. Behind this are impressive new premises for the **BBC**, by *DLA Architecture*, 2002–4 [89], with a generous curved front behind thin louvres. It swings round the corner to link with the almost hidden **College of Music**, a contrasting block in buff brick with curved roof by *Allen Tod Architects*, 1997. Next to it, and nearing completion, their 13-storey teaching and accommodation block, a dark masonry base and dominating glass-panelled tower.

The Academic Quarter

Introduction

Woodhouse, NW of the city centre, was an area of open fields in the medieval period with the Lord's waste on higher ground to the N. The Kirkstall Abbey estates extended into the area from the W. The sale of the abbey's land after the Dissolution changed the landscape and by the mid C17 many small fields had been enclosed. Ancient rights of pasture on Woodhouse Moor were, however, protected and the area used for markets and fairs, with coal mines and quarries at its NW fringes. During the later C18 merchants built houses on the lower S-facing hill slopes of Woodhouse, several of which survive, but planned development of residential squares near the town developed slowly in the area known as Little Woodhouse. The moor continued in common use, while in 1835 a fashionable private cemetery was opened on St George's Fields E of the moor. Clarendon Road was laid out in 1839 between it and St George's Church in the town. Architectural fashion changed in the mid C19 as the town's wealth increased; detached villas were built beyond the moor, at Headingley (*see* p. 245) and the area around Clarendon Road became a popular residential area in the 1860s. A site W of Woodhouse Lane was purchased in 1877 for the Yorkshire College, later the University of Leeds. It marked a profound change in the character of the area as the buildings erected by the university, in three main and distinctive phases, imposed a new pattern, eventually extending as far S as the General Infirmary (*see* p. 83), to which it is umbilically connected. Numerous early C19 terraces and villas survive, however, adapted for residential and teaching purposes. Rising inflation and declining building impetus in the 1970s encouraged the University to preserve these enclaves within its campus. Simultaneously the conservation movement also re-awakened interest in the important early Victorian survivals of Hanover and Woodhouse Squares. Closer to the centre and just inside the sunken inner Ring Road, the city's Central Colleges (now Leeds Metropolitan University) were amalgamated onto a new campus during the 1950s and 1960s creating a continuous academic quarter between the city centre and Woodhouse Moor.

Leeds University

Of all Britain's universities, Leeds has grown most rapidly since 1945, and by 2004 had 31,500 students. Its origins were modest, however, and it had only 1,750 full-time students in 1939. It began as the Yorkshire College of Science in 1874, inspired by Owens College in Manchester, and first took rented premises in Cookridge Street. Medical students took classes from 1875 and College and Medical School (*see* p. 87)

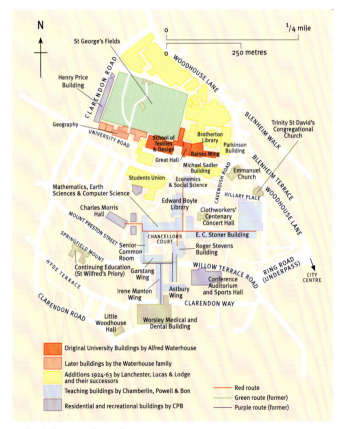

Legend:
- Original University Buildings by Alfred Waterhouse
- Later buildings by the Waterhouse family
- Additions 1924-63 by Lanchester, Lucas & Lodge and their successors
- Teaching buildings by Chamberlin, Powell & Bon
- Residential and recreational buildings by CPB
- Red route
- Green route (former)
- Purple route (former)

90. Leeds University Central Precinct

amalgamated in 1884. In 1887 it joined Manchester and Liverpool as the smallest element of the Victoria University, an association that lasted until 1904 when Leeds assumed independent university status.

The university has overlain Woodhouse in three main phases of building, each the work of a single firm, first *Alfred Waterhouse* and his descendants in 1877, then *Lanchester, Lucas & Lodge* in the 1920s–50s, mainly to the N and E, and finally *Chamberlin, Powell & Bon* to the s. The phases are distinctive for their very different sizes, scales and especially materials: red brick giving way to Portland stone and then to concrete. Pevsner complained of Waterhouse's dryness and considered that Lanchester, Lucas and Lodge's classical revival style 'achieves nothing'; now we are more sympathetic to their rich materials and grand spaces, particularly of the interwar work that gives the university its greatest landmark. Chamberlin, Powell and Bon's work has no such fine finishes, but has an epic monumentality and genuine flexibility that withstands accretions – though had all their scheme been built too many good buildings would have been lost. All these architects were initially welcomed enthusiastically by the university, but in the course of their subsequent long building campaigns this was replaced by a mistrust that Leeds was not getting its due, and then a means was sought for a clean and uncontested break. Most recently the University has preferred to work with local architects.

Instead of a conventional tour, this guide looks at each of the three phases of university expansion in turn and then at the surviving pre-university buildings.

Early Buildings

In 1877, with *Alfred Waterhouse*'s plans for Owens College, Manchester, to hand, Yorkshire College appointed him as architect. A fund-raising campaign had yielded only £20,000 of a hoped for £60,000, and building was made possible only by the munificence of the Clothworkers' Company of London, anxious to improve the scientific basis of their industry after the Paris International Exhibition of 1867. The first building was thus the **School of Textiles and Design (Wool Division)**, in **University Road** (1879), a blind red brick façade with Spinkwell Quarry stone arcading; open trusses and N lights to the weaving sheds and lecture theatre behind. In 1880 Sir Edward Baines, Chairman of the College Council, donated £3,000 towards the long range to the E, the three-storey **Baines Wing** of 1881–5 (dated 1883) with regular gables and a stubby tower with one of Waterhouse's steep pyramid roofs. More utilitarian ranges to the rear were demolished in 1936. In between these long ranges Waterhouse inserted the **Great Hall** in 1890–4 [91], banded in stone with a large Perp traceried window flanked by towers with tall pyramidal roofs and bartizans. Inside, the well-lit first-floor hall is used for meetings and examinations, reached up a staircase lined with Burmantofts tiles [17], an effect Waterhouse later repeated at University

91. Leeds University, Great Hall, by Alfred Waterhouse, 1890–4

College Hospital, London. A refectory was originally set below. The hall has a s gallery, columns with floral capitals, and 'YC' monogrammed in the cornice. In 1902 Waterhouse abdicated his practice to his son Paul, with whom he designed the modest Proctor Leather Department (1905, demolished). Also by *Paul Waterhouse*, an E extension to the Baines Wing completed in 1908 and a w extension to Textiles of 1909–12, ending in a short tower and again paid for by the Clothworkers. Fine cast-iron staircases, Art Nouveau capitals and a museum with stained glass roundels to its windows. A link building between the Great Hall and Baines Wing, 'Swiss Cottage', was also completed in 1912. The Neo-Georgian **Agriculture Building** (now Geography) [92] was funded by the Board of Agriculture following a donation by Walter Morrison in 1913, but not built until 1923–5 at much inflated prices and amid rising concern at the efficiency of *Michael Waterhouse*, Paul's son.

92. Leeds University, Geography Building, by Michael Waterhouse, 1923–5

Interwar and Early Postwar Buildings

A move NW to suburban Weetwood was considered in the 1920s but instead a limited competition was held in 1926 for a new master plan, to bring belated civic dignity to the institution. *Paul Waterhouse* was one of eight firms invited to submit plans, but the winners were *Lanchester, Lucas & Lodge*, who from the first proposed an imposing landmark clock tower on the curve of **Woodhouse Lane**. In 1927 the chemical manufacturer Sir Edward Brotherton offered up to £100,000 for a library, and promised his private book collection on his death (duly donated in 1935).* Opened in 1936, the **Brotherton Library** has a circular main reading room 160 ft (48.8 metres) in diameter, with a gallery and Swedish green marble columns supporting a concrete dome [93]. Oak panelling and fittings, with carvings of the University and Brotherton's arms, and symbols representing Arts and Science; the dome has further symbols in plaster. The Brotherton Library has no street presence; it was always intended to be set behind a central arts and administration block, and in 1936 Frank Parkinson offered £200,000 for its construction. The **Parkinson Building** has a monumental E front with recessed portico up a wide staircase [18]. The landmark clock tower, faced in good Portland stone, in four stages with a

*From Roundhay Hall, Gledhow, *see* p. 243.

low-pitched pyramid roof, is in the distinctive Greek Revival style of *Thomas Lodge*, the university's relations with *H.V. Lancaster* having quickly soured. Inside, the grand entrance hall was intended as a meeting place. The 1926 plans were revised to incorporate a council chamber, committee rooms and offices; it was formally opened in 1951 having served as a Ministry of Food store in the war. Meanwhile, in a sequence marching up Woodhouse Lane, *Lanchester & Lodge* (as the firm became in 1930) produced buildings for Mining (1928–30), followed by Physics (1932) and **Chemistry** (1934), with a wide apse decorated by attached columns. In the centre of the site, s of University Road, the **Students' Union** by *J.C. Procter* was opened in 1939, the first of a more utilitarian Portland stone sequence continued after the war by the adjoining **University House** refectory and senior common room in 1955, and opposite by **Man Made Fibres** of 1954–6 combining stone with brick. All these were conceived by *Thomas Lodge* with his assistant *Allan Johnson* as executive architect. After Lodge's retirement in 1957 responsibility passed to *Allan Johnson*, who completed the **Michael Sadler Building For Arts**, s of the Parkinson Building. This contains in its entrance hall a war memorial of 1923 by *Eric Gill*, depicting *Our Lord driving the Money Changers out of the Temple* [94]; also glass by *Mark Angus*, 1989. Johnson continued the line of science and engineering buildings up Woodhouse Lane, with extensions to Chemistry and Physics, and the **Houldsworth School** in 1958, **Civil Engineering** in 1960, **Mechanical Engineering** in 1961 and **Electrical Engineering** in 1963. Mechanical Engineering has a powerful fibreglass relief designed by Johnson and made by *Alec Dearnby* over its entrance.

93. Leeds University, Brotherton Library, by Lanchester, Lucas & Lodge, 1935–6

94. Michael Sadler Building, war memorial, by Eric Gill, 1923

The Work of Chamberlin, Powell and Bon

The University used Lodge's forthcoming retirement, announced in 1956, to rethink its strategy for the teaching precinct, seeking advice from Leslie Martin and J.M. Richards, the latter then teaching here. A limited competition resulted in the appointment of *Chamberlin, Powell & Bon (CPB)* in 1959, preferred to *Denys Lasdun* after interview. Except where noted, *Peter (Joe) Chamberlin* can be assumed as the lead architect. Their work extends southwards down the steep slope to the inner Ring Road, sunk below ground as part of the firm's recommendations so that the university retained its link with the Infirmary and the city. The changes in level informed the circulation pattern of the new work. *CPB*'s detailed report, published in 1960 and revised in 1963, was based on interviews with staff and flow charts of student movements through the precinct and offered a model throughout the 1960s for subsequent studies of university campuses, old and new. The architects recalculated projected student numbers, estimating in the 1960 plan that they needed to build for 7,000 by 1970, subsequently raised to 10,000 as a result of the Robbins Report, and looked closely at the relationship between departments as well as their individual needs. They identified, for example, that Mathematics (with a service role to other departments) needed a lot of lecture theatres, whereas science subjects needed very few. From this CPB evolved the **plan** of the built portion of their scheme: a central block of communal lecture theatres and the disposition of the other departments around it. CPB considered that university accommodation was of three kinds: one-off buildings that would not change; laboratories and teaching space that might change; and flexible laboratories with large, heavy equipment that changed regularly. A multi-storey car park was set under the most heavily serviced research laboratories, which otherwise would have had to be free-standing. More car parking was intended under the deck which, at their suggestion, spanned the Inner Ring Road s of the precinct.

The buildings were all based on a modular tartan grid based on the unit of the Forticrete concrete blocks with which they were clad (painted in 1996–7), which allowed subdivision for partitioning at 1 ft 8 in. (50 cm.) intervals. A system of internal block partitions allowed the occasional flexibility required as departments changed or lecturers moved on. Clustered beams and columns at 40 ft (12.2 metre) intervals allowed the distribution of services; in an architecture entirely of grids, the junctions assumed great importance, especially in the hands of *Christoph Bon*. The other flexible element was what Powell called 'the joker in the pack', teaching units or flats on the top floor of the blocks into which departments could expand over time. Finally, there were internal walkways between the buildings at three levels across and down the hillside – red, green, and purple in descending order.

The main buildings are grouped around **Chancellors Court**, re-landscaped in 1995 with sculptural interventions by *Lorna Green*: *Meet, Sit and Talk* of 1995 and *Conversation* of 1999. A broad flight of steps links it externally to the hub of the precinct at Beech Grove Terrace. The first perspectives of the buildings show CPB repeating the shell domes they had used at New Hall, Cambridge, but the form eventually adopted emerged only around 1963, inspired by Louis Kahn's Alfred Newton Richards Medical Research Laboratories in Philadelphia. First came **Mathematics, Earth Sciences and Computer Science**, completed in 1966. At right angles, the **Senior Common Room** of 1964–7, denoted by its external staircases and with a suite of lounges and bars on its principal second floor; the main bar at the southern end with large windows on three sides had a sunken dance floor. The (former) dining room above has a timber ceiling and long, narrow mural. Across the main axis is the **E.C. Stoner Building** for physics, much the longest of the spine ranges; fourteen slightly irregular bays long (mainly five storeys topped with vents); its elegance shows the hand of *Geoffry Powell*. The centrepiece of Chancellors Court, however, into which the walkways all debouched, is the **Roger Stevens Building**, 1968–70 [19, 95], with sixteen small raked lecture theatres on four levels, and nine larger theatres at right angles over a glazed café and television studio. The external ventilation pipes to the lecture theatres follow the rake of the building. This is the core of the CPB campus, where the red and green routes met. Inside, the raked theatres are set directly off staircases with doors off every step so latecomers can sneak onto the rear benches; it was a prototype for the planning of CPB's Barbican Theatre in London. The concrete beams which form the seats and benches constitute the structure of the floor and ceiling of the lecture theatre below. The benches in the glazed ground-floor café are also by *CPB*. Refurbishment by *Braithwaite & Jackman*, 1998. To the s, towards Clarendon Way, are the spines of **Garstang** and **Irene Manton** for biophysics and biological sciences, completed in 1969–70. Irene Manton was extended by *Ellwood Hooson* for biology, and linked to Garstang in 1995–7 by a research building (Astbury) that repeats the fenestration of the old but uses modern metal cladding; it was extended again in 2000 to accommodate microbiology. Links were also provided to the Worsley Building, s of Clarendon Way (*see* Leeds General Infirmary p. 87). N is

95. Roger Stevens Building, by Chamberlin, Powell & Bon, 1968–70

the **Edward Boyle Library**, completed by *CPB* in 1975 and extended by *Jackson & Calvert* in 1994 by infilling the space deliberately left for this purpose, part of which was occupied by cluster columns supporting a suspended sculpture by *Quentin Bell* (now in the Baines Wing courtyard). The plan is an open well surrounded by reading cubicles, stepped towards the windows; changes in technology prompted Jackson & Calvert to opt for a contrasting design. The final block, for **Economics and Social Science** was handed over in 1978 but its N and E elevations remain uncompleted. A second court intended SE of here, Convocation Court, was never built. *CBP* also extended the **Students' Union** with a partly submerged structure down the side of the hill that ended in a glazed pyramid over a debating chamber. This was extended again in 2001 by *Farrell & Clark*. Also by *CPB* was the original sports complex at the southern end of the precinct, remodelled and extended by *Jones Stocks & Partners*, 1986. For twenty years Leeds Playhouse occupied the adjacent building, by *William Houghton Evans*. It had been intended to convert this into a further sports hall, but by the time the University took the building over there was a greater need for more teaching space, and the building was put to use as a conference centre, remodelled in 2003 by *Farrell & Clark*.

The University long had a policy of building **Halls of Residence** on cheaper land away from its main precinct. *CPB* looked into the cost of laying on transport and duplicating facilities, and recommended building high-density student flats within the precinct. These included the

96. Charles Morris Hall, Mount Preston Street, by Chamberlin, Powell & Bon, 1964–6

'joker' flats, and two new blocks. The **Henry Price Building** is a 'flying freehold' across the cemetery wall on Clarendon Road (*see* below), with a distinctive water tower. Built to *Christoph Bon*'s designs in 1963–4, it was followed by **Charles Morris Hall** in Mount Preston Street (also by *Bon*) in 1964–6 [96], linked to the 'red' route across the precinct, with two tall blocks originally for men and a lower range for women containing dining and common room facilities. Accrington brick was used for the purely residential blocks, to contrast with the concrete finish of the teaching buildings and in homage to the red brick terraces they replaced.

Pre-University and Other Buildings*

The N part of the university precinct is dominated by **St George's Fields** between University Road and Clarendon Road. Originally the Leeds General Cemetery, opened 1835, won in competition by *John Clark*, who designed the central **chapel** as an Ionic temple. This has columns at the entrance, and at the other end an arcade of square columns infilled with large sash windows. In the porch a **statue** of Michael Sadler (linen merchant and supporter of the Ten Hours Bill) by *Patric Park* of London, 1837; originally at Leeds Parish Church. Massive grey cemetery walls relieved by two small entrances on the w side (one original) and the

*The names and dates in this section come from Professor Maurice Beresford's *Walks Round Red Brick* (1980)

gatehouse on the N side – Greek Revival, with giant Doric columns *in antis* on the exterior and flanked by projecting lodges within, with battered pilasters and urns. Next to it a fine monument to heroic Leeds firemen, their gallantry recorded on an obelisk shielded by a fireman's hat and columned canopy, with a carving of a C19 fire engine. The cemetery was acquired by the University in 1965 and largely cleared of gravestones. 'May it always be treated with sympathetic respect,' Pevsner pleaded in 1967. *Chamberlin, Powell & Bon* wanted to preserve more gravestones, and to create a small lake and open-air stage, but excavation was impossible, the University demanded clearance, and the stones were used in 1965–8 to form mounds within the resulting greensward. On the SE side an area had been set aside in 1842 for cheaper graves, recorded by vertical slabs each bearing twelve names. In 1968 these were reused as paving; when they ran out CPB used concrete slabs marked with hieroglyphs.

Building w of Woodhouse Lane began in the 1790s. Preserved within the University precinct are numerous houses associated with the development of Little Woodhouse from the late C18. The first houses acquired by the Yorkshire College have been demolished, others purchased in 1896 survive and form a cordon between the phases of purpose-built development. Most of the housing dates from the 1820s and after. It is of only minor interest but several buildings should be mentioned. **Beech Grove House**, whose driveway formed the basis of **University Road**, was built of ashlar in 1799 for Abram Rhodes. Symmetrical with a central bow; in 1840 it was sold to an ironfounder, John Ogden March, who probably added the Norman porch and plate-glass sashes.

Between Clarendon Road and Hyde Terrace is **Little Woodhouse Hall**, described in 1741 as a 'new house empty' and available for letting with magnificent views. Its plain three-storey façade built for Christopher Thompson, gentleman, can be seen on the s side, flanked by later C18 shallow two-storey canted bays. *John Clark*'s new entrance range with pillared porch was added on the E side *c.* 1840, for the sons of the industrialist John Atkinson who inherited in 1833; interiors remodelled in 1847 by *William Reid Corson & Edward la Trobe Bateman*. They had advice from *Owen Jones*, whose influence is obvious in the circular staircase hall, paved in blue, brown and yellow mosaic to a geometric pattern around an eight-pointed star. The staircase has a cast-iron balustrade of scrolls and flowers, top-lit dome with interlacing ribs [97]. Six lunettes painted by *John Everett Millais* are now in the City Art Gallery. Behind, in **Hyde Terrace**, the remnants of **Springfield House**, built in 1792 for Thomas Livesey, a cloth dresser. Once a gracious two-storey brick house with central pediment and pedimented doorcase.

97. Little Woodhouse Hall, Hyde Terrace, staircase hall, by W.R. Corson & E. la Trobe Bateman, 1847

98. Clothworkers' Centenary Concert Hall, by J.B. Fraser, 1870

In **Springfield Mount** to the N is the former **Priory of St Wilfred** (now **Continuing Education**), a hostel of the Community of the Resurrection founded in houses here in 1892 by Charles Gore of Mirfield, to enable men too penurious to enter Oxbridge to read theology at Leeds. Designed by *Temple Moore*, and built in two phases: 1907–10 and, supervised by *Leslie Moore*, 1927–8. Dormers in the high roof are oddly domestic in this context. Inside, chapel, refectory and meeting rooms, with panelling, fireplaces and a fine staircase, and to the rear a cloister-like rear courtyard garden.

Grand mid-C19 houses survive in an enclave off the W side of **Woodhouse Lane**, which is dominated by three former churches. **Emmanuel** was built in 1880 by *Adams & Kelly*, a body of rock-faced ashlar and a smooth massive tower spire over the crossing, remodelled in 2004 by *Halliday Clark* to provide seminar rooms and accommodation for the Chaplaincy. Behind it the **Emmanuel Institute**, the former Chaplaincy, internally remodelled by the *University Estates Department* with a first-floor workshop theatre. Further s downhill, **Trinity St David's Congregational Church** of 1898 by *G.F. Danby*, subdivided in 2004, when it (and its attached Sunday School of 1901) were adapted to nightclub and café-bar.

At the s end of **Cavendish Road** is the landmark tower of the former Presbyterian Church of 1870 by *J.B. Fraser*, converted to the **University Clothworkers Centenary Concert Hall** in 1974–5 by the *University Surveyor* [98]. Restored in 2004 by *Harrogate Design*, when the basement was converted to form additional practice rooms and the concert hall capacity increased. A glorious entrance, giant stone steps below a brick tower flanked by stone parapets and urns. **School of Music** behind, by *Harrogate Design*, 2003.

Nearby, on **Woodhouse Lane**'s E side, **Blenheim Terrace** was built in phases from 1824 to 1839 by *T.E. Upton*, a local solicitor and building speculator. It is an unusually long row of over twenty brick two-bay houses of three storeys and basement (now offices, flats, shops and university premises) set behind long, narrow front gardens with tall stone gate piers. Downhill, on the corner with Blackman Lane, the former **Blenheim Baptist Church**, *c.* 1858 by *William Hill*. Nave and aisles under one roof and a large traceried three-light w window; lancet windows in brick panels, NW tower with lucarnes. The classical **Friends' Meeting House** by *Edward Birchall*, 1866–8 has an arcaded porch with Tuscan columns and an arcaded pediment.

On **Blenheim Walk**, N, **Blenheim Building** (Jacob Kramer College), 1981–4 by *M. Thurmott*, City Architect, project architect *R. Shepley*. Eclectic Arts and Crafts style, an early example of what became known as the 'Leeds Look'. Banded brickwork in bold colours extends to paving and flanking walls; L-plan on a corner site (Woodhouse Lane and Blenheim Walk), four storeys, bold entrance and staircase tower with bullseye glazing. Long bands of windows light the top-floor studios, under deep eaves.

Elain Harwood

Little Woodhouse and Hyde Park

The small cluster of buildings shown on the Giles map of 1815 developed along an ancient lane leading to the medieval open fields. Mr Kendall, a merchant, built a house here in about 1588, and in the early C18 Ralph Thoresby wrote that Little Woodhouse was 'one of the pleasantest hamlets'. Seven fashionable villas were built in this area between 1740 and 1790. Others followed in the early C19, providing homes for merchants, industrialists, clergy and physicians. Many of these survive within the precincts of the University (*see* p. 184) and along Clarendon Road (laid out in 1839). Further w, however, a less exclusive district emerged on land sold by the Earl of Cardigan's estate in the 1860s and built up with streets of standard rows of back-to-backs served by new churches and schools. It extended N to the suburb of Hyde Park NW of Woodhouse Moor. A walk is only justified for a small part of Little Woodhouse. Other significant survivals are listed by street.

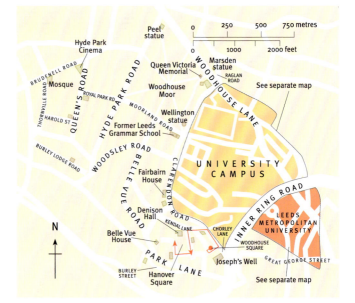

99. Little Woodhouse and Hyde Park

Woodhouse Square, Hanover Square and Neighbourhood

Proposals were first made in 1825 to lay out **Woodhouse Square** in the grounds of the C18 villa-mansion of Claremont (*see* below) but building began only after the mill owner John Atkinson purchased the house in 1840, by which time the fashion for such planned developments was dissipating and the square was never completed. The earliest building is **Waverley House**, W side, by *John Clark* for Atkinson, built in 1840 as two houses with an entrance on the S side. Solid, six bays, three storeys over a basement and exceptionally shallow pediment. Warm orange brickwork, heavy pilastered doorcase, stone sill bands and recesses below the windows. Originally intended as the end of a row of four, climbing uphill on this side of the square. Instead its neighbour is the functional red brick **St Anne's (R.C.) School** *c.* 1900 by *J.H. Eastwood*, contemporary with his cathedral (*see* p. 54). Two storeys and five bays, segmental windows and two small stone crosses on gablets. Now along the S side, Nos. 2–9, a row of red brick houses by local architect and builder *Richard William Moore*, 1845–6, built just after he had completed his pupilage with Robert Chantrell [100]. Moore lived at No. 3. Two storeys, Nos. 6–7 are higher, intended as the centre of a symmetrical design, undone when the W end of the row was not completed. An attractive group, somewhat weighed down by the early Victorian flamboyance of rusticated quoins, doorcases with deep entablatures and margin-light windows. The heavy console brackets at Nos. 6 and 7 are probably later. Now, the square's E side, open to **Clarendon Road**: No. 12 is of 1868 by *George Corson* for George Herbert Rayner, an importer of valonia (acorn cups for tanning and dyeing). Baronial Gothic, in red brick with blue brick decoration. Strong corner emphasis with bulky

100. Nos. 2–5 Woodhouse Square, by Richard William Moore, 1845–6

101. Statue of Sir Peter Fairbairn, Woodhouse Square, by Matthew Noble, 1868

stone columns (the capitals left uncarved), and a round tower with curved window glass and pointed roof, s gable decorated with short turrets. It stood alone until 1902 when its Queen Anne-style neighbour (No. 12a) was built. At No. 14, Gothic again, 1869, by *Corson* for Mr Atkinson, a mill owner, the stonework here carved with shamrock and thistle emblems.

The garden within the square was originally sloping but levelled to hold a water tank in 1941. At its SE corner, set on a high granite plinth, a bronze **statue** of Sir Peter Fairbairn, engineer and Mayor at the time of the Town Hall opening, by *Matthew Noble*, 1868 [101]. He faces the town, his left hand resting on a column covered with symbolic cloth, cog-wheel and chain of office, a scroll in his right hand. His pose is also symbolic, his right shoulder aligned southwards in the direction of his works on the Aire, his left directed uphill towards his home on Clarendon Road (*see* below).

N of the square, in **Clarendon Road,** is **Claremont** (No. 23), from whose gardens the square was created. s-facing, pedimented Georgian house of two storeys, described as 'new built' in 1772 for the Quaker merchant John Elam. The character was changed by the addition of an entrance porch and large bay windows after 1856 by *George Corson* for Dr John Deakin Heaton, physician and co-founder of the Yorkshire College. Inside, the rooms are substantially C19 but there is a fine cantilevered stone staircase with knopped balusters. Good Minton floor tiles. Since 1968 the house has belonged to the Yorkshire Archaeological Society and the Thoresby Society who have incorporated fabric from other buildings: a 1740 doorcase from Scarcroft Grange and library furniture of 1925 by *Kitson, Parish & Ledgard*. Upstairs, two white marble fireplaces from Osmondthorpe Hall, Whitkirk, the carving thought to be by *Flaxman*. Terraced houses ('The Claremonts') were squeezed into the garden after the sale of the grounds in 1894. The rear outbuildings and garden wall line the narrow **Kendal Lane**, which divided the Little Woodhouse Hall (*see* p. 184) and Claremont estates in the C18.

John Wilkinson Denison, one of Leeds' wealthiest merchants, acquired Claremont in 1786 and divided its estate for the construction of **Denison Hall** (now flats) [102], which stands prominently to the W on the N side of Hanover Square. It was designed by *William Lindley* of Doncaster and built of local Potternewton stone in less than four months. Lindley had designed houses on Park Place in 1777 (*see* p. 112). The house is typical of Lindley's work for a wealthy but conservative client (Denison is thought to have built cloth-finishing workshops as well as stables to the rear), following the Adamish style of his master John Carr. Three-storey, five-bay centre flanked by bowed two-storey wings, given increased grandeur by the sloping site. The round-arched recesses to the central three bays, giant Ionic pilasters and pediment with urns are in the style of James Paine. Modest pedimented E entrance, with Doric columns and delicate carved swags. Typical Neoclassical entrance vestibule screened by columns *in antis* and central oval staircase hall. Dramatic cantilevered staircase with wrought-iron balustrade of S-scrolls and ribbon-like motifs, the work of *John Rogers*, a pupil of ironsmith *Maurice Tobin* (who worked regularly for Carr and made the ironwork for his Leeds Infirmary in 1770). The stair design is similar to Carr's at Norton Place, Lincolnshire, itself a variation of Inigo Jones' Tulip staircase at the Queen's House, Greenwich. Adam-style plasterwork in the dome above and in the former music room above the entrance, Corinthian pilasters and wind instruments on the ceiling. At the W end of the house a cantilevered stone staircase with plain square-section balusters extended from ground floor to attics, probably inserted *c.* 1824–6 when the house was divided in two by the new owner, George Rawson, stuff merchant.

Soon after acquiring Denison Hall, Rawson commissioned *Henry Teal* to survey his grounds for residential development as **Hanover Square**. Its private garden was promoted as an important attraction, advertised as 'Hanover Square Park' in 1828 by *Joshua Major*, landscape gardener of Knostrop (and the designer of Manchester's first parks), as

a pleasure ground with flower beds, shrubs and forest trees.* The design for the buildings was undertaken by *Charles Watson* (a pupil and partner of Lindley) and *J.P. Pritchett* of York. Like Woodhouse Square, this speculation was a failure and only two blocks of houses were built, on opposite corners of the new square. No. 11 (NE corner) was designed as two houses, built 1826–30. Smooth red brick, six windows wide and three storeys high over stone cellars, the area protected by railings. Stone steps to a tall entrance doorway with fanlight and stone cornice supported by Pritchett's characteristic slim console brackets. Recessed panels below the ground-floor windows, stone first-floor sill band. The second entrance and discreet blind windows face Denison Hall. The house was occupied by a Rawson relative, J.P. Clapham. He advertised a 'capital family house' to let in the *Leeds Intelligencer*; it had a detached kitchen with hard and soft water, and conveniences with laundry and washhouse. In 1836 Clapham proposed to build a row of seven 'genteel houses' here, but his plans were never realized. Instead plots filled a generation later with less prestigious terraced houses, typified by those on the E and S sides of the square. On the S side a Sunday School built *c.* 1900. At the S end of the W side are Nos. 37–40, the second block completed by *Pritchett* (in John Clark's style) for two semi-detached pairs. They were promptly occupied by George Rawson Jun., Edward Baines Jun. (editor of the Liberal *Leeds Mercury*), and Robert Perring (editor of the Tory *Leeds Intelligencer*). Nos. 37 and 38 have an attractive wide

*The garden remained the property of Denison Hall until gifted to Leeds City Council, who made it public in 1958.

102. Denison Hall, s front, by William Lindley, 1786

103. Hyde Park Picture House, Brudenell Road, by Thomas Winn & Sons, 1914

entrance framed by paired attached Tuscan columns supporting a heavy entablature. One of these would have been the 'substantially built house' advertised in March 1831 by John Standish, plumber and glazier of Hunslet Lane. It contained breakfast, dining, and drawing rooms, a library and seven 'lodging rooms' as well as kitchen and laundry, cellars, stable and coach house. Uphill, a terrace built 1880–93, with rear extensions for workshops added *c.* 1889 for the use of travelling drapers trading with surrounding villages.

The remaining buildings of note in Little Woodhouse are now described by street, arranged alphabetically:

Belle Vue Road was made in 1860. Terraces on the w side display classical and Gothic detailing. At the s end **Belle Vue House**, built for cloth merchant Michael Wainhouse in 1792. A small red brick Palladian mansion standing on an ashlar plinth. Pedimented, five bays, two storeys over basement, ornamented with carved stone console brackets supporting a pedimented doorway, sill bands to the front. Venetian stair window to rear. Wainhouse had workshops and a warehouse at the end of its curving drive from Park Lane. The grounds were built up with back-to-back houses in the 1860s, and now by late 1970s housing. The extensive view remains.

Brudenell Road belongs to the area developed from the 1860s as Hyde Park, a socially less select district than Headingley to the n. Here is one of the best-preserved early cinemas in Britain, the **Hyde Park Picture House** of 1914 by *Thomas Winn & Sons* [103]. It stands at a junction with a canted corner under a Dutch gable with ball finials. Free

Ionic columns of Burmantofts white 'Marmo' to the entrance with an attractively lettered glazed terracotta frieze above and dressings of the same, all contrasting nicely with red brickwork. Staircase window with timber columns and coloured glass. The fittings are splendidly well preserved including the kiosk and mosaic lobby floor, while the auditorium has moulded plasterwork, a decorated barrel-vaulted ceiling and a balcony with a frieze of plaster festoons, brackets and shields. Even the original screen is preserved (hidden behind its modern successor) painted directly onto the wall with surround of gilded cherubs, swags and festoons. Art Deco wooden panels on the rear wall of the balcony are a subsequent addition. Uniquely, the cinema is still lit by gas 'modesty' lighting to avoid complete darkness. Nearby is the **Makkah Mosque** of 2003, designed by Atba Al-Samarraie of Archi-structure. Bright yellow brick relieved by bands of blue. Two towers face the road in addition to the usual dome and minaret.

Burley Street. **St Andrew's Vicarage**, *c.* 1860 Gothic by *G.E. Street*, now a solicitor's office. Street used contrasting stones here, buff for walling and grey for quoins and details. Original entrance obscured by a glazed porch but the picturesque grouping of entrance, stair window of three cusped lights, external chimney and steeply pitched roof with small dormers can still be appreciated.

Burley Lodge Road. Named after Burley Lodge, built *c.* 1794 on the vast Cardigan estate. A fragment of the front of the house is visible between Kelsall Terrace and Road, named after the Lodge's last occupant, William Kelsall, mayor of Leeds in 1859. James Strickland bought the property in 1886 and built streets of back-to-back housing in its grounds. Like the 'Harolds' (*see* Queen's Road, below) they were built in blocks of six or eight houses with outside toilets ('closets') in small yards between, a layout little altered since the Leeds Improvement Act of 1866. Renovation in the 1960s provided inside toilets and in 1995–2002 an Urban Regeneration Scheme included grants to upgrade the former closet areas as bin yards and social spaces using attractive artwork.

Chorley Lane was created in 1742, as a drive for Little Woodhouse Hall (*see* University Precinct, above) from Park Lane. Chorley Mill stood at the s end in 1818; and it was developed from *c.* 1840. On the w side is **Joseph's Well**, a vast clothing factory built 1888–1904 by Sir John Barran, an expansion of his ready-made clothing business. Four and five storeys in brick and terracotta, typically freely styled for its date. The E warehouse wing is most ornate, the main business entrance under a deep segmental arch and the basement storey rusticated, with great use of heavy mouldings and huge keystones; impressive cast-iron columns in the entrance hall which has a staircase enclosing an elevator shaft. The five-storey N range, which contained workshops behind rows of large windows has a prominent stair-tower with a steep slated roof. The workers' entrance was on the w side from Hanover

Lane, close to their homes. The factory employed over 2000 people and continued in use until the mid 1960s. Converted for offices in the 1990s when the single-storey sheds were demolished for car parking and sympathetic new-build created on the s side.

Clarendon Road was laid out by John Wilkinson in 1839. It is nearly one mile long and was infilled first by fashionable houses in spacious grounds, then by semi-detached houses and terraces. N of Woodhouse Square and Claremont (*see* above) on the E side, behind a high wall with narrow front gateway, is No. 20, **Clarendon House**, built 1853–7 for William Braithwaite, surgeon. Solid, two-storey, Italianate. Neat oriel window over the entrance, deep cornice, ornate chimneys. Round the corner, on Hyde Street, there is a blocked street entrance with segmental pediment and walling buttressed by brick pilasters. Nos. 22 and 24 are a semi-detached pair by *Isaac Dixon*, 1859, originally named Albert Villas. Central three-column portico, the column capitals lavishly carved with eagles and grapes. Wide hipped roof. James Bedford, chemical works owner, was one of the first occupants. Further up the hill on this side, a group of detached houses in a mixed, gabled Gothic style with projecting porches carried up to small turrets: No. 40, **Southfield House**, built 1867–70 for James Reffitt, dyer, with ornate tower, scrolled gable and a stone roundel carved with plants. For contemporary developments E of Clarendon Road *see* University, above.

On the W side at this point, No. 67, **Oak Villa** with a cheerful oriel window above the front door. Uphill **Fairbairn House** (Nos. 71–75) is a fine brick Italianate mansion of 1840–1 by *John Clark* for the engineer Peter Fairbairn [104]; the first house to be built on the new road, which must have functioned almost as a private drive for a brief period. Close to the road, a shallow curved driveway guarded by two pairs of monolithic pedimented stone gatepiers, side panels ornamented like rivetted steel plates. Two storeys and seven windows wide, ashlar plinth and giant Corinthian pilasters, a small pedimented doorway and an attic storey behind heavy balustraded blocking course. Clark's preferred Greek ornament is extravagantly used inside where fluted columns *in antis* screen a fine Imperial staircase with scrolled iron balustrade. Some of the heavy plasterwork was probably added in 1858 when Queen Victoria and Prince Albert stayed here when they came to open the Town Hall. Secondary oval newel stair with Egyptian lotus balusters to the basement, fire-proof construction of cast-iron beams and segmental brick arches. Occupied from 1873 by John Gott, vicar of St Peter's. Later converted into a clergy training school, with red brick pilastered N extension. Tall **chapel** on the s side, by *Temple Moore*, 1896. Blocked round gable window; three-light cusped tracery on the s. Inside, ribbed barrel-vaulted ceiling.

Furthest N at the corner with Woodhouse Lane, the former **Police Station, Fire Station and Library**, dominated by its landmark leaddomed clock tower. Dated 1901, in the extravagant free Italianate style

104. Fairbairn House, Clarendon Road, by John Clark, 1840–1

105. University Business School, former Grammar School, by E.M. Barry, 1858–9; additions by Carey Jones Architects, 1995

of *W.H. Thorp*. Red brick, carved Bradford stone dressings including pickaxes and hoses on the keystone of the traceried central window. Granite columns with Ionic and Corinthian capitals and a segmental pediment with coat of arms. Now a pub.

Moorland Road. The **University Business School** [105], is the former **Leeds Grammar School** and headmaster's house. The earliest part is by *E.M. Barry* (brother of the headmaster), 1858–9. Decorated Gothic to a long, cruciform plan, with gabled flanks and a spirelet over the 'crossing'. Barry built a small detached **chapel** on the street corner in a slightly thinner Gothic in 1862–3. Large additions to the w are by *Austin & Paley* from 1904–5. Adapted in 1995 by *Carey Jones Architects*, who added the **Innovation Centre** fronting Clarendon Road, 2001 and glazed arcade along the s side of the school.

Queen's Road was laid out by the Cardigan Estate as a long *cul-de-sac* off Alexandra Street c. 1865. A single building is shown on a map of 1866, probably the modest rendered two-storey house, twin gabled and with round-arched openings at the e end of Harold Street, one of nine e–w streets known as '**The Harolds**' on the w side of Queens Road. Their alignment follows old field boundaries, each with rows of brick back-to-backs in blocks of eight, built by 1881. A tenants' strike in 1913 contributed to the City Council's decision to build affordable houses. Further N and on the e side of Queen's Road the former **Board School** by *William Landless*, 1892, now the Royal Park Primary School. Its scale

must have intimidated its small pupils. Red brick classical style planned around a central hall (a plan-form which Landless introduced to Leeds' schools) flanked by adjoining two-storey wings. Two enormous porches for the boys' and girls' entrances, each topped with balustrades. The sides are broken up by brick pilasters. Tall roof ventilator. The most striking feature of all, the truly monstrous gateposts with rock-faced rustication, provide an element of the sublime.

Victoria Terrace: Highfield House, on the corner with Belle Vue Road, was built in 1862 for George Hirst, whose dyeworks stood near Wellington Bridge. Possibly by *David & John Eastwood*. Conservative classical, two storeys and three bays, console brackets over the entrance, flanking bay windows.

Woodhouse Moor was the only public space in Leeds until the later C19 and has been the site of numerous public and political meetings. Acquired in 1855 by the Corporation who had already established their waterworks on the Moor's E side. The reservoir has been covered over but the **North Lodge** of *c.* 1850 survives, a picturesque single-storey Gothic cottage built of edge-tooled gritstone ashlar. Four **statues** have found their way to the moor, all re-set from city centre sites. The best, rather side-lined on the N side and deserving of a more prominent site, is the stately memorial to **Queen Victoria** by *George Frampton*, 1903 [106]. Portland stone base and bronze figures, the Queen in coronation robes flanked by 'Peace' and 'Industry'. Coats of arms, and radiant sun

106. Queen Victoria, Woodhouse Moor, by George Frampton, 1903

carved on the back. Originally unveiled outside the Town Hall as the centrepiece of Victoria Square, moved here in 1937. There are two Victorian statesmen: N by St Augustine's church (*see* p. 254) at Hyde Park Corner is a bronze statue of **Sir Robert Peel** by *William Behnes*, 1852, from outside the (dem.) Court House in Park Row. On the s corner, the **Duke of Wellington** in bronze by *Marochetti*, 1854. It stood outside the Town Hall until 1937. On the E side of the moor, at the corner of Clarendon Road and Raglan Road, is **Henry Rowland Marsden**, 1878, by local sculptor *John Throp*. Carrara marble whiskered figure in mayoral robes, its high plinth carved with interesting reliefs: 'Education', 'Benevolence' and 'Industry', the latter represented by the stone-crushing machine developed by Marsden after emigrating to the United States in 1848. He returned to establish the Soho Iron Foundry in Hunslet.

Leeds Metropolitan University, City Campus

The cluster of blocks between Calverley Street and Woodhouse Lane were commissioned in 1951 to amalgamate on one site the City's Colleges of Technology, Art, Commerce and Housecraft (renamed Leeds Central Colleges). By *Yorke, Rosenberg & Mardall* built between 1955 and 1969. Refounded as Leeds Polytechnic in 1970, and Leeds Metropolitan University, 1992.

YRM's bold original scheme for a single campus with shared Assembly Hall, Students' Union and Library had to be altered mid-stream and although Pevsner noted 'the style of the c20 at last belatedly recognized in the centre of Leeds' the results are disappointing. The original approach was from **Calverley Street**, with buildings set into the sloping ground. A long block on pilotis was planned to bridge the entrance approach but instead only the range fronting Portland Way was completed in 1955. Three storeys with thin concrete piers and panels of light aggregate facing. Rising behind is the ten-storey **Teaching Block**, completed in 1958, originally curtain-walled but re-clad in 2000 by the

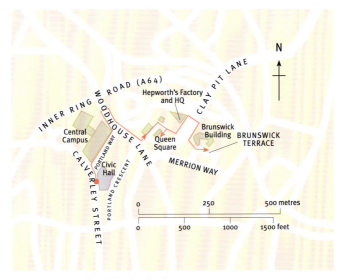

107. Leeds Metropolitan University, City Campus

108. Engineering & Teaching blocks, Portland Way, by YRM, 1951–8; altered 2000

Bowman Riley Partnership with a sharp, if rather dark, glazed façade [108]. YRM's original scheme continued the slab NW to three times its present length; but a design for three towers in pre-cast concrete was substituted in 1966–9. The overall height remained the same, but the result is undermined by its lack of unity, emphasized by the recent refurbishment of the earlier block. Each of the towers (Buildings D, F and H) have tight grids of grey pre-cast aggregate cladding and are similarly treated. They group around a low podium containing the refectory. At the NW corner, the tower which contained the College of Art has larger windows. The NE corner of the campus to Woodhouse Lane was substantially altered and re-clad in 1999–2000 by the *Bowman Riley Partnership* to create the lively **Leslie Silver Building**, which incorporates the main entrance and Learning Centre [109]. Five storeys in yellow brick and aluminium cladding with a curved glass entrance screen flanked by high brick stair-towers. In the entrance lobby: 'One Hundred Books' by *Stephen Hurrel*. Ten paired glass shelves support sheets of blue glass etched with the author and title of a book selected by staff. At night they are back-illuminated. Inside, the lobby opens into a light reception area, the Learning Centre is glazed in alongside a corridor to the original S entrance.

109. Leslie Silver Building, Woodhouse Lane, by Bowman Riley Partnership, 1999–2000

LMU has also taken over much of **Queen Square**, a modest Georgian oasis of red brick houses built up on the w side of Claypit Lane by developers *John & George Bischoff*, 1806–22. The houses are on three sides, the earliest on the NW of three storeys. Nos. 1–3 are pedimented with three-quarter Tuscan columns flanking the doorways and an elliptical window in the pediment. Original railings to Nos. 3–4 with cupand-cover finials. The rest are smaller, many with stone wedge lintels and fanlights. As at Park Square, the rows were built with access to warehouses and workshops at the rear. No. 8 (N side) has a carefully preserved shopfront *c.* 1900 for Kayll & Reed, stained glass makers and signwriters, with gilded lettering on the fascia. The houses on the sw have doorways with wooden reeded pilasters. Late C19 gas lampposts with fluted shafts and a small central garden complete the scene. Just behind, in Claypit Lane, stands Joseph Hepworth's late C19 clothing factory and its seventeen-storey headquarters of 1973 by *K. Peers* of the *P-E Consulting Group*. Marble-faced podium and curtain-walled slab with reflective bronze windows in a crisp and clean interpretation of late Le Corbusier.

Across Claypit Lane, stands the **Brunswick Building** (Faculty of Environment, Construction and Design), planned in 1969 when Patrick

Nuttgens was the Director of the college. Executed 1973–9 by *David Wrightson* and *Christopher Kaye* working for *E.W. Stanley*, of Leeds City Council. A grand but compromised scheme of three, linked four-storey blocks built on one of the city's highest points, and canted around a stepped courtyard in the form of an amphitheatre (originally designed to be covered by a glass roof). The composition is monumental with buff tile-clad walls pierced by vertical and horizontal openings; the inner faces of the buildings are glazed, the outer walls to the busy roads left impressively blank and boldly sculptural. The planned Engineering Block on the E side of the courtyard was never built, its steel connecting rods left exposed. Also redundant is the first-floor bridge between the stair-tower close to the entrance and the studios on this side; originally intended to provide a continuous link through the building between the Merrion Centre to the S and a car park to the N. Less impressive interior, with an awkward subterranean lecture theatre. Ground-floor exhibition space with the eccentrically placed, circular **Pearson Room**, screened by tall round-arched windows crammed with stained glass, the gift of Lord Cowdray.

Outer Leeds

JOHN MINNIS

Armley

Armley, rising up steeply w of the city centre and forming a ridge along the s side of the Aire Valley, was a small cloth-making village with its own chapel in 1630. Scattered groups of houses (some of which survive) were built from the C17 in Upper Armley. The Leeds–Liverpool Canal (opened from Shipley to Leeds in 1777 and throughout in 1816) encouraged the growth of cloth mills, notably those of Benjamin Gott at Armley Mills. Winker Green Mills were established at about the same date. Gott leased a villa on the Armley Estate on the high ground to the w of the village and commissioned Repton to landscape the surrounding park. Main line railways through the Aire Valley and to Bradford led to the opening of heavy engineering works. In 1847, Armley Prison, still a significant landmark, was opened. In the next decades, large numbers of back-to-back houses were built and churches and other institutions followed in their wake. The population trebled from 9,200 in 1871 to 27,500 in 1901. Although now engulfed by the city, Armley still has surprisingly rural patches left around Hill Top and Armley Moor, an open space where horses graze, in close juxtaposition with tight rows of

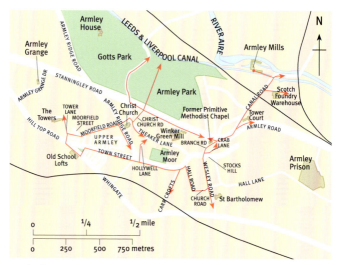

110. Armley

111. Armley Mills, Mill managers' houses, late c18

back-to-backs and council tower blocks. The earliest housing to the E has been replaced with low rise and tower blocks, that to the w largely remains.

The circular walk begins in **Canal Road** at **Armley Mills** (the Leeds Industrial Museum since 1982) which are picturesquely sited on sharply falling land between the Leeds–Liverpool Canal and the River Aire. Corn and fulling mills were erected here in the c16. In 1788, the fulling mill was rebuilt by Colonel Thomas Lloyd, a Leeds cloth merchant, as the largest woollen mill in the world. At the same time, the corn mill was rebuilt; it was rebuilt again after it burnt down in 1797. Benjamin Gott rented the Armley Mills c. 1800 while his Bean Ing Mill (*see* topic box, p. 138) was being rebuilt and in 1804 agreed their purchase, transforming the mill into one of the most technically advanced of its kind. The 1788 woollen mill was destroyed by fire in 1805 and replaced with one of fire-proof construction, one of the first examples in England and the earliest surviving in Yorkshire (*see* topic box, p. 206). Powered by two water wheels, whose gearing enabled them to outperform steam engines until c. 1840. The corn mill was converted to textile production, c. 1810.

The **Main Range**, as rebuilt by Gott in 1805, is L-shaped with a long four-storey N–S wing straddling the mill race; the E wing incorporates the 1797 former corn mill, built into the slope of the canal embankment. Regular façades of coursed stone, punctuated by small windows. A beam engine house was added *c.* 1854 with an imposing tapering chimneystack on a panelled pedestal. Inside, fulling stocks originally extended down the centre of the ground floor, with scribbling and carding machines on the second and third floors and mechanics' workshops at the top. The lower floor of the former corn mill has cruciform cast-iron columns but the top floor retains a small portion of the original sheet-iron nailed to the underside of joists for fire-proofing in 1807. Throughout the main range, the fire-proofing is more conventional: jack-arches of shallow brick supported by cylindrical cast-iron columns and T-section cast-iron beams.

Fire-proof Construction

The insurance of industrial buildings against fire became an important aspect of Leeds' commercial prosperity in the C19. Before the late C18 textile mills were traditionally built with stone or brick outer walls and timber internal structures, including floors. Mills were highly vulnerable to the risk of fire, either from oil lamps and candles or from sparks produced by mill machinery which ignited accumulated fibres on the floor. In the case of woollen mills, fire spread easily through the wooden structure, which was often saturated in oil and animal fat. The Navy advocated thin iron plates fixed to a wooden structure as a fire deterrent on ships in 1782 and in 1790 James Watt proposed replacing floorboards in mills with iron plates or covering exposed timber with a layer of plaster. Benjamin Gott used iron not only to fire-proof his Armley Mills and Bean Ing Mills in the early C19 but also his own villa at Armley. From the 1790s innovative mill builders and engineers developed cast iron for construction; intending it not only to prevent or slow the spread of fire but also to support heavy machinery, resist vibration and halt the penetration of damp. The technology was brought to Leeds (and Yorkshire) in 1802 by *Charles Bage*, designer of Ditherington Mill, Shrewsbury (1796), whose flax mill at Holbeck (dem.) for T. & B. Benyon used the same structure of cast-iron columns and beams supporting floors on brick arched vaults. John Marshall, also a partner at Ditherington, followed the design for his flax mill, of which the warehouse (1806) and later buildings survive at Holbeck (*see* p. 131–2). By 1870 concrete vaults were used in combination with iron structures but a few small mills still had timber supports and flooring after 1875. The introduction of stronger steel frames in the last years of the C19 brought an end to the use of cast iron for fire-proof construction.

N of the mill, a long low cloth **Drying House** of the 1820s with a roof composed of strikingly curvaceous cast-iron roof trusses, the w end formerly housing a gas plant (the main range had been gas lit from 1809, an exceptionally early use, with apparatus by *Boulton & Watt*). Raised up on the embankment facing the canal to the N, a semi-detached pair of **Mill Managers' Houses**, here by 1793 [111]. Quite plain with mullioned windows but with tall round-arched stair windows to the rear. Lower wings resemble Pennine weavers' cottages, with first-floor loomshops attached on each side. Adjacent, a mid-C19 nine-bay **warehouse**.

s along **Canal Road** are further buildings associated with Armley's industrial past. On a wharf known as Botany Bay (Australian wool was unloaded here), survives a very decayed timber **Loading Bay** with a canopy over the canal. High above the valley to the E, can be seen the warehouse of the former **Scotch Foundry** of Mathieson, Wilson & Co. (general ironfounders) of 1897 (dated 1888, the year of the company's foundation), a most ornate red brick block by *Walter A. Hobson* with extensive iron cresting along the roof parapets. Canal Road passes over the Midland Railway main line. On the right, the former **Armley Canal Road Station**, opened 1847. Only the booking office survives, a stylish pavilion of 1909 by the company's architect *Charles Trubshaw* (designed before his retirement in 1905) with his usual refined detailing. Opposite, the office block of the former **Carlton Works** of 1898 (also owned by Mathieson, Wilson), almost certainly by *Walter A. Hobson* with enrichment of decorative cut brick panels and banding, nicely carved timber mullions between large paired windows, a Flemish gable and a corner turret. Utilitarian workshop ranges behind. Cast-iron firegrates were made here. On the right, the former **Midland Asbestos Works** of J.W. Roberts Ltd of *c.* 1886, stone, single storey with some attempt at show on the Aviary Road façade. To the left, Nos. 6 and 8, a pair of three-storey stone cottages built *c.* 1840 into sloping ground with steps giving access to the rear on the first floor.

s is the busy **Armley Road** and the beginning of the compact C19 town centre. Prominent to the E of the junction, **Tower Court**, the former Armley Board School of 1878 by *Richard Adams*. A grand thirteen-bay composition in an elaborate but decidedly wayward Italianate. The front is articulated by projecting end bays with pediments and a central clock tower but these are insufficiently weighty to provide the emphasis needed to balance the over-busy treatment of the bays, each of which is delineated by stone pilasters. Closer to the junction, the former **Primitive Methodist Chapel**, 1905, by *Thomas & Charles Howdill* makes skilful use of its prominent corner site. Red brick and terracotta in a Free Renaissance style with a splendid Venetian window flanked by prominent twin ventilation towers. The interior has cast-iron columns with Ionic capitals separating the side aisles. Its Neo-Romanesque predecessor of 1877 by *Thomas Howdill* stands behind in

112. Armley Branch Library, Stocks Hill, by Percy Robinson, 1901

Branch Road, concealed by an incongruous classical façade of 1910, added on conversion to a cinema. Immediately N on **Stanningley Road**, the red brick four-storey former **Dress Warehouse** of Lutas Leathley & Co., 1891, by *James Fawcett*, a good example of a small cloth warehouse with retail premises on the ground floor, the frontage decorated with incised stone bands at lintel level. Fire-proof construction of concrete floors and steel beams. The old commercial centre of Armley is **Town Street**, reached along **Branch Road**. It begins with a good group of commercial buildings. To the left, **HSBC Bank** (formerly London City & Midland) of 1909 by *Sydney Kitson*, single storey and basement, with a curved façade of white faience with classical motifs, its flat roof hidden behind a parapet, originally balustraded. Facing it the **Yorkshire Bank**, 1936, by *C. Medley* in a simple but dignified moderne style, stone-faced and curved to its corner site. Opposite in **Stocks Hill**, the exuberant **Armley Branch Library** of 1901 by *Percy Robinson* [112]. Flemish Renaissance with two big shaped gables and plenty of ashlar channelled rustication to contrast with the brickwork. The city arms are in the centre of the gables. On the corner a low clock tower, topped by a louvred cupola, seems out of scale with the curved entrance loggia which wraps around its base. Interior with a gentle top-lit barrel-vaulted ceiling, mosaic floors and a handsome glazed screen with Art Nouveau glass. An extension (One Stop Centre) added in complementary style 2003. In **Crab Lane** to the N, the **Malt Shovel**, a C18 pub with mullioned windows, is a lone survivor of the old village.

Returning to the beginning of Town Street, s up **Wesley Road**, the former **Temperance Hall and Mechanics' Institute** of 1866–7, built by the Armley Temperance Society, founded in 1836. Chapel-like, gable facing the street, with deep round-headed windows contrasting with segmental-headed ones with marginal lights on the ground floor. At the top of the road, at the highest point in Armley and visible from much of the city, looms the unmistakable if forbidding profile of one of Leeds' finest Victorian churches. **St Bartholomew**, of 1872–8 [14] replaced the C17 Armley Chapel, enlarged in 1825 and 1834–5 by *R.D. Chantrell*. Its replacement by the little known *Henry Walker & Joseph Athron*, their sole large-scale work, is a colossal church of Horsforth sandstone in E.E. style with a tower on the crossing and lancet windows, conforming in every way to the Tractarian ideal. Pevsner thought the crossing tower (not completed until 1903–4 and built to a modified design, replacing the intended saddleback roof with a squat pyramidal spire) was so tall and the transepts and polygonal apse kept so close to it that the effect was reminiscent of the Rhineland. But the influence of such High Victorian churches as Street's St Philip and St James, Oxford (1860–6), Burges' St Finn Bar, Cork (1863) and, especially, Teulon's St Stephen's Hampstead (1869) are equally evident in the massing of the E end. Goodhart-Rendel said of it 'This is a very great effort . . . credit is due in every direction. But I can't find any idea in it . . . one does feel that the architect tried *so* hard.' The awkward detailing of the tower (which is larger than the crossing and has to be supported on small retaining arches between the nave and transepts), the undersized spirelets and a certain thinness apparent in the aisle elevations may be criticized but the magnificent scale of the building overcomes any lingering doubts. Minimal later additions include a gabled and arched lychgate of 1888 and choir vestry of 1896.

The lofty **interior** [113], faced with Ancaster limestone, is 73 ft (22.3 metres) high but seems, if anything, taller because of the spacious clerestory. The nave of six bays has quatrefoil piers clasped in the centre and plain capitals. The N transept is almost entirely filled by the organ case with an arcaded timber screen below enclosing the N chapel. Nave roof with tie bar trusses on attached columns with large part-gilded angels holding shields. Apse, short chancel and crossing, all rib-vaulted. **Reredos**, 1877, by *Thomas Earp* appropriately large and architectural in form, the lower part of alabaster with a carved representation of the Adoration of the Magi, the upper of Caen stone, arcaded, with painted tiles depicting the Crucifixion by *Powell Bros.* **Font**, octagonal and arcaded with rich red and black marbles. **Pulpit** (1884) by *Adams & Kelly* of alabaster and grey marble, with a small sculpture of St Bartholomew copied from that by Peter Vischer (c. 1460–1529) at the shrine of St Sebald in Nuremburg. **Choir stalls**, carved by *Earp* to the design of *Walker & Athron*. Exceptionally grand **organ case** by *Walker & Athron* housing the celebrated organ by *J.F. Schulze*, installed in 1879

113. St Bartholomew, Wesley Road, crossing by Walker & Athron, 1872–7

but originally built for a summer house in the grounds of Meanwood Towers (*see* p. 265). Gothic in detail but Baroque in inspiration with carved angels crowning it. The case, carved locally, has panels based on Morris' Acorn and Strawberry Thief wallpaper designs. **Mosaic panels**.

E end: seven panels under the E window of 1879, partly obscured by the reredos. Below these, tiled figures Praise and Prayer and SS Luke, John and Bartholomew, executed 1925–34. W end: *opus sectile* work of 1884 [114], the Baptism of Christ, mainly British saints except, on the right, Bishop Selwyn and Dean Hook, the latter seemingly an afterthought. All these by *Powell & Sons*, who intended to continue the scheme above the arcading in the nave. **Stained glass**. In the apse and S transept of 1878–80, the W windows of 1881, all by *Clayton & Bell* and those in the nave by *Powell Bros* of 1882–3. An understated and delicate scheme with no single colour predominant. **Monuments**. Benjamin Gott Jun. (d.1814 while in Greece on the Grand Tour) by *Joseph Gott* (a distant relation), a weeping figure in antique dress with a funerary urn and a standing figure of Faith representing the triumph of Christian Piety over Grief. Benjamin Gott Sen. d.1839 also by *Gott*. Comfortably semi-reclining figure on a mattress rolled up at the top. He is realistically depicted, wearing a woollen cloth jacket of the highest quality to signify his role in the development of the woollen industry. N of the church are the foundations of the C17 church as an enclosure for the Gott family graves.

In **Church Road** to the NW, Nos. 4–14 are the Gothic **Walker's Almshouses** of 1883, two storeyed, the central pair of houses brought forward and given a large gable. Forming part of Armley Medical Centre, **Redcourt**, a substantial red brick house *c.* 1900 with a big hipped roof, mullions and leaded lights. Right into **Hall Road** and the red brick former **Methodist Free Church** of 1898–1900 by *Walter Hanstock & Son* in an odd amalgam of styles mixing Wrenaissance with Florentine windows in the nave. Two stocky towers flank the W front which is topped by an oversized rounded broken pediment. The interior retains plaster pilasters formerly flanking the rostrum. In the parallel **Carr Crofts**, the Neo-Georgian **Swimming Baths** of 1929–30 by the *City Architect*, part of the Armley Leisure Centre, have a monumental quality, with small window openings and bands of brick rustication.

Town Street retains the air of a village street with groups of small C19 shops but little individually of note other than on the N side the **Denison Hall Club**, a Conservative Club of 1890 by *Charles Thornton* in a simple Renaissance style. Then the open space of Armley Moor marks the start of Upper Armley. Opposite the Moor, just off Town Street, No. 1 **Roscoe Terrace**, a late C17 house with quoins and mullioned windows, altered in the C18. Possibly a former farmhouse. On

114. St Bartholomew, Wesley Road, *opus sectile* panel by Powell & Sons, 1884

115. Edinburgh Place, back-to-back houses, late C19

Town Street's N side are further remnants of Armley's pre-industrial past with **Moor View**, three early C19 houses and, down a footpath, Nos. 2 and 3 **Hollywell Lane**, a pair of early C19 houses, given dignity by quoins and deep round-headed staircase windows but still retaining plain cottage-like window and door surrounds. Beyond Wortley Road on the S side of **Town Street**, **Weavers Court**, a row of late C18 two-storey weavers' houses with a communal loom room occupying a third storey and a large archway providing access to the rear. Large paired windows of equal size on each floor. Two larger three-bay early C19 houses abut them at right angles. Opposite, **The Barleycorn**, early C19, with a lively front added in 1898. Two small mills face each other across Town Street. **Westfield Mills** (N side) has a little-altered early C19 four-storey hipped roof block to the rear. Paired windows, divided by stone mullions. It was used as a tannery in the late C19. Pair of two-storey blocks end on to Town Street, now rendered and altered. Opposite, **Shaw Mills** has a mid-C19 three-storey brick block with Dutch gabled-ends and broad segmental windows. A house, possibly the owner's, links it with a lower block at right angles.

The streets N and S of Town Street are tightly packed with rows of late C19 back-to-back and blind-back houses [115]. In **Edinburgh Grove** and Edinburgh Terrace are what appear to be straightforward back-to-backs of the 1890s with a mere six-inch gap between them. They are in fact two parallel terraces of blind-backs, marking successive phases in the development of the area. At the W end, near the junction of Town Street with **Whingate, Old School Lofts** was the West Leeds Boys' High School of 1906–7, by *William Broadbent*. The epitome of up-to-date school design and claimed to be the first building in Leeds to have all the floors of reinforced concrete. A symmetrical twenty-six-bay frontage in Free Baroque style with a centre raised on a basement and two three-storey wings, each with a cupola. Big windows, attached columns and rusticated pilasters in abundance and two ornate projecting porches with paired Ionic columns and segmental open pediments.

To the NW of Town Street, off **Hill Top Road**, are **The Towers**, a group of *c.* 1870 villas set back down a long drive. No. 21 has a very thin tower with fish-scale slated roof, Nos. 23–25 are double-fronted with oriel windows in the centre, an ogee-shaped gable above and exaggeratedly tall but thin towers with inset round-headed windows and surmounted by iron cresting. Gateposts topped by impressive carved lions. Off **Tower Lane** just to the E is a much altered C17 house, Nos. 40 and 42 **Westville**, with plain stone mullions containing later sashes and a large carved lintel over the entrance.

Now into the heart of Upper Armley, along **Moorfield Road**. A long row of blind-backs in **Moorfield Street** to the left present a cliff-like expanse of absolutely plain brickwork to the rear. In **Armley Ridge Road**, the landmark is the large **Christ Church** of 1869–72, by *Adams & Kelly*, in well-executed but slightly mechanical E.E. with paired lancets to the aisles, tripartite clerestory windows and a tall w tower. Interior much altered by reordering in 1983 by *Kitson & Partners* which cut off the two w bays of the nave to form a narthex. Inside, the **reredos**, arcaded with cusps and crocketed pinnacles, fills the width of the chancel. **Stained glass**. E window of 1884 in memory of William Gott, chancel s windows of 1885 and w windows of 1890 all by *Clayton & Bell*, N aisle, fourth window by *E. Pickett & Son*, 1948 and the seventh of 1951 by *Harry Stammers*. s aisle, seventh and eighth windows by *Charles E. Steel*, 1950. The adjacent brick Gothic **Church Hall** of 1905–6 by *Beckwith & Webster* has a medallion 'Little Children Come Unto Me' dated 1860 inserted in the gable. Behind the church in **Theaker Lane** is the **school** of 1871, single-storey Gothic, U-shaped with a central entrance and additions of 1895 by *Smith & Tweedale* and of 1992 to the rear. Early C19 **Farfield House** is now a club.

N now down **Christ Church Road** and on to **Stanningley Road** before entering **Armley Park**, opened in 1893. A Jubilee **Fountain** of 1897, paid for by William Gott. Fluted pilasters, a reeded stem and a gadrooned bowl. The **First World War memorial** is in the form of a Gothic wayside cross with an octagonal arcaded base bearing the names of the fallen surmounted by an open-sided shaft.

On the s side of Stanningley Road, the impressive complex of **Winker Green Mills** is an early example of a factory used for cloth production with several processes being carried out on one site. A mill had been established *c.* 1803, which was acquired by William Eyres & Sons in 1824. The earliest surviving building is the stone four-storey s range of 1825–32, probably used for hand spinning and handloom weaving, the two E bays are later extensions. Paired almost square windows, separated by a mullion (cf. Westfield Mills, Town Street, *see* above). Taking-in doors to the first and second floors. A fire in 1833 destroyed all but the engine house of the original mill, which was replaced by the large (nineteen-bay) four-storey brick and stone steam-powered mill. Its internal construction is of timber beams supported by cast-iron columns but part of the ground floor, which housed the willey machines, is fire-proofed. Some further fire-proofing can be seen in its E extension (of six bays), built in 1836 and incorporating the earlier engine house. At the same time, a second engine house was added to the S elevation. Later buildings include a warehouse block (shortened in length) c. 1840 with a rounded arch over a cart entrance, a single-storey N shed with north-light roof of the 1870s–80s and a further single-storey weaving shed. A chimney and one of three reservoirs survive. To the N on Stanningley Road, **Armley Park Court**, a former Board School of 1900 in an elegant and competently handled Neo-Jacobean by *W.S. Braithwaite*. Two gables in the centre and two domed ventilation towers project from the symmetrical façade, the detailing of which resembles that of Braithwaite's contemporary Pupil Teachers' College (*see* p. 153).

Return down Canal Road to Armley Mills or to the city centre along Armley Road.

Armley House

Gott's Park, off Armley Ridge Road, now a clubhouse for the golf course.

The Armley Estate was the property of Thomas Woolrich, a Leeds merchant who in *c.* 1781 built a villa here, facing E down the Aire Valley towards Leeds. Its style was that of John Carr with a big canted bay and low pavilion wings. Woolrich subsequently leased the estate to Benjamin Gott, the owner of Armley Mills (q.v.) who purchased the property in 1803 and soon turned to *Humphry Repton* for advice in remodelling house and grounds as his principal residence (Gott previously resided at his town house close to the Bean Ing Mills). Repton declared that the house 'may be compared to a good story told in ungrammatical language' and his Red Book of 1810 shows a proposal for raising the canted bay with an attic and remodelling the pavilions with pediments and Venetian windows. Replanting of the grounds began at once. Gott moved permanently to Armley in 1816 and appears almost immediately to have commissioned *Robert Smirke* to remodel and enlarge the house in a Grecian style. This was Smirke's first domestic work in this style and probably amongst the earliest use for a house not only in Yorkshire but also in England. It was quickly influential in Leeds. The house became the setting for Gott's collection of Greek and Roman antiquities, some of which were acquired by his son on the Grand Tour, but also included busts of contemporary engineers, among them John Rennie.*

*Gott commissioned Rennie to design Wellington Bridge over the Aire in 1817–19, for access to his Bean Ing Mills.

116. Armley House, by Robert Smirke, *c.* 1817. From J. P. Neale, *Views of the Seats of Noblemen and Gentlemen*, vol. 5 (1821)

The main E front [116] has a grand tetrastyle temple portico, in Smirke's favoured Ionic order from the Temple on the Ilissus, into which projects the canted bay of the earlier house, an unusual combination. Steps up to the portico give it an elevated position. This central block is flanked by low wings, curving to the w, that formerly linked it to plain two-storey pavilions (dem. in the 1950s), the absence of which unbalance the composition. The interior was innovative, Gott displaying the same interest in fire-proof construction as he had at Armley Mills, with cast-iron beams supporting vaulted masonry floors, a cast-iron service stair and cast-iron panelled doors. Some of this may still be seen; a faux timber panelled door leads to the basement while the cast-iron ribs of the roof to the wings are also exposed internally. The Prussian court architect Schinkel visited the house in 1826, while investigating the new mills of northern England, and praised it in his journal as 'a splendid construction . . . in the best style both inside and out', its interior 'sumptuous' and 'exceedingly tasteful'.

Repton's landscaping exploited the visual relationship between Gott's villa and the source of his wealth at Armley Mills, creating a setting in which mills and house would be seen together by travellers along the Kirkstall Road. From the house, the mills became the focus of the view E towards Leeds, while making an opening in a plantation provided a suitably picturesque vignette of Kirkstall Abbey to the w. In spite of much later building these views are still framed by a screen of trees in front of the house.

To the s in Armley Grange Drive, surrounded by 1930s suburbia, **Armley Grange**, a large ashlar early C19 house of seven bays, the central three projecting. Porch with Doric columns *in antis*.

117. Armley Prison, by Perkin & Backhouse, 1843–7

Armley Prison

Set amongst low rise 1970s council housing, the massive and forbidding **Armley Prison** dominates the skyline [117]. The prison was built as the borough gaol in 1843–7, the competition for which had been won by *Hurst & Moffat* of Doncaster. Negotiations broke down and *Perkin & Backhouse* took over the design, although they may have produced a new plan to accommodate more prisoners. The style is the favoured castellated type with a mighty gatehouse with splayed and battered towers and corbelled crenellated parapets flanking a large round-arched doorway. Its grimness is emphasized by the tooled ashlar facings and rock-faced dark gritstone of the walls which have corner turrets. Armley Prison is one of the earliest to follow the model radial plan established by Joshua Jebb at Pentonville in 1840–2: only Reading precedes it in date. The gatehouse fronts an entrance court behind which is a central hall from which radiate four three-storey wings. The plan, on the separate system, i.e. of prisoners with individual cells and exercise yards, was a half-cartwheel. It accommodated 291 prisoners. Women and children were originally held in two of the radial wings which had cells on one side of the corridor only. These were doubled up *c.* 1856 and in the 1870s. All the cell blocks were extended in the 1880s.

The Bank and Burmantofts

The Bank rises steeply above the River Aire to the E of the city centre; to its N, beyond the York Road, Burmantofts occupies a gentler slope. Until the early C19, it was open country. The Bank was home to much of Leeds' Irish Catholic population which grew substantially following the potato famine of 1846–7, reaching almost 15,000 in 1861, over 12 per cent of the population, mainly employed in flax spinning and plaid weaving. It was once an area of tightly packed housing, developed from the 1820s, consisting mostly of back-to-backs and including some of the worst slums in Leeds. The inhabitants were the object of much attention by the different churches, including one of the earliest High Anglican missions. Three major churches, St Saviour, St Hilda and Mount St Mary occupy

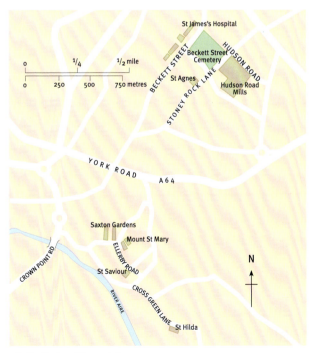

118. The Bank and Burmantofts

ground at the top of the Bank and originally towered over surrounding terraced housing in the manner typical of big Victorian town churches. Housing at Burmantofts was interspersed with factories and brick-works, including Wilcock & Co. established in 1842 which, following its acquisition by James Holroyd in 1879 and the discovery of a seam of fireclay in a local coal mine, became a nationally famous producer of decorative architectural faience and terracotta (*see* topic box, p. 225). Clearances in both districts began in the early C20 until the vast major-ity of housing in the area was demolished, some of it replaced by indus-try, some by flats, such as Saxton Gardens (*see* below) and more recently by new estates of semi-detached houses looking oddly suburban in such a setting. Although the area contains several churches of exceptional quality and one of national importance, much of it is open space, semi-derelict industrial land or is decimated by road schemes. The surround-ings discourage walking but the buildings of interest in both the Bank and Burmantofts are quite close to each other.

The Bank

St Saviour, Ellerby Road. The most important Victorian church in Leeds, and the beginning of Anglo-Catholicism in England. Built 1842–5 by *John Macduff Derick* for Dr E.B. Pusey, Regius Professor of Hebrew at Oxford University and one of the founders of the Oxford Movement. Pusey as 'Mr Z' paid for the whole church and insisted on it bearing the words 'Ye who enter this Holy place, pray for the Sinner who built it' incised in the floor inside the w doorway. It was to be a monument of renewed Anglican faith in a district with a population described by Sabine Baring-Gould as of 'gross profligacy combined perhaps with attendance at socialistic meetings'. St Saviour's encom-passed much of the turbulent history of the Church of England in the mid C19; as the prototype Oxford Movement church at which most of its leaders preached; as the first post-Reformation parish in which the daily mass was restored; and as one of the first to be opened without pew-rents. Its clergy twice defected to Rome; in 1847 and 1851. Its archi-tecture is as splendid as its history has been stormy. A remarkably seri-ous piece of design, both scholarly and emotionally potent. Prominently sited high above the River Aire with a tall flight of steps leading to its w end. Tall, not long, with transepts, N porch and cross-ing tower of 1937 by *Leslie Moore* following Derick's design. The origi-nal design envisaged a rich and splendid spire modelled on that of St Mary, Oxford and pinnacles along the eaves of the roof. Tracery in the style of *c.* 1300. Five-light E, W and transept-end windows. Tall three-light windows in the chancel. Two lights in the aisles. Small clerestory. Carved corbel heads were added to the doorways in 1866 by *G.E. Street*, among them Queen Victoria and C.T. Longley, Bishop of Ripon on the w door and Dr Hook at the N transept door. Inside the w door are heads of Dr Pusey and Charles Marriott, vicar of St Mary, Oxford.

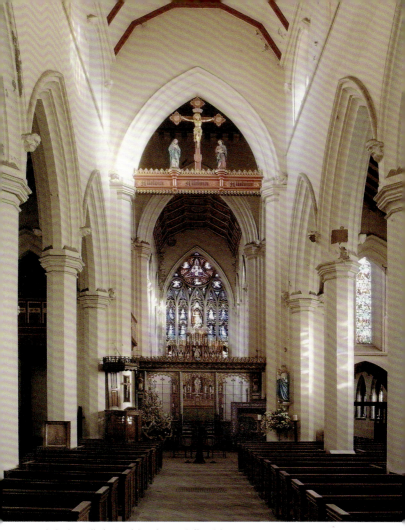

119. St Saviour, Ellerby Road, by John Macduff Derick, 1842–5

The **interior** [119] has undergone three major refurbishments. The first in 1866–7 by *Street* who raised the altar, replaced the original pulpit and had *Clayton & Bell* decorate the roofs and paint frescoes on the chancel walls. The second was by *G.F. Bodley* in 1888–90 who built the Pusey Memorial Chapel and carried out the stencilling on the nave roof. The third in 1963 by *George Pace*.

It is of lofty proportions, especially in the aisleless chancel and at the crossing. Windows fill almost all the wall surfaces. Tall octagonal piers with no mouldings in the nave. Double chamfered arches. The overall effect today is undeniably drab, largely due to *Pace*'s painting in white which obliterated the chancel frescoes and *Bodley*'s stencilling. There are plans in 2005 to reinstate the C19 decorative scheme. **Reredos** by

Bodley, part of the 1890 scheme but not installed until 1902, tripartite, richly carved in deep relief, the statuary added 1902–12. **High altar**, mensa of grey marble with oak legs, part of the original furnishings, with retable containing a central tabernacle by *Bodley*. **Chancel screen** also by *Bodley*, as is the **rood**, both of 1890. The central part of the former chancel screen is now in the N porch. In the Pusey Chapel, the painted **reredos** by *Frances Darlington*, 1922, depicts St George and St Joan and forms the War Memorial. **Statues** in wall-mounted niches by *Thomas Garner*. Oak cupboards by *Bodley* contain Dr Pusey's robes. **Pulpit** of 1899 by *Bodley*. **Statue** of Our Lady by *Temple Moore*, painted and gilded, on the site of the original pulpit. **Font**, circular with four leaf-shaped panels, inlaid with white marble by *Street*, 1871, the **cover** of 1885 by *J.T. Micklethwaite*, decorated and gilded in 1923 by *Frances Darlington*. **Stained glass**. An important scheme that cost 17 per cent of the total cost of the church. Windows in the nave, clerestory and chancel executed by *Michael O'Connor* to Pusey's directions and worked out by him with Benjamin Webb of the Cambridge Camden Society. The E window, the Ascension, is also believed to be by *O'Connor*. The glass, completely preserved in the four five-light windows, is of great merit, in the style of the C13, and of glowing colours, predominantly blue and green – Pevsner saw nothing yet of what he viewed as Victorian insipidity. The W window [9] originally depicted angels catching the blood of Christ in chalices and had to be altered before the bishop would consecrate the church. This and the N and S transept windows are by *A.W.N. Pugin*. Several windows by *Morris & Co.*, with green again the dominant colour. The N aisle N window of 1868 is by *Morris* himself. Single figures of saints and amongst them, to one's surprise, Fra Angelico – a sign of the respect of the Pre-Raphaelites for the most Christian of Pre-Raphaelite painters. N aisle fourth window by *Morris* and *Burne-Jones*, 1870. In the porch, 1878 by *Burne-Jones*. In the S aisle, fifth window by *Ford Madox Brown*, 1872 fourth window, 1872 by *G.J. Baguley*. Pusey Chapel windows all of 1890 by *Powell Bros*. Large Gothic **Clergy House**, its eaves punctuated with gabled half-dormers, adjacent to the church.

St Hilda, Cross Green Lane. Built 1876–82 by *J.T. Micklethwaite*, the distinguished archaeologist-architect. A daughter church of St Saviour and built in accordance with the same High Anglican principles with an austere but powerful brick exterior, reminiscent of James Brooks' London churches. High nave and chancel under one roof. Double bell-cote. Thin stair-turret on the N side at the junction of nave and chancel with a romantic conical spirelet. Lancets, paired in the clerestory, and simple Geometrical tracery. The elevated setting, clear glass and white walls give a wonderfully light **interior** that emphasizes the richly painted furnishings. Octagonal piers and double-chamfered arches. Chancel with piscina, credence and sedilia. The segmental curved and

120. St Hilda, Cross Green
Lane, Font Canopy
by C. Wood, sculpture by
Alfred Southwick, 1936–8

closely panelled roof was intended to be decorated with striking gilded sun-rays. Micklethwaite wrote 'money is scarce, therefore the outside of the church will be perfectly plain. We will concentrate on making the interior as beautiful as possible.' The present appearance of the church is witness to his ambition. The painted wooden **furnishings** in late Perp style by *W.H. Wood* of Newcastle were not installed until the C20 and display the continued vitality of the Gothic tradition. Magnificent **rood screen** of 1922–3, based on Micklethwaite's original proposals but modified by Wood, with seven statues by *Alfred Southwick* in canopied niches, and with bas-relief panels of the Incarnation and Resurrection by *J.T. Ogelby* of Newcastle added in 1924. **Rood** of 1904 by *Micklethwaite* on a separate beam, the figures carved in Oberammergau, embellished and painted in 1912. **Reredos** of six painted panels, the pictures by *Percy C. Bacon*, with an elaborate frame of 1927 and a canopy arching forward over the high altar. The octagonal **pulpit** of 1882 was given a sounding board and decorated to match the screen in 1917. Handsome **font** of Frosterley marble, the bowl octagonal on a fine base under a 25 ft (7.6

metre) high **canopy** [120] (inspired perhaps by the great Perp canopies of Trunch, Norfolk and St Peter Mancroft, Norwich) by *C. Wood* of 1936–8, the sculpture by *Alfred Southwick*. **Statues** of St Hilda above the main door by *George Hodgson Fowler*, 1903 and, holding a model of the church, by *Alfred Southwick*, 1938. **Stained glass** by *Burlison & Grylls*. E window inserted in stages 1891–1902, s window of Lady Chapel 1905. Attached **Clergy House** by *Micklethwaite*.

Mount St Mary (R.C.), off Ellerby Road. Built 1853–7, and financed as a mission by the French Order of the Oblates of Mary Immaculate, no doubt as a challenge to Dr Pusey's St Saviour. It remained in their hands until closure in 1989. Massive in appearance (188 ft (57.3 metres) long, 60 ft (18.3 metres) wide and 83 ft (25.3 metres) high), it occupies a very prominent position on the hill facing the city. The design was by *Joseph Hansom* but later handed over to *W. Wardell*. Only the nave and aisles were complete in 1857, the chancel and transepts added in 1866 by *E.W. Pugin*. A NW tower with a 300 ft (91.4 metres) spire, even higher than that intended at St Saviour, was planned but not built. Geometrical tracery, w front with eight-light window and a narthex rather than a porch. Cross-gabled aisles and transepts with rose windows. Very tall circular piers with four detached shafts with shaft-rings. Polygonal apse with three thin tall two-light windows. Lady Chapel and five other altars. The church's recent history is a sad tale of theft and vandalism. **Stained glass** in the apse by *J.H. Powell* is extant but boarded up, the Pugin tabernacle and Hardman altar rails have been recovered and are in store but other fittings including the carved oak altar by *Benedict Labre* are still missing. The **presbytery** was built in two phases. The first follows *Wardell*'s designs, the later extension differs slightly in style. The adjacent **St Mary's Convent** of 1861 is by *M.E. Hadfield* and has a low tower with a spire placed almost inconsequentially at one end. A **college** was added in 1901. Built around a courtyard with the college on the NW side. All are in a simple Gothic style, the convent walls buttressed.

Saxton Gardens, 1955–8 by the City Architect, *R.A.H. Livett*, who had been responsible for Quarry Hill before the Second World War. Early C19 working-class housing had been largely cleared in 1936–8 and a scheme prepared but the war intervened. A total of 448 flats in seven long parallel slabs, five to ten storeys high, rising in height as they climb the Bank. Reinforced concrete frames clad in buff and dark brown facing bricks. Pairs of flats on each floor shared a lift and, as at Quarry Hill, were originally provided with Garchey refuse disposal whereby rubbish was ground up and passed through chutes to a boiler house where it was burnt to provide power. The flats represent a move away from the formal enclosure of the Quarry Hill scheme to the more relaxed planning of postwar London developments which eschewed the existing street patterns. Renovations in 2004 added new balconies.

Burmantofts

St Agnes, Stoney Rock Lane. Built 1886–7 by *Kelly & Birchall*. Nave and chancel in one with aisles continued unbroken to form a vestry, built of coursed rock-faced stone. A slender turret with an octagonal top, which Pevsner thought 'silly', emerges from the aisle roof on the s side between nave and chancel. Five-light E window with Geometrical tracery. Paired flat-headed windows to the aisles, two-light windows with Y-tracery (circular in the chancel) to the clerestory. **Reredos** made in 1891 of Burmantofts faience, now painted white, three canopied niches. There is also a memorial **wall tablet**, set in a faience surround, to James Holroyd d.1890, 'the founder of the Burmantofts Faience Works', erected by his workforce. **Stained glass**: the richly coloured E window and those in the N aisle by *Charles E. Steel*, 1930–3, those in the N aisle, w and s aisles by *Powell Bros*, 1903. Also by *Powell Bros*, the s aisle w window of 1889. The four-light w window has figures by *William Wailes* of 1867, formerly part of the E window of St Stephen, Burmantofts and re-set after its closure in 1939.

Beckett Street Cemetery. Leeds was the first of the great industrial towns to take civic responsibility for providing burial space. In 1845, the Corporation set up a Burial Grounds Committee which spent £25,000 establishing three cemeteries, of which Beckett Street, opened in the same year, was the largest. Sixteen acres of land were purchased from William Beckett M.P. The cemetery was equally divided between Anglicans and Nonconformists and has over 180,000 burials. The almost square site encouraged a grid plan but the layout becomes less formal near the entrance where paths wind sinuously. The original chapels were demolished in the 1960s but the twin Tudor-style **lodges** of 1880 by *W.S. Braithwaite*, possibly his earliest work, remain. **Monuments**. The most intriguing, off Anglican Walk to the right, is that to Sarah Kidney (d.1895), wife of the 'oldest steeplejack in England' which was in the form of a factory chimney 8 ft (2.4 metres) high, sadly vandalized in 2004. Christopher Burn (d.1849), (to the right of Dissenters' Walk) a ship's master, has a fine carving of a Humber keel in its pediment. The Hodgson and Galli memorials of 1858 and 1896 are large Gothic monuments, as is the Marks memorial of 1891, surmounted by a carved angel. Among many notables buried here is Sir John Barran, (1821–1905) clothing manufacturer and twice mayor. He has a plain but dignified pedimented granite tombstone off Dissenters' Walk near the entrance. Many 'guinea graves' with shared headstones, inscribed on both sides. **First World War Memorial** of standard *Blomfield* design.

St James's Hospital, Beckett Street. The core of 'Jimmy's' is the former **Workhouse**, built in 1858–62 by *Perkin & Backhouse*, architects of Armley Prison. The original building (now the Thackray Medical Museum) is T-shaped with service buildings to the rear. Three-storey in red brick Neo-Jacobean with shaped gables, a pierced parapet, the central part projects with a central tower with corner turrets capped by ogee-shaped roofs. Its long façade is broken by shallow projecting bays and deeper three-storey bay windows in the centre. Entrance hall with ribbed plaster ceiling and later Art Nouveau dado band above green tiles. The **Southside Building** pre-dated the Workhouse, and was built as a Moral and Industrial Training School by the Leeds Guardians in 1846–8 for 499 children aged between seven and nine to learn practical trades and domestic work. The style is broadly similar but projecting gabled bays are emphasized by slender octagonal flanking turrets which terminate in ogee domes high above shaped gables. Later converted to infirm wards, it was altered in 1904–5. The former '**Idiotic**' **Wards**, 1862 by *Perkin & Backhouse*, are two storeys, of matching style but less elaborate.

The contemporary Workhouse **chapel** [121] is an eclectic and busy mix of Romanesque and Lombardic Gothic. Red brick with polychromy of blue and white brick around the window heads. Cruciform with pedimented gables, a prominent cornice and a tall clock tower at

121. St James's Hospital Chapel, Beckett Street, by Perkin & Backhouse, 1858–62

The Burmantofts Pottery

The successful mass-production of terracotta and faience ceramic wares at Burmantofts began in 1859 when a seam of fireclay was discovered in the coal mine of William Wilcock and John Lassey. In 1863 John Holroyd, a Woodhouse clothier, bought Lassey's share of the business which was renamed Wilcock & Co. Holroyd's premises in Infirmary Street were used as its store and offices. From *c.* 1879 James Holroyd expanded production to include decorative bricks and tiles in terracotta, glazed bricks for architectural work and faience 'art pottery'; in 1880 *Maurice Bingham Adams* (architect and editor of *Building News*) was commissioned to design stock architectural features for the firm's catalogues. The firm supplied faience facings and tiles for *Alfred Waterhouse*'s Yorkshire College [17] in 1883 and an important partnership developed. By 1885 Burmantofts architectural faience was on sale in London, Paris (where it was used for Baron Rothschild's bathroom) and Montreal. Following amalgamation in 1889 with businesses in Wortley, Halifax and Huddersfield the firm became 'The Leeds Fireclay Company Ltd', the largest clay-working company in the country. This period was the peak of terracotta's popularity as an alternative to stone for building and decorative work. It was highly favoured not only because it resisted the effects of smoke and soot (some of it, ironically, produced by the potteries themselves) but also because a high standard of architectural detail could be achieved by skilled craftsmen. From 1890 *E. Caldwell Spruce* was the principal modeller at Burmantofts (he went to Paris in the mid 1890s; on his return to Leeds he set up a studio in Cowper Street, Chapeltown). Terracotta and faience also made possible colourful surfaces and by the end of the C19 Burmantofts work was thrillingly varied, as demonstrated by *Matcham*'s County Arcade [12]. Pottery production at Burmantofts ceased in 1904 but in 1908 an imitation white marble – known as 'Marmo' – was perfected and widely used either as a tile facing or in block form for construction. An early example is Atlas House, King Street [53]. The Burmantofts works was closed in 1957, the site (which then comprised sixteen acres of buildings, ninety kilns and mountains of waste coal and old plaster moulds) developed for housing.

the NW angle of the transepts with an arcaded belfry and a slated spire. The W front has a large round-arched recess with paired doors, blind arcading above them and a rose window. A shorter round tower at the SW angle. The interior again displays extensive polychromy, capitals to the piers are carved with flowers, birds and animals. Broad chancel arch with chevrons, the chancel top-lit and apsidal. **Stained glass** E windows by *Celtic Studios*, 1952.

Chapeltown, Chapel Allerton and Gledhow

Chapeltown and Chapel Allerton pose problems of nomenclature; both were originally called Chapeltown. The ancient village centre is at Chapel Allerton on Harrogate Road three miles N of Leeds city centre where a small community grew up around the chapel in the C17. Late in the C18, the high ground around Potternewton to the S of Chapel Allerton became favoured as a place for the well-to-do to build mansions away from the smoke of the city. These included Potternewton House and Newton Hall (both dem.), Gledhow Grove, Gledhow Mount and Harehills Grove. The village of Chapel Allerton was acclaimed as 'the Montpellier of Yorkshire' in 1767 and, in 1834, was described by Edward Parsons as 'by far the most beautiful and respectable in the Parish of Leeds'.

Chapeltown today encompasses several phases of unrelated C19 suburban development S of Harehills Lane which began as estates and were parcelled off for building. The earliest parts were closest to the city centre at the S end of Chapeltown Road. In 1826, 55 acres (now bounded by Spencer Place, Cowper Street, Leopold Street and Chapeltown Road) were sold by Earl Cowper to developers who planned to create New Leeds, a suburb to rival Bath or Edinburgh New Town. The purchasers were bankrupt within three years and Earl Cowper bought the land back in 1829. Only a few houses of the grand scheme were built, some surviving in Spencer Place. The remainder of the area was filled in the late C19 by large terraced houses. The Newton Park Estate, developed from the 1870s, emulated Headingley in the quality of its houses and layout of broad tree-lined roads. A gap remained between this and New Leeds until the Harehills Grove Estate (formed by John Brown of Harehills Grove) was laid out from 1886 with a grid of good quality semi-detached and terraced houses. The part of the estate to the E of Roundhay Road (the district generally known as Harehills) was developed with small terraced houses and back-to-backs for artisans. Along the tramway-served Roundhay Road, a shopping centre grew up. Potternewton, which had vied with Headingley as the most desirable suburb in the city, suffered a decline after 1918. As its large houses became relatively cheap, it became home to successive waves of newcomers to the city: in the 1920s to the Jews who moved from the Leylands just N of the city centre and since 1945 to Poles, West Indians,

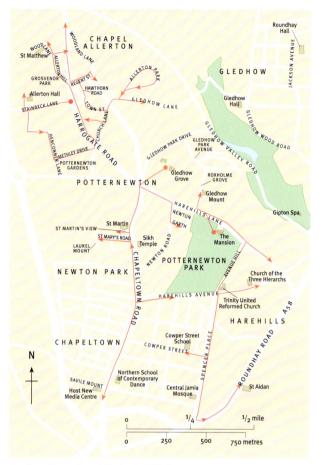

122. Chapeltown, Chapel Allerton and Gledhow

Asians and refugees from the Balkans and the Middle East, reflected in the changing uses for many buildings.

In Chapel Allerton, following the enclosure of Chapeltown Moor to the s of Stainbeck Lane in 1809, a great variety of houses were built but the centre remained largely undeveloped until the arrival of the electric tram in the early C20. Large houses went up around Allerton Park and the remaining fields were built over in the 1930s. To the E, Gledhow Hall with its great park remained largely untouched by development until the 1900s when a grid of roads lined with small semi-detached houses was built to the N. From the 1930s, further building has filled much of the farmland but the environs of the Hall retain their rural character, the roads bordered by high walls and thick woods partly preserving the isolation of the area known in the C19 as 'Little Switzerland' due to its hilly and picturesque appearance.

a) Chapeltown Road, Potternewton & Newton Park

The walk begins in Potternewton at the junction of Chapeltown Road and Harehills Lane. Here in Mansion Drive, is its grandest surviving C19 mill owners' house: **Gledhow Grove**, of 1835–40 by *John Clark* for John Hives, partner in Hives & Atkinson, flax spinners of Bank Mills. He moved here from the Park Square area. A remarkably stately Greek Revival mansion: eleven bays wide, two storeys, stone-built with a broad eaves cornice, deep entablature and corner pilasters. Generous portico of two attached giant fluted Ionic columns *in antis*. Inside, a spacious staircase covered by a shallow tunnel vault, Ionic columns to the ground floor, Corinthian to the first. The **stables** form a U-shaped group with an Egyptian-style clock tower as the centrepiece. Battered walls, roll mouldings to the edges and an arched recess surmounted by a deeply coved cornice. The front in ashlar, the rest in coursed rubble. Gateposts topped with Soanian caps. The chimneys have unusual stacks shaped like Ionic columns, a feature shared with the **lodge** which adjoins the gates on Harehills Lane.

To the SE, off Newton Road, **Newton Garth**, a housing scheme of 1969 by *Derek Walker Associates* with terraces set around a communal garden originally separated from them by private gardens, a reversal of the traditional Georgian square where the road is placed between the houses and the gardens. The houses, built of blockwork, austere and flat-roofed, have balconies facing the square and are built above garages opening straight on to service roads behind, a concept developed by Walker at Milton Keynes in the late 1970s. From Harehills Lane, turn left into Chapeltown Road.

The **Newton Park Estate** was laid out to the w of Chapeltown Road by the Lupton family who lived at Newton Hall (now dem.). Francis and Darnton Lupton engaged *George Corson* to draw up plans for the estate at the beginning of the 1870s but building was eventually begun by the Newton Park Building Club to plans by *Chorley & Connon* (who designed most of the houses) in 1879.

The former **lodge** of 1856 and **gateposts** of **Newton Hall** survive on Chapeltown Road next to **St Martin's Church**, built for the estate in 1879–81 by *Adams & Kelly* of Potternewton stone in the Dec style [123]. Its intended w tower with spire, commenced in 1898, was truncated a little above the nave roof giving the w end an unfinished look. Heavy buttresses to the tower, nave and chancel, the latter topped with finials. Six-bay clerestory with four-light windows, E window with Geometrical tracery. The plain exterior scarcely prepares one for the riches inside. Six-bay nave with double-chamfered arches on tall quatrefoil piers, the capitals carved with foliage by *Thewlis & Co.*, not completed until 1901. The roof trusses continue as shafts with capitals and brackets, alternately decorated with foliage and heads. Splendid and well-preserved **murals** of 1913 by *Hemming & Co.* cover the whole of the chancel walls and the chancel arch. Paintings on a 'Te Deum' theme are set in

123. St Martin, St Martin's View, by Adams & Kelly; stained glass by Kempe, 1890; murals by Hemming & Co., 1913

canopied panels divided by chevrons. Above them, angels, who include both black and oriental figures, carry scrolls. A **reredos** of carved and gilded wood replaced the original stone piece between 1898 and 1905. The painting of the Nativity in the centre, two further paintings each side, in traceried panels and in a highly naturalistic style. The lower side panels, each with paintings of four northern saints, were added by 1913. Ornate **choir stalls** with poppyhead ends, metal **gates**, brackets carved with angels and encaustic floor tiles. Caen stone **pulpit** by *J. Throp*, a demi-angel supporting the desk, and with cusped openings set in ogee arches on four short columns; enlarged 1898. **Stained glass.** A fine set by *Kempe*: E window, 1890, N aisle; War Memorial window, 1921 with roundels depicting the Calvary against a realistic and moving depiction of the shattered trees and mud of the western front and soldiers receiving field communion; S aisle of 1903 and 1909, W window of

1898. s chapel s window by *William Pape*, 1956. N aisle w of 1894 by *C. E. Tute* and that in the porch by *Charles Powell* of 1893. In **St Martin's View**, the **Church Institute**, a large and ornate Perp-style hall of 1902 by *Percy Robinson*.

The Newton Park Estate centres on **St Mary's Road**, approached from Chapeltown Road through gateposts with pedestrian entrances to each side. On the right, Nos. 1–10, a terrace of 1894 by *Smith & Tweedale* [124], the houses with similar plans but varied façades whose attractive detailing includes half-timbered gables, paired windows with deep sashes and shell-like porches. **Eltonhurst** and **Oakfield** of 1885 are semi-detached Domestic Revival houses by *Chorley & Connon* with the full gamut of fish-scale tiling, applied half-timbering, decorated plaster coving below big gables, their roofs continued as catslides to ground-floor level. Their largest house on the estate is the twin-gabled **Rockland** of 1886 for Francis Lupton, for whom they also built at Headingley. The most attractive is **Penraevon** of 1881 in **Laurel Mount**. Again Domestic Revival but in stone, with a half-timbered gable above an oriel window, leaded lights and a pretty timber porch.

Back on Chapeltown Road, the former **Union Chapel** was built for shared use by Baptists and Congregationalists in 1887 by *Archibald Neill*. A prominent porch, in shape a half octagon, heavily buttressed with an open balustrade and crocketed pinnacles, projects from a gabled clerestoried lantern to which it is linked by flying buttresses. Above perches a low tower. Gabled transepts flanking the short nave provide yet more complication. Centrally planned interior. Behind and linked to it, a Congregational Chapel (gutted by fire 2003) of 1870–1 by *W.H. Harris* that later became a meeting hall and then in turn, a synagogue and a Hindu temple. Steep roof with a rose window in the gable.

124. Nos. 1–10 St Mary's Road by Smith & Tweedale, 1894

The Union Chapel later became a Sikh temple but since replaced by the new **Temple** of 1998–2000, by architects Singh & Partners, on the E side of Chapeltown Road. Large, quite boxy in yellow brick. The central part, which has a large round-headed window, is brought forward to form a porte cochère. Octagonal turrets topped by small onion domes flank the façade and a larger dome at the centre.

The estate was given a highly original shopping parade at Nos. 168–176 **Chapeltown Road** in 1890 by *Archibald Neill*. Not quite as wild as his Union Chapel but bizarrely detailed, the first floor of the central pair of shops set back behind large arches, banded attached columns between each shop transmute above capitals to form tapering buttresses rising above the eaves. Two splendid carved lions on their haunches perch above the shopfronts at each end. Coursed stone and mullions throughout.

Then E of Chapeltown Road, tree-lined **Harehills Avenue**, is the centrepiece of the Harehills Grove Estate. Set back behind long gardens, are Nos. 1–12 **Newton Grove**, a handsome terrace of broadly Italianate three-storey houses of the 1850s by several hands and variously treated. In the centre is a detached villa with a pediment above all three bays, reminiscent of Brodrick's Oakfield, Headingley (*see* p. 251) but without his powerfully outsized detailing.

Moving s down Chapeltown Road is another shopping parade on the w side, Nos. 213–229 of 1906–7 by *Carby Hall & Dalby* with alternating rounded and pedimented gables, again with corner turrets. On the E, the **Holy Rosary Church** (R.C.) of 1936–7 by *Marten & Burnett*. Large, of brick in a sparing simplified Romanesque style. Then two buildings that reflect the area's early C20 Jewish past and its C21 regeneration. On the E side, the dramatic Neo-Byzantine former United Hebrew Congregation Synagogue of 1929–32 by *J. Stanley Wright*, very successfully adapted as the **Northern School of Contemporary Dance** in 1995–8 by *Allen Tod Architects* [125]. A massive central dome, a lower dome at the E end and small domes above stair-towers either side of the w entrance. Tall triplets of round-arched windows set in buttresses which break through the curve of the central dome. Browny brick on a concrete block foundation. Jazzy Neo-Egyptian Portland stone portico with tulip-capitalled paired columns and topped by vases. The spacious octagonal former prayer hall adapts well to use as a dance auditorium. It retains a marble Ark and a Star of David at the apex of the roof from which a bronze pendant light is suspended. The women's gallery is supported on octagonal stone piers. Stained glass with Star of David motif. The conversion added the large but not overbearing brick and glass extensions for studios with a library and offices in the basement. The new work incorporates a rare survival of 'New Leeds', No. 98 Chapeltown Road, a three-bay villa of 1835 with a plain Doric porch with attached columns. To the w in **Savile Mount**, the **Host New Media Centre**, converted by *Bauman Lyons Architects* in 2000–1 from the for-

125. Northern School of Contemporary Dance, Chapeltown Road, by J. Stanley Wright, 1929–32, converted by Allen Tod Architects, 1995–8

mer Jewish Institute and Jubilee Hall, by *G. Alan Burnett*, 1934. Three storeys and basement, well-detailed brickwork, the key motif narrow oriels (in shape like those on Norman Shaw's Swan House, Chelsea) on the upper floors spaced at regular intervals along the façade. The conversion to studios and workspaces has provided a new entrance on the site of a demolished extension, set at an angle, in modish horizontal timber boarding, brightly coloured render and exposed steel. Staircase hall running the full height of the building lit by one of the oriels. Finally an early C20 shopping parade, Nos. 97–117 in coursed stone with mullions, shaped gables and a corner turret, injects a last satisfying dose of urbanity before the complex road junctions at Sheepscar which cut Chapeltown off from the city centre.

Buses run to the centre along Chapeltown Road.

b) Potternewton Park, Harehills and the remains of New Leeds

The walk begins at **Potternewton Park**, Harehills Lane, created in 1906 after Leeds City Council purchased the estate of **Harehills Grove**. The house (now Potternewton Mansion) was built *c.* 1817 for James Brown, a wool merchant. Elegant and refined in a Neo-Grecian style, the height of fashionable taste. Seven bays, two storeyed with the roof hidden behind a balustraded parapet. The centre with a curved Ionic porch with a tripartite window over. Circular top light to the staircase and fine iron balusters, cornices and moulded door surrounds survive inside. Leaving the Park, in **Roxholme Grove** to the NW off Harehills Lane, is **Gledhow Mount**, another of the early C19 houses on the hill overlooking the city. Almost square and severe with a Doric porch, pilastered quoins and bands the only decoration. Retracing one's steps along **Harehills Lane**, No. 89 is the appropriately named **Corbie Steps** [126], with a projecting crowstepped central gable, mullioned windows and a corner entrance, a quaint amalgam of Arts & Crafts and Scots Baronial by *J.S. Brocklesby*, 1914.

From here, the walk includes a great variety of places of worship from the C19 to the C21, which reflect the changing population of the area over successive decades. First, further SE on **Harehills Lane**, the **Baptist Church**, a red brick Italian Romanesque design of 1928 by *Herbert J. Manchip* with big corbels and a rose window on the W front. Three-bay nave with broad rounded arches and domed E baptistery as the focal point. To the SW on the corner of Avenue Hill and **Harehills Avenue**, the **Trinity United Reformed Church** (formerly Presbyterian) of 1906 by *W.H. Beevers*, paired lancets and buttresses with a chunky SW tower on a good corner site and nearby the Greek Orthodox **Church of the Three Hierarchs** (originally Primitive Methodist), 1902, by *W. Hugill Dinsley* of Chorley, Lancs. Broad fronted and including a NW tower with a short spire and three windows below a relieving arch, the central of two lights. A school, lit by a continuously glazed clerestory, is behind the church.

This part of Harehills Avenue is lined with substantial houses reflecting the high status of the area in the C19. S down Spencer Place and up **Cowper Street** to the W is **Hillcrest Primary School** (the former Cowper Street Board School) [16] opened in 1905, the last to be built by the Leeds School Board, and in scale, decoration and massing, the grandest. The architect was *Philip Robson*, the son of the noted school architect E.R. Robson, who entered practice the year the school

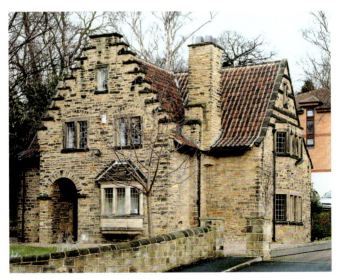

126. Corbie Steps, No. 89 Harehills Lane, by J.S. Brocklesby, 1914

was built. Largely red brick Queen Anne (his father's style) but incorporating Free-Baroque domed corner turrets and giant pilasters. The great shaped gable of the central hall is balanced effectively by two lower gables flanking it on the Cowper Street elevation; the entrance has Ionic columns. Infants were housed in a separate block (since dem.). The arcaded basement of the main block provided for covered play sheds, unique in Leeds at the time. **Spencer Place** was the E boundary of the 1828 New Leeds Development. Three houses survive: **Newton House**, No. 54, restored in 2003, is the most handsome. Fine ashlar façade of five bays, the central three brought forward slightly and the ground-floor windows set in arched recesses either side of a Doric porch, corner pilasters and a parapet. **Spencer House**, No. 52, is rendered with a bow-fronted bay in the centre, No. 50 is slightly fussy, the combination of a tripartite window below a pediment, ground-floor bow windows and a big porch too much for its modest size. Then the **Central Jamia Mosque** of 1997–2000 by *Finn & Downes Associates* [127]. Steel-framed and clad in polychrome brick. Large central dome and minarets, round staircase towers at the angles of the building. Three floors, the lower forming a basement, the top floor is a gallery below the dome giving all worshippers a good view of the Mihrab. At the rear is the former **Chadssidishe Shul Synagogue**: a brick box of 1935.

Roundhay Road divides the smarter enclave of the Harehills Grove Estate to the W from the artisan streets to the E. This district is now known as **Harehills**. Its key building is **St Aidan's Church**, built at the request of Dr Jayne, vicar of Leeds, to serve this working-class district. It is a massive basilica, externally gaunt but with a rich interior [128],

127. Central Jamia Mosque, Spencer Place, by Finn & Downes Associates, 1997–2000

won in competition in 1889 by *R.J. Johnson & A. Crawford Hick* of Newcastle and largely complete by 1894. *Chorley & Connon* had earlier produced a design for an Early Christian basilica but only the hall and schoolroom to the N of the church was erected to their design. The Romanesque style is a scholarly hybrid, drawing equally on sources from Italy, France (Johnson had produced a series of lithographs of French Romanesque architecture in 1885) and Germany. Some of the external decoration, notably the corbel table, is based on that of Lund Cathedral, Sweden. Johnson died within months of his design being accepted and much of the detail work is by *Crawford Hick*. Of red brick, the curved apse flanked by a small sw tower and the lower part of an unbuilt NW tower which would have been 200 ft (61 metres) tall. Paired windows in both aisles and clerestory, the walls articulated by pilasters. Apsed w baptistery. Inside, a broad nave and narrow aisles with long arcades of circular columns and arches. The richly foliated carving to the capitals, Byzantine in style and each different, was completed in 1902. The apsed SE Chapel has a carved timber screen in C17 classical style. In the same style is the panelling in the w apse, carved and with biblical scenes depicting children. The **mosaics** in the chancel [15], unveiled in 1916, are by *Sir Frank Brangwyn*: *Sylvester Sparrow* superintended the work which was executed by *Rust & Co*. Scenes from the life of St Aidan are set in a poetic landscape under an agitated streaky sky. Tall slender trees with long bare trunks – a motif beloved of Arts and Crafts artists and designers. The figures mostly in white, but some accented in vehement scarlet. The chancel and nave are separated by *cancelli* on which a procession of white-robed neophytes moves towards the opening in the centre, eager to be baptized by St Aidan. The donor was Robert H. Kitson, nephew of the architect Sydney, and for whose Sicilian villa Brangwyn had designed a dining room with furniture and painted frieze. The St Aidan's work too was to be in *tempera* but in 1913, after three years' intermittent work, Brangwyn feared the effects of pollution and suggested mosaic. Sumptuous **furnishings** including a **pulpit** of Caen stone on Italian marble columns with an almost Moorish arcade of 1895, designed by *Crawford Hick*, with modelling, sculptured panels and carving by *John Roddis* of Birmingham. **Altar rails** of alabaster with brass infill also of 1895, those in the SE chapel of 1909 by *Sydney Kitson*. Massive **font** of Mexican onyx with Irish green marble columns of 1896 and an equally immense wrought-iron **font cover** designed by *Sydney Kitson* and made by *Silas Paul* of Leeds School of Art in 1914. The **rood** was carved by a *Mr Hedley* of Newcastle in 1898. Choir Stalls in C17 classical style and similar organ case. Painted **Stations of the Cross** of 1950 and **statue** of the Redeemer in N aisle by *Josef Heu*. **Stained glass** mainly by *Percy Bacon & Bros*. SE chapel, two windows of 1906–7, s aisle, w window, 1893, Baptistery, 1895.

128. St Aidan, Roundhay Road, by R.J. Johnson & A. Crawford Hick, 1889–94

c) Chapel Allerton and Gledhow

The centre of Chapel Allerton is strangely lifeless, having lost as its visual focus a large Methodist church of 1874 by *C.O. Ellison* which was regrettably demolished in the early 1980s. Late C20 buildings predominate and the feel is that of a suburb rather than a village. The walk begins at the junction with Stainbeck Lane and Harrogate Road. On the corner, the **Yorkshire Bank** of 1937 with a Portland stone façade. On **Stainbeck Lane**, the oldest house in the area is **The Mustard Pot**, originally Clough House. Early C18 of five bays, similar in style to the great merchants' houses then being erected in central Leeds and, as there, with a former workshop range to the left, possibly used as a cloth-finishing shop. Brick with a stone slate roof, a moulded eaves cornice and flush timber window frames. The much altered interior retains two fireplaces, one with a stone surround with a shouldered architrave and the coat of arms of the Henson family above it, the other generally similar but with early Delft tiles decorated with small figures representing games, pastimes, churchmen, etc. On the s side of Stainbeck Lane, **Stratford House** is early C19, large and plain of three storeys in ashlar with two later projecting two-storey wings on each side. Attached Doric columns to the doorway. Extensive additions of 2004. Further w, **Allerton Hall** is of several dates and in a mixture of styles. It began as a sprawling brick C18 house with a handsome bow-fronted three-storey wing and a stable block behind, the latter incorporated into the house in 1898. Extensive late C19 additions to the w with a jettied black and white gable and coved cornice were followed by the long N wing of 1898–1901 by *Temple Moore* in a highly convincing Queen Anne style with modillion eaves and some circular windows. In **Henconnor Lane**, some late C18 houses: **Newton Villa**, ashlar with a Diocletian window within a pediment and the very handsome **Rose Mount** of *c.* 1780, also pedimented but in red brick with a wide five-bay front and a Doric porch.

Off Henconnor Lane, **Potternewton Gardens** by *Yorkshire Development Group*, 1973, an infill estate in an area of terraced houses and retaining existing street patterns. Mixed development with two-storey houses, flats and patio houses, each with private gardens and open entrance courts. Carried out in white brick and well detailed and landscaped.

Returning to the centre via Methley Drive to **Harrogate Road** and **Chapel Allerton Primary School** of 1878 by *Richard Adams*. Single storey red brick with twin gables flanking a long central section. Cusped tracery in the upper lights of the mullioned and transomed windows, the upper parts of the gables divided into panels with brick nogging. Approaching the centre, on the right, the **Public Library**, **Police Station and Fire Station** of 1904 by *W.H. Thorp* form a fine group of public buildings, done with gusto. Only the first named is still used for its original purpose. The style is broadly that of the later C16, with shaped gables, mullions and transoms and obelisk pinnacles but with early classical details such as rounded open pediments and Tuscan columns on the doorcases and Ionic pilasters to the first floor. Jolly touches such as the oval windows in swirling cartouche surrounds in the gables and a tall chimney on the library with corner pilasters. N of Stainbeck Lane on the left is the former **Yorkshire Bank Computer Data Centre** of 1968 by *Braithwaite & Jackman*, a crisp sculptural composition in ribbed *in situ* concrete and brown brick with an oversailing upper storey (re-clad in dark glass) and shallow strip windows. Its chunkiness is very much of its period but the deft handling of the two thin asymmetrical towers flanking the entrance is exceptional. Up **Allerton Hill** to the left is **Grosvenor Park**, an attractive *cul-de-sac* of *c.* 1920. Arts and Crafts houses of stone with roughcast walling and leaded mullions. The view is closed by two three-storey houses each with deep, steeply pitched roofs which are placed at an angle at the end of the road.

In **Wood Lane** stands the noble and spacious parish church of **St Matthew** of 1897–9, a late work by *G.F. Bodley* [129]. It was built on a new site to replace the old parish church (*see* p. 243). Constructed in Bath stone and Ancaster stone ashlar, its most striking feature is the bold and sturdy detached SW tower over the porch which is linked to the nave by a low passage. The tall chancel and nave are under one roof, the aisles lean-to but without a clerestory. Refined Perp elevations with simple, sparse mouldings and narrow buttresses. The tower has mouldings only at plinth level, the belfry sills and below the battlements, the buttresses forming the sole decorative element. Sculpture of St Matthew set in a niche above the porch. Simple three-light windows, Perp in character, like the rest of the church. Four-light E window. Austere and undeniably sombre interior with dark oak panelling and much stained glass. The porch has a vaulted ceiling with a central octagonal boss. Six-bay nave with slender quatrefoil piers of C14 type with plain moulded capitals. Timber tunnel-vaulted ceiling, ribbed and panelled in the chancel. Stone corbels and timber brackets to the aisle ceilings, painted with badges and chevrons. Timber **reredos** of Christ in Glory, the Annunciation and Saints, under traceried canopies. A gilded and traceried **screen** with an **organ loft** and **organ case** separates nave from chancel, dominating the interior, and adds the one note of richness. **Font**, dated 1637, is from the old church, a small polygonal bowl with inscription and very elementary ornament on the underside. **Stained glass** in the chancel, S chapel and second window in the N aisle by *Burlison & Grylls*, the E window of 1900 designed by *Bodley*. That in the S aisle 1915–22 by *Clayton & Bell*, S and N aisles W windows of 1923 by *Shrigley & Hunt* and in the porch by *Maile & Son*, 1948.

Wood Lane leads back to **Harrogate Road** where there is **Westfield Terrace**, very large three-storey houses of *c.* 1870 with canted bays, set back from the road on a private driveway with massive round gateposts, quite unlike anything else as far out in the suburbs as this. Opposite,

129. St Matthew, Wood Lane, by G.F. Bodley, 1897–9

and in scale a great contrast, Nos. 150–170, a handsome ashlar early C19 terrace, two storey with console brackets and corniced hoods over the doors. Continuing on similar lines, Nos. 198–218 and Nos. 226–230, a long row, mostly double-fronted, ashlar façades, not a formal terrace but individual houses very similar in design. Nos. 204–206 have marginal lights, No. 208 an ornate Edwardian rendered façade. In **Regent Street** are two early C19 houses, No. 7 and **Hawthorn House** both have Diocletian windows in the end gables, seemingly a favourite feature in the area (cf. Newton Villa, Henconnor Lane), the former in coursed stone, the latter larger and rendered. A most elaborate group of late C19 shops at Nos. 51–55 **Woodland Lane** with much use of heavy shouldered arches in the window detailing, the rock-faced stone enlivened by bands of red brick. Four houses at Nos. 57–63 (much altered) with Gothic doorways are evidently by the same hand. Opposite to the s, the

Alcuin School, formerly St Matthew's Parish Hall of 1912 by *Sydney Kitson*, a suave design in red brick with buttresses topped by urns at each end and much use of circular windows in lower wings.

To the s on **Hawthorn Road**, in **Hawthorn Mount**, **View and Vale**, are terraces of small cottages of *c*. 1900 with applied half-timbering, tile-hanging and gabled dormers, far more elaborate than the Leeds norm. Then **Town Street** and the former **Wesleyan Sunday School** of 1794, converted to a school in 1878. Two storeys of coursed stone, the central part of the front projecting slightly with a pediment. Tall round-headed windows and a pedimented doorway with attached Doric columns. Next to the excellent **Town Street Housing** of *c*. 1970 by *E.W. Stanley*, City Architect assisted by *D.M. Wrightson*. It replaced decayed early C19 cottages but retains the curve of the original road as a pedestrian path with small squares leading off it. A varied building line and extensive planting add charm. The grey brick houses have mono-pitched roofs and simple elevations.

An area of high-class housing is centred on **Allerton Park**. Laid out with large houses by *Bedford & Kitson* at the beginning of the C20, there has been some interesting redevelopment, including Nos. 2 and 2A, striking houses by *Bauman Lyons Architects*. No. 2 of 1995 is of conventional brick construction, its dominant motif a clerestory running the length of the house. Full-height entrance hall in the centre. In contrast, No. 2A, built 1998, has a timber frame on a 3.3 metre grid, rendered externally. Two wings meet at an oblique angle, extensively glazed on the principal s-facing elevations. Mono-pitched roofs with deeply over-hanging eaves. Double-height living space in the shorter left-hand wing, split-level bedrooms with balconies and service areas to the right. **Webton Court** (No. 7) is a fine Domestic Revival house of 1902–3 by *Bedford & Kitson* for W.J. Cousins. The garden front nicely balanced, almost symmetrical, close-studded half-timbering above a stone ground floor, other elevations tile-hung. The entrance door recessed and set in a screen with Art Nouveau stained glass. Remarkably well-preserved interior with restrained plasterwork of flowing foliage designs to the ribs of the drawing room ceiling, an arched inglenook and well-crafted fittings e.g. door handles. Cottage and stable in similar style but altered. Nos. 11a–c, a trio of self-build eco-houses of 1993–6 by *Jonathan Lindh*, three-storey, timber-framed with roofs partly sedum-clad, a prominent timber balcony and steps. Garden ponds have reed beds for sustainable waste water treatment. Return now to **Gledhow Lane** and **Chapel Allerton Hall**. In the C19 this was the home of Sir John Barran, the clothing manufacturer, twice mayor of Leeds. At first sight a rather shapeless red brick house of the 1860s with an elaborate fretwork porch, it incorporates work of *c*. 1830 at the rear. The C18 stables have been unsympathetically converted to residential use.

The highlight of Chapel Allerton, best seen from Allerton Park, is **Gledhow Manor** (Nos. 350–352 Gledhow Lane, built as Red House) of

130. Gledhow Manor, formerly Red House, Gledhow Lane, by Bedford & Kitson, 1903

1903 by *Bedford & Kitson*, a large and ambitious Neo-Georgian mansion (now flats) [130], built for Commander Bernal Bagshawe, proprietor of the Kirkstall Forge. U-shaped front, the centre filled in on the ground floor to form an outer hall. Red brick with Ancaster stone quoins and bands, roofed in red slates with a timber modillion eaves cornice. A broad semicircular portico with paired Ionic columns *in antis* of Hopton Wood stone with a pecked surface which forms a balcony for the first floor. Front door in an ashlar surround with a fanlight and flanked by two deep windows also with fanlights. Canted bay windows and hipped roofs. Planned around an enormous square top-lit central hall that extends the full height of the house. At first floor is a gallery, built to exhibit Bagshawe's collection of c18 prints. Much of this is preserved including the staircase and gallery with column-on-vase balusters, the gallery reached through fluted Ionic columns *in antis*. Fine woodwork, original tiling and light fittings. Stained glass in the vestibule and staircase probably by *George Walton.** The service quarters are in a NE wing. Impressive **stables** (also converted to houses), off Allerton Park with more of an Arts and Crafts feel, the upper floor

*I am grateful to David Boswell for this information.

roughcast, broad sliding sash windows and a big carriage arch with a deeply moulded cornice on one side and tile voussoirs on the other.

Back down **Church Lane** for **The Elms**, a house built in several phases, the earliest of *c.* 1730, cottage-like and now rendered, extended at right angles *c.* 1750 by five bays in brick with a pedimented doorcase, itself enlarged with a taller wing, the front canted, in the early C19.

Return to the centre through the **graveyard** of the old parish church (dem. 1935), which was superseded by Bodley's St Matthew in 1899 (*see* p. 239). The church was possibly of C17 origin but completely rebuilt in 1737 and again in the C19. The graveyard contains a number of early C18 gravestones and the table **tomb** of John Hives of 1843 in the form of a Roman altar. Scrolled ends to the top slab, below a dentilled cornice and Doric frieze with guttae and triglyphs with paterae.

Gledhow

Gledhow is separated from Chapel Allerton by the heavily wooded Gledhow Valley and is best visited by car. It was just fields until the beginning of the C20 when extensive building took place to the NE of **Gledhow Hall**, Gledhow Lane. This was constructed soon after 1766 for Jeremiah Dixon and is attributed to *John Carr*. Two storeys, ashlar with a hipped roof behind a balustraded parapet. The w front has a central door with a Gibbs surround and pediment between a pair of two-storey canted bays, all suggestive of Carr's style. A third broad bay on the s front. Rear extensions and alterations of *c.* 1885–90 by *Chorley & Connon* for Sir James Kitson M.P., later first Lord Airedale, who acquired the house *c.* 1880. Two projecting bays and an entrance with two pairs of decorated Ionic columns *in antis* forming a loggia. Corner entrance porch with Tuscan columns. A service block to the left. Panelling in the library, morning room and dining room of 1911 by *Sydney Kitson* who also remodelled the inner and outer halls in the manner of Carr, on whom he was an authority. Fine tiled bathroom in Burmantofts faience of *c.* 1885. Gritstone **stables** with a cupola and a lodge, mid C19, with additions by *Chorley & Connon*. Early C20 motor house with glass roof with cast-iron trusses within the stable yard. Coursed rubble **foot-bridge** dated 1768 built across Gledhow Lane to Home Farm.

More impressive is the Neoclassical **Roundhay Hall** (a private hospital since 1989), in Jackson Avenue, slightly NW [131]. Built 1841–2, originally called Allerton Hall, by *Samuel Sharp* for William Smith, a stuff merchant. Between 1916 and 1930, it was owned by the chemical manufacturer Edward Allen Brotherton (later Lord Brotherton of Wakefield) who donated his magnificent collection of books to Leeds University (*see* p. 178). Finely proportioned with a giant four-column Corinthian portico, the pediment with acroteria. Very broad corner pilasters. The s front has a bowed central ground-floor bay with Corinthian pilasters and a tripartite window over. Grecian detailing. Much originality in the treatment of the chimneys which are paired

131. Roundhay Hall, Jackson Avenue, by Samuel Sharp, 1841–2

with cylindrical moulded shafts. Splendid oval entrance hall with a mosaic floor and a handsome T-plan staircase under a coved dome. Wall niches with casts of Canova's 'Venus' and 'The Shepherd Boy' by Bertel Thorvaldsen, added by Lord Brotherton. Vaulted landing on the first floor leading to rooms with elegant Neoclassical plaster decoration including guilloche panels, moulded capitals and egg-and-dart cornices. **Lodge**, in Thorn Lane, with bowed centre, and projecting roof supported on square columns.

To the w on **Gledhow Lane**, **Hillside**, a pair of c19 cottages altered and extended in 1901–3 by *Sydney Kitson* for his own occupation. He added a columned loggia with views down the Gledhow Valley. At the s end of the woods on **Gledhow Valley Road**, is **Gipton Spa**, a small gabled bath-house reputed to have been built in 1671 by Edward Waddington but probably rebuilt *c.* 1800. Attached to it is a high wall enclosing an open-air bath with a platform on three sides. The bather would plunge into the ice-cold water brought from a nearby spring and then sweat by the fireplace inside.

To the e, on **Gledhow Wood Road**, *J.S. Brocklesby* was commissioned in 1914 to design an estate of smart houses set in a well-wooded landscape. Only six houses were built before war intervened, one pair (Nos. 37–39) semi-detached, the others detached including **Stone House** (No. 3 Coppice Way) with a crowstepped gable and No. 47 **The Cairn** with a mansard roof. All are in the local stone and have dormers and pantiled roofs, a style later employed by Brocklesby at Merton, South London. To the n, **Gledhow Lodge**, mid c19, three bays, stone with a curious timber-framed and rendered extension of 1906 by *Sydney Kitson* (now **The Croft**) to provide staff quarters for Sir James Kitson of Gledhow Hall.

Headingley

Headingley has the most important group of large and small villas and mansions in the city, set on ground which rises steadily N of Woodhouse Moor with a sharp dip on the E to the narrow Meanwood valley. Here Meanwood Beck provided power for industry, notably leather tanneries for which Leeds was an important base. In the C17 Headingley was open country with huddles of cottages and a few larger houses, amongst them Headingley Hall, which dominated Headingley itself, and Kirkstall Grange to the N at Far Headingley. In the C19 this came into the possession of the Beckett family, whose patronage played an important part in the later development of the suburb. The well-to-do of Leeds had already begun to move on to the higher ground of

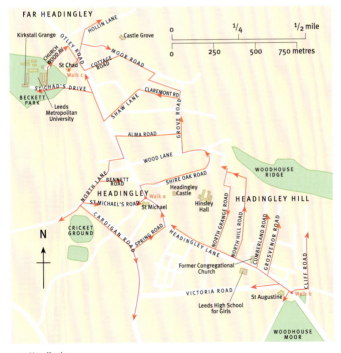

132. Headingley

Headingley during the late C18 and early C19, driven there by the increasingly smoky atmosphere of the town. They built villas on the s-facing slopes of Headingley Hill adjoining the Otley–Leeds Turnpike, opened in 1754 (now Headingley Lane). 'In no village in the parish are the effects of the prosperity of Leeds more visible than in Headingley, Chapeltown only excepted,' wrote the Leeds historian Edward Parsons in 1834. Development was slow, with only a few villas along Headingley Lane before 1850 but in the second half of the C19, the area between the Lane and the Ridge was filled with villas, many of them of considerable architectural distinction. Headingley, its exclusiveness preserved by tightly drawn restrictive covenants, became the prime residential area of Leeds.

Further smart development took place to the w along Cardigan Road but by the late C19 a social division had grown up s of Headingley Lane below which grand houses would not sell. In their place came modest but respectable terraced housing, including some back-to-backs. Superior development continued instead northwards, extending towards Far Headingley where the enclosure of the remaining part of Headingley Moor in 1829 had been followed by an expansion of cottage building N of Shaw Lane with varieties of smaller terraces mixed in with large villas. Far Headingley's centre remains village-like to the present day but Headingley itself is now a busy shopping centre, dominated by the ugly Arndale Centre. The expansion of the Leeds universities at the end of the C20 has led to the building of student residences and the conversion of much of the housing to student flats but this has not lessened the appeal of the narrow, heavily wooded roads between Headingley Lane and the Ridge which still look much as they did when they inspired the paintings of Atkinson Grimshaw in the 1870s.

The walks are divided into three areas, beginning with central Headingley, then Headingley Hill, Far Headingley and three important outlying mansions in Meanwood.

a) The Centre

The centre of Headingley is along Headingley Lane and its continuation, Otley Road. Its principal ornament is **St Michael** by *J.L. Pearson* of 1884–6 [133], a typically proud and prosperous church for the suburb. It is the third church on the site. Its predecessors were a chapel-of-ease, erected in 1626, which was replaced by a church by *R.D. Chantrell* in 1837. This became too small and Pearson was engaged to design its successor, in which he was aided by the local architect, *C.R. Chorley*. Pearson had by this time perfected his version of C13 Gothic at Truro, with which St Michael has much in common; in particular the thin 200 ft (61 metre) w tower and spire (completed in 1890) which are reminiscent of the twin towers of Pearson's original design for Truro. The broach spire has tall octagonal pinnacles at the angles. A strong vertical emphasis both outside and inside, achieved externally by tall thin

133. St Michael, Otley Road, by J.L. Pearson, 1884–6

buttresses and internally by the height of the nave and the chancel arch. Two rows of triple lancets at the E end. The N porch (added 1890) has five carved figures by *Thomas Earp* of Our Lord in the centre flanked on the left by SS Peter and Paul and on the right by Daniel and Isaiah.

Fine but not over-rich interior with a three-bay nave with round columns and shallow transepts. As Anthony Quiney has noted, Pearson here used for the first time on a large scale a timber roof resting on pointed stone transverse arches, a device he would later employ at St John, Redhill, Surrey and, most notably, All Saints, Hove, Sussex. These handsome but sober arches frame the chancel, lending a monumental quality that acts as a foil to *Pearson*'s iron **screen** (executed by *White & Sons*) of 1891–2 and *Temple Moore*'s gilded and carved wooden **reredos** of 1905, executed by *Thompson & Sons*. It depicts Christ in Glory flanked by St George and St Michael and eighteen figures influential in the history of the Church in the N of England, set in canopied niches. Painted **altar** by *Hardman & Co.*, 1891. In the Lady Chapel, a **triptych** by *Pearson* added in 1897. **Pulpit**, alabaster and marble, richly carved with figures in arcaded niches, on short granite columns. **Lectern** by *Pearson*, executed by *Hardman & Co.*, 1889. Octagonal **Font** of alabaster carved with panels of biblical scenes. **Organ case** of 1890 by *Pearson*. **Sculpture** of Virgin and Child in the Lady Chapel and **screen** enclosing the children's corner by *Robert Thompson*. **Stained glass**. E and W windows of 1886 by *J.H. Powell* for *John Hardman & Co.* Some N and S aisle windows were reused from the previous church. First N aisle window from E by *Wailes & Strang*, 1889, second of 1871 and third of 1866 by *William Wailes*. The central S aisle window and right-hand light of first window from E were part of the 1879 E window by *Powell Bros.* S aisle fourth, 1886 by *T.W. Camm* for *Winfield & Co.* Porch windows by *Hardman*, 1890. In the Lady Chapel, three windows by *J.H. Powell* for *Hardman & Co.* of 1887–8. Next to the church, on the corner of **St Michael's Lane**, the former **Headingley National School** of 1834, in the usual Gothic with a pretty bellcote, extended by *Chorley & Connon* in 1889 and 1893.

Opposite St Michael's, on **Headingley Lane**, is the **War Memorial** of 1922 by *Sydney Kitson*, a plinth and obelisk. Also two early C19 pubs, the **Skyrack** and the **Original Oak**, scanty remnants of the old village. On opposite corners of Shire Oak Road, the former **Yorkshire Bank** of c. 1932 by *Chorley, Gribbon & Foggitt*, classical in red brick and Portland stone and the **HSBC Bank**, 1913–14 by *Sydney Kitson*, ashlar-fronted with pilasters and a secondary order of attached Doric columns.

Down **Shire Oak Road**, to the E of Headingley Lane, on the left is **Headingley Hall**, which was in existence by 1649, when John Killingbeck, Mayor of Leeds set his initials in a keystone on an archway. The present Hall, the earliest building in the area, was erected c. 1795, enlarged in the 1830s and again in the 1880s when a billiard room and a two-storey bay window were added. Plain exterior with coped gables and kneelers. Shire Oak Road was laid out with half-acre plots in 1885–6 by *George Corson*, with the intention that purchasers would put up houses to his design. In the event, development was slow and several of the houses are by other hands, including Nos. 4–6 **Shire Oak Dene** by *F.W. Bedford*, an urbane pair of large Neo-Georgian houses of 1894, an early use of the style, designed to look like one large house with a central doorway. Double-height bay windows, sash windows and a hipped roof with dormers half hidden behind a parapet. The effect more reminiscent of Hampstead than the industrial north. Some houses by *George Corson* display a variety of styles; the former Bellamona and Ravenstone of 1887, now a hotel, have applied half-timbering and corner turrets and Nos. 21–23 are heavy-looking stone semi-detached houses of 1884 with a big central gable. Then the two high points of the road. On the right, **Arncliffe** of 1892–4 by *F.W. Bedford,* his first recorded work and for his brother. An early example of the butterfly plan, with a central hall flanked by a dining room and a drawing room, the stairs behind the hall and a service wing to the rear. Its style is broadly C17 Flemish with mullioned and transomed windows and a little strapwork decoration. The interior retains its fireplaces and panelling and has plasterwork by *George Bankart*, including one ceiling

Bedford & Kitson, architects

The partnership of *Bedford & Kitson*, which lasted from 1897 to 1904, united two old Leeds families whose fortunes were made in industry. *Francis W. Bedford* (1866–1904) was the son of James Bedford, manufacturing chemist. He trained with *W.H. Thorp* (perhaps working with him on Quarrydene, Weetwood, and the Art Gallery in the mid 1880s) and in the office of *Ernest George & Peto*. By the early 1890s, he was in practice in London and Leeds, where he designed several beautiful Arts and Crafts houses for his family. *Sydney Decimus Kitson* (1871–1937) was a member of a prominent engineering family and the youngest son of James Kitson of Elmete Hall, Mayor of Leeds (1860–2); his brother James (later Lord Airedale) was the city's leading Liberal businessman and first Lord Mayor in 1897. Sydney became a pupil of the important Arts and Crafts architect *E.J. May*, protégé of Norman Shaw. The partnership provided Leeds with some of its finest buildings, in a mixture of vernacular and Shavian Queen Anne styles, beginning with Lincombe, North Hill Road, Headingley, and detached houses such as Redhill, Headingley (1900–1) and Red House (1903, now Gledhow Manor) for the owner of Kirkstall Forge. Their domestic work caught the attention of the hugely influential Hermann Muthesius, author of *Das englische Haus* (1904–5), who noted their traditionally-designed exteriors and more independent interiors, impressed by their comfort and quiet refinement. Their major buildings in the city demonstrate an understanding of new materials and technology, notably the School of Art (1903) and North Street Public Dispensary (1904).

This account is based on David Boswell, 'The Kitsons and the Arts', unpublished PhD thesis, University of York, 1996

loosely based on the Plantin House, Antwerp. A charming **Summer House** with conical roof and Venetian window survives from the former Dutch garden. A little to the NE, **Redhill** (No. 33) of 1900–1 by *Bedford & Kitson* for Joseph Nicholson, with additions of 1911 for Edward Audus Hirst. Tile-hung and half-timbered, a particularly successful rendering of Shaw's Old English style. Nicely balanced garden front with two tiled gables and a much larger projecting half-timbered one. Inside, an Art Nouveau chimneypiece and stained glass by *George Walton*.

Turn down a path to the left to join **Wood Lane** which runs parallel back to Otley Road. On the left, several large houses, including **St Ives**, Gothic of 1869 by *George Corson* and on **Grove Road**, **Ashfield**, a tall 1860s Italianate house, possibly by *Cuthbert Brodrick*, with large eaves brackets and a semicircular window; the porch, with its paired square columns joined by a central band, exhibits his characteristic tough detailing. On the corner of Grove Road with Alma Road, **Wheatfield Lodge**, is an 1880s Italianate house with unusual additions of 1892 by *T. Butler Wilson*, including a bow window and two towers that bulge out from the retaining wall to Alma Road on the N side. The entrance hall has a tessellated floor and a first-floor screen of coupled Tuscan marble columns. Ionic columns support an entablature with carved frieze in the principal ground-floor room. Also on Alma Road, the impressive stables by *Wilson* with rusticated banding, modillion eaves and semicircular fanlights above each window.

On the N side of **Alma Road**, the large **Moorfield Court** of 1855–6, Gothic with an octagonal three-storey tower with octagonal corner

134. No. 7 Alma Road, by Cuthbert Brodrick, 1859

turrets, built for William Joy, a chemical manufacturer. The decoration is sumptuous. An elaborate porch has crouching dogs carved in the architraves and male and female heads as label stops. Above the entrance bay, a spire. The interior has a hall with cusped arches on polished granite columns, panelled rooms whose ceilings have pendants and a vaulted octagonal chapel. No. 9 of *c.* 1860 is broadly classical, yet in no sense 'correct'. It has a boldly modelled doorway, the surround decorated by large bosses, the type of oversized detailing suggestive of Brodrick's hand. Façade with four broad pilasters, the windows round-headed and paired under segmental mouldings. *Cuthbert Brodrick* was the architect in 1859 of nearby **Oakfield** (No. 7, now Brodrick Court) [134], an idiosyncratic Neo-Grecian design, three bays wide topped by a pediment with a circular window extending the full length of the façade with exaggeratedly broad overhanging eaves on large coupled brackets. Grecian doorway.

Back to **Otley Road** where on the w side survive some remnants of the agricultural past of the area with some much-modified c18 farm buildings. In stark contrast, the horribly out of scale **Arndale Centre** of 1965, a group of shops originally built with a bowling alley above and a tall slab at the N end, recently re-clad. To the s on the w side of Otley Road, is the **Wesleyan Church** of 1844–5 probably by *James Simpson*, the first Methodist chapel in Leeds to be built in the Gothic style. Transepts, side galleries and an apse of 1862. A Sunday School opened in 1857, rebuilt in Chapel Street in 1908–9. Surrounding the chapel, an interesting group of mid-c19 workers' housing. First to the N are **Alma Cottages**, semi-detached Tudor cottages with bargeboards and gables of *c.* 1860 that have what must be some of the grandest outside privies in England; in blocks of two with crenellated parapets set some distance from the cottages. Then Nos. 1–9 **Chapel Terrace** and Nos. 1–8 **Chapel Square**, two stone terraces of *c.* 1850 back-to-backs linked at right angles. These retain Georgian proportions. More through terraces in similar style nearby.

On **North Lane** stands the finely detailed Jacobean style former **Pumping Station** of 1860 for the Leeds Corporation Waterworks, extended in 1866 and again in 1879, now a pub. U-shaped with two tall wings, each with a flèche and the rear part under a steeply pitched roof with dormers. Elaborately shaped gables. It originally had a tall chimney. To the rear in **Bennett Road** is the former **Parochial Institute** of 1883–4 by *George Corson*. It draws attention to itself by its heavy and ornate porch which has short columns with naturalistic foliage and a dramatic sculpted panel of St George defeating the dragon on the front, royal arms to the side. Asymmetrical twin gable façade, the smaller to the left projects forward with a quatrefoil window, the larger with a big five-light traceried window. The hall roof is tunnel vaulted with decorative wrought-iron trusses. Back into **North Lane** for **The Lounge Cinema**, built in 1916 by *C.C. Chadwick & William Watson*, originally

135. Nos. 49–51 Cardigan Road, formerly The Old Gardens, by F.W. Bedford, 1893.
Perspective from *The Builder*, December 1904

seating 782. Long street façade with much faience, extended N with a
sweeping parabolic glass front. In **St Michael's Road**, Nos. 76 and 78 are
elegant small 1830s houses that have sophisticated Neoclassical porches
and margin lights (cf. Harrogate Road, Chapel Allerton). **South Parade
Baptist Church** was built in stages. The earliest part, the Sunday
Schools on the corner of South Parade and Water Grove, is by *Percy
Robinson & W. Alban Jones*, 1909. Red brick, late Gothic style with a
tower originally intended to link it to the planned church. This followed
in 1924–7, designed by *Jones & Stocks*, in a free Gothic style with steel
roof trusses, hidden above a suspended ceiling. Reordered in 1999,
including a s porch, by *Robert West*. Further along North Lane is
Headingley Cricket Ground, established in 1888 and the headquarters
of the Yorkshire Cricket Club since 1903. All that needs to be mentioned
are the **Sir Leonard Hutton Memorial Gates** of 2001 by *Chrysalis Arts
Ltd* which depict scenes from his life.

The area to the s of the Cricket Ground along **Cardigan Road** was
the site of the short-lived Leeds Zoological and Botanical Gardens
which opened in 1840 and were managed by a society founded three
years earlier for the purpose. The gardens, designed by *William
Billington*, a Wakefield engineer and *Edward Davies*, landscape gardener, were surrounded by a 9 ft (2.7 metre) high stone wall, part of
which survives near the junction with Chapel Lane. Following the
gardens' failure, the site was sold in 1848 to become a tip. All that
remains is the **Bear Pit** on the E side of Cardigan Road. Built of large
blocks of rusticated masonry with two circular castellated viewing
turrets. The circular pit had a gateway in the form of a Serlian arch
and cages in the basement in which eagles were reputedly incarcer-
ated. The Botanical Gardens Estate was eventually sold for building
and high-quality mansions covered the ground by 1893. The first

house to be built was **Manor Court** (No. 43, originally Clareville), Cardigan Road, of 1868 by *George Corson*, a heavy design with round-headed dormers, much red brick cogging and stumpy columns to the porch. On the w side **Cardigan House** (No. 84), 1870 by *Edward Birchall*, is larger with a corner turret resting on a massive shaft and quatrefoils in the staircase window. By contrast, Nos. 49–51 (originally The Old Gardens) by *F.W. Bedford* of 1893 [135] is in the tile-hung Old English style, designed to look like a single house but completely asymmetrical with a large end chimney and two big gables that are slightly jettied. Now flats, it has been much extended. Next the Bear Pit (*see* above) then two more striking mansions of 1894, almost identical, both with tall central towers, **Sandholme House** (No. 114) and **Leefield House** (No. 116) by *Daniel Dodgson* who had carried out much work for their owners, the speculative builders Benjamin and William Walmsley.

Return to the centre of Headingley via Spring Road. On the right, by the junction with Headingley Lane, **Spring Bank** of *c.* 1857 by *John Fox* for Robert Ellershaw is large with shaped gables of C17 type. Enlarged in 1877–8 by *C.R. Chorley* for the prominent locomotive manufacturer Sir James Kitson M.P. (who later moved to Gledhow Hall, *see* p. 243), and again by *William Thorp* who added the left half of the garden front for William Harvey in 1885–6, to include a library with an oriel above a children's playroom. Across Headingley Lane, on the N side, **St Columba United Reformed Church**, of 1964–6 by *W. & J.A. Tocher*. Striking design on sloping ground with a meeting room on the s side raised on concrete columns over a car parking area. Multi-gabled roof, peaked at each end. The brickwork of the E end is canted rather like the bows of a dreadnought.

Next, hidden down a long drive and announced by a Gothic **lodge** of 1866, is **Headingley Castle** of 1843–6 by *John Child*, the largest of his Tudor Gothic houses, for Thomas England, a wealthy corn factor. Symmetrical with a three-storey tower whose octagonal corner buttresses transmute into panelled turrets on the upper storey. Battlemented throughout. Central porte cochère with a broad Tudor arch, an oriel window above. An octagonal rib-vaulted entrance hall with a big central pendant and niches sets the tone for the restrained Gothic detailing of the interior. It leads to a staircase hall rising the full height of the house, lit by a lantern. Fire-proofed basement construction of brick vaults sprung from cast-iron I-beams. Now flats.

b) Headingley Hill

The walk begins at **Hyde Park Corner** at the N end of Woodhouse Moor, marked by a brick and terracotta **Shopping Parade** of 1906. To the N in **Woodhouse Street**, a former **Post Office**, also of 1906, with a very busy Neo-Baroque façade. Splayed entrance front, Gibbs surrounds and open pediment over the door and exuberant terracotta decoration veering towards Art Nouveau. Large round-headed windows with prominent mullions that slope outwards and merge into the sills. Then into **Cliff Road** to the N. On the right in **Woodhouse Cliff**, Nos. 1–4, a terrace of substantial three-storey early C19 houses and **Cliff House** (Nos. 5–5A), possibly late C17 or early C18, vernacular with two light mullioned windows save for a Gibbs window surround above the door, a remarkable survival so close to the city centre. Further up **Cliff Road**, Atkinson Grimshaw lived at No. 56, then the former **Headingley Home for Girls** of 1873 by *W.H. Thorp* with additions of 1876. Long symmetrical red brick front with projecting wings at each end, porches with pointed arches, and blue brick diapering.

The key building here is **St Augustine**, Hyde Park Terrace to the s, a big church of 1870–1 by *James B. Fraser* [136] with a 186 ft (56.7 metre) tall SE tower and spire, pierced pinnacles on the angles of the octagonal top stage, completed in 1878. Dec style with Geometrical tracery. It has N and s chapels in the position of transepts but these are roofed parallel to the nave to allow the clerestory lancets to run through from the chancel to the w end. Well-preserved **interior** retaining pews and encaustic tiles. Arcading of five arches with label stops of carved heads of apostles with shields bearing their emblems. Polished red granite columns, excellent carving of leaves of hawthorn, ivy, etc on the capitals. Impressive clustered columns at the junction of the transepts and the chancel arch responds, the latter of grey as well as red granite. Tall chancel arch on short black marble shafts, angel capitals. Trussed spur roofs, that in the chancel boarded with bosses depicting the symbols of the Passion. **Reredos** of 1882, probably by *Fraser*, of pink veined marble, mosaic of the Last Supper in the centre, canopies above and flanked by panels with biblical passages. **Altar** of cedar, richly decorated, arcaded with grouped ebony shafts. **Pulpit** executed by *Charles Mawer*, in Caen stone, square with two marble shafts on dark serpentine and Irish green marble bases. Three circular mosaics on a gold background with richly diapered spandrels by *Simpson*. **Font**, carved with angels holding crosses, texts, etc., also by *Mawer*. Timber cover. Early C20 Arts and Crafts style **electric light fittings** are a rare survival. They comprise brass orbs from which extend pendants with leaf form decoration in brass on square plaques. **Stained glass**. Five-light E window, the Doctrine of the Atonement by *C. E. Kempe*, 1883. Two windows in the s transept of 1900 by *Powell Bros*, two in the N transept by *Kayll & Co.*, 1909.

On **Headingley Lane**, a group of early C19 semi-detached villas on the N side and on the s, **Victoria Road** veers off. Nos. 3–7 Victoria Road of *c.* 1840 have simple but handsome ashlar façades while Nos. 27–29 have the central ground-floor portion recessed behind Doric columns. The **Bethel Pentecostal Church** (formerly the Free Methodist Chapel) by *W.S. Braithwaite* of 1885–6 slots into the terrace, a violently Gothic interjection. Braithwaite made the most of a tight site employing a tall gable with a large w window with geometrical tracery flanked by

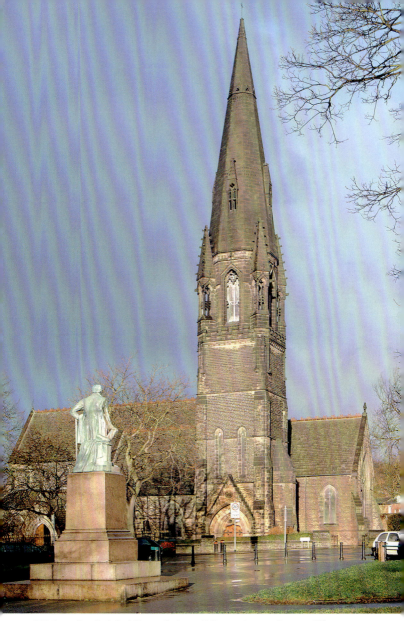

136. St Augustine, Hyde Park Terrace, by James B. Fraser, 1870–1 and statue of Sir Robert Peel by William Behnes, 1852 (*see* p. 198)

smaller two-light windows on each side. A portal with twin doorways crashes into the lower part of the w window and a tall thin tower with triple bell openings, a narrow pediment and tall spirelet with two further sets of openings and conical top is to the left. The remainder of the church is of brick with a clerestory with timber quatrefoil openings.

Internally, iron columns and galleries on three sides with a curving front. Sunday School and classrooms below.

Returning to Headingley Lane, we should now explore the various dead end roads leading up Headingley Hill to the Ridge. Each is lined with C19 villas, set well back and partly hidden by the mature planting: the following is a selection. The first is **Grosvenor Road**, with **Grosvenor House**, an elegant three-bay Neoclassical house of *c.* 1840 with pilasters only on the corners of the ground floor and a porch with fluted columns and anthemion mouldings to the capitals. Greek key decoration below the first-floor windows. At the top is **Hilly Ridge House** of 1839, classical and plain. Back on Headingley Lane, **Rose Court** is a fine five-bay house of *c.* 1842 by *John Clark*. The central bay brought forward with a broad tetrastyle portico with a pediment on Tuscan columns. The garden elevation visible from Victoria Road has its entrance recessed behind four Tuscan columns *in antis*. The **interior** is equally elegant with a tiled circular staircase hall (cf. Clark's Little Woodhouse Hall, p. 184) with attached columns and pilasters with Corinthian capitals and a vaulted ceiling. The octagonal ground-floor central room, which also has a vaulted ceiling, has niches and a frieze of palmettes with masks flanking the garden doors. Music room to the left with excellent plaster decoration to the paired composite order pilasters, a frieze of putti with lyres and a coved and panelled ceiling. The right-hand room has a bucranium frieze, although composed of living bulls rather than skulls. The Leeds Girls' High School, founded in Woodhouse Lane in 1876, moved here in 1905–6. Of that date, impressive Neo-Georgian **School Buildings** by *Chorley & Connon*. Long s range, two floors and an attic of six bays, divided by rusticated pilaster strips, the end bays brought forward and given open pediments. The upper parts roughcast, the lower embellished by much brick banding. Tall thin windows closely spaced. Internally planned around a central two-storey hall with galleries giving access to classrooms. Now part of the school, **Buckingham Villas**, a pair of particularly large and ornate Gothic villas of 1870 by *S.E. Smith* with a billiard room and stabling behind. Opposite is **Headingley Terrace**, a group of five three-bay houses of the 1840s with broad bracketed eaves, the end and centre houses brought forward and gabled.

Now up **Cumberland Road** where on the right are two contrasting villas, **Elmfield** and **Spring Hill**, the first debased and asymmetrical classical, the second Gothic, both of 1846 by *Thomas Shaw*, a graphic illustration of his eclecticism. On the left, **Devonshire Hall** (Leeds University halls of residence), created from Regent Villas, two pairs of mid-C19 semi-detached houses. The w pair (now Old Hall) have a fine interior, possibly by *John Child*. Behind is the former gatehouse which has a large rounded arch topped by a pierced parapet and a pair of single-storey wings whose eaves cornice extends to form imposts to the central arch. The houses are now incorporated within a formal

137. Devonshire Hall, Cumberland Road, by J.C. Procter & F.L. Charlton, 1928

arrangement of 1928 by *J.C. Procter & F.L. Charlton*, with L-shaped wings extending around a courtyard from a five-bay central hall. Free Scottish Baronial, of two storeys, rendered above a stone ground floor. The hall has a two-storey oriel that rises above a balustraded parapet to form a crenellated clock tower [137]. Residences of three storeys with dormered attics and an arcaded ground floor with four-centred arches. Just beyond, **Cumberland Priory**, a small and pretty Gothic house of *c.* 1841 with a projecting central gabled bay with an oriel, probably by *John Child* for himself.

Back down Cumberland Road, on the corner with Headingley Lane, the former **Headingley Hill Congregational Church** of 1864–6 by *Cuthbert Brodrick* [10], his only church (converted to offices in 1981 but now a church again). Superficially conventional with a sw tower but with characteristically original detail. Elevated for impact above a basement with six prominent gabled bays on the N and s sides, each with a tall two-light window within a pointed head and buttresses topped by a crouching beast. The w front has a double pointed arch doorway under a gable enriched with carved rosettes. The capitals, which have red sandstone colonettes, are described by Derek Linstrum as 'a sort of Gothic Corinthian'. Topping the tower is a spire of obelisk form, pierced with the architect's favourite rosette motifs. Next to the church, **Ashwood Villas**, a planned development of semi-detached and terraced villas, *c.* 1870 and mainly Gothic, Nos. 3–5 with shaped gables, the remainder quite plain. Then two of the finest villas on Headingley Hill, best viewed from North Hill Road. First, No. 48 Headingley Lane, **Ashwood** (now Hilton Court), of *c.* 1836 for Joseph Austin, probably by *John Child*, classical in form, its roof hidden behind a parapet but with traceried windows, some in large canted bays, drip hoods and tall grouped octagonal chimneys. Next door, **Headingley Hill House**, of similar date, a symmetrical Greek villa with two projecting bays flanking an Ionic porch and a balustraded balcony above. It closely resembles a design in Francis Goodwin's *Domestic Architecture* (1833–4).

North Hill Road showcases the two principal phases of Headingley Hill development. Some building took place in the 1830s but subsequent development took place on land purchased in 1897 by Norris Hepworth, the clothing manufacturer. On the w side, **Holmfield**, a

138. Lincombe, North Hill Road, by Bedford & Kitson, 1898–9

rambling Tudor villa of 1835 with an oriel and timber porch with cusped lights. Nos. 3–5 are probably by *Bedford & Kitson*, tile-hung with big half-timbered projecting gabled bays in the Shaw style. *Bedford & Kitson* also designed **Lincombe** (No. 7) for H.M. Hepworth in 1898–9 [138]. The house is clearly influenced by Voysey in the use of roughcast surfaces, windows with leaded lights and ashlar mullions, iron eaves brackets and dormers in the hipped roof. But it is boxy, lacking the low, rooted look of the best of Voysey's work. Interior with simple timber fire surrounds with tiled inserts and much white timber panelling. Divided into flats in 2001 with a highly sympathetic rebuilding of the coach house by *David Cook* of *C.R.L. Architects*. Also by *Bedford & Kitson*, **Highgarth** (No. 9) is a simpler roughcast Arts and Crafts essay of 1901–2 with plain timber mullions. No. 17, an early C19 picturesque Tudor villa, is twin gabled and has an embattled parapet, its chimneys linked by cornices.

At the top of North Hill Road turn left past extensive blocks of student accommodation in James Baillie Park to join **North Grange Mount** which was developed *c.* 1910 by Robert Wood with semi-detached houses and, unusually for the suburbs, a block of flats, Grange Court (*see* below). But what catches the eye is the extraordinary **North Hill House**. A strikingly original Neo-Gothic house built for William Walker in 1846, now in a bad way. Symmetrical, its predominant motif is the pair of very broad five-light full-height bay windows with Perp tracery over each light, the ground floor given a double dose with heavily cusped quatrefoil top lights. The windows are tall, the lower ones extending almost to the ground. Equally extravagant is the entrance, slightly projecting with a four-centred arch below a panel of contorted tracery, flanked by two pilasters which rise to become pinnacles. A castellated parapet completes the composition. Inside, the hall and one of the main ground-floor rooms have friezes of pointed arch arcading. A panelled billiard room was added by *S.E. Smith* in 1881. **Grange Court** of 1911–12 by *Joseph J. Wood* was the first block of mansion flats to be erected in Leeds. U-shaped, built on sloping ground so that there are four storeys to the front and five to the rear. Built of red brick, the top floor rendered but with floors of Hennebique concrete. The principal entrance in ashlar inscribed RW and 'Parum Sufficit'. External balconies run across the façade on elegant curved brackets. Jolly plaster decoration of birds and fruit in the tympana of the windows, together with similar panels in the rendered top floor. Pitched roof with attic dormers. Most flats have two or three bedrooms, unusually the basement had communal dining and recreation rooms together with caretaker's and maid's flats. A further block of 1923 in slightly simplified style to the E.

Return to **Headingley Lane** down **North Grange Road** past more early C19 Neoclassical villas and on the W side, **Lyndhurst** (No. 13) of 1887 by *Chorley & Connon*, with an irregular half-timbered front and angled porch. Moulded brickwork window surrounds. Continuing on the s side, **Buckingham House**, is substantial and elegant Neo-Grecian of *c.* 1840 with a porch with Ionic columns *in antis* and corner pilasters. The former **Church of Christ Scientist** (now the Elinor Lupton Centre of the Girls' High School) is of 1912 by *William Peel Schofield*. At first, only the school to the right was constructed, the church following in 1932. A low Portland stone block sparsely decorated with Egyptian pilasters flanking shallow but broad windows with circular glazing bars. The porch projects slightly and is surmounted by an urn. Large simply-furnished auditorium, little altered for its new use. On the N side, a long driveway leads to **Hinsley Hall** (now a R.C. Diocesan office). Built in 1867 as Wesley College by *Wilson & Willcox* of Bath. Low, a little starved, and symmetrical, with a middle tower with a large and prominent conical roof. Geometrical tracery in the ground-floor windows, on the upper floor steeply gabled windows, rising as dormers into the roof. *Cuthbert Brodrick* had submitted a castellated design. Enlarged 1902 by *Danby & Simpson* with a tutor's house and chapel in Perp style to complete a rear courtyard. Refurbished 1998–9 by *Abbey Holford Rowe* who added a top-lit octagonal chapel with ashlar walls.

From here, it is a short walk to the centre of Headingley or to return to Hyde Park Corner.

c) Far Headingley

The walk begins at **St Chad's Church** set back on the w side of **Otley Road**. St Chad was built in 1868, paid for by the Becketts of Kirkstall Grange (*see* below) who offered the land and £10,000. The design was laid down by *Edmund Beckett Denison* (later Lord Grimthorpe, now usually remembered for his drastic restoration of St Alban's Cathedral in 1879) but largely executed by *W.H. Crossland*. Very handsome tall w tower of three stages with Dec traceried windows, clock and three belfry openings. The slender, finely proportioned spire has diaper-patterned bands at intervals. Originally the church had a polygonal apse of French inspiration but in 1909–11 this was replaced by the young *J. Harold Gibbons* with the present structure, which incorporates a Lady Chapel on the N side and an organ chamber on the s. When seen from the s Gibbons' chancel, continuing the line of the nave roof unbroken, is of the highest quality and in the tough unmoulded style which one associates with his master Temple Moore. The E wall is divided into two panels by a pilaster, the E window high-set and flanked by buttresses. Rich **interior**, immensely long, the nave, choir and chancel each distinguished by differing roof treatments – the nave with exposed trusses, the ribs in the choir continued as shafts and the chancel with thin decorative ribs – yet preserving the essential unity. Arcades of circular columns support narrow pointed arches with lush carving, the bossy Dec-style foliage on the capitals is by *Mr Ruddock* of London, inspired by Selby Abbey choir and the Percy Shrine at

139. St Chad, Otley Road, E window, by Margaret Rope, 1922

Beverley. Narrow aisles with moulded stone trusses. A fine tall arch with four orders leads to the baptistery below the tower with mosaic paving of 1896. The clerestory windows have Gothick glazing bars. The originality of Gibbons' detailing is striking. A favourite motif is the shouldered arch, used in the wall passage that runs at high level below the E window behind the reredos, a device he was to use again in St Cyprian's, Frecheville, Sheffield (1952), and in the curious pierced piers (each adorned with a small carved lizard) that divide the Lady Chapel from the nave. The Lady Chapel, with a vaulted stone ceiling above the sanctuary and internal arcading to the small N windows, is lined with plain painted panelling and displays an innovative handling of Gothic forms. Extremely tall circular piers on the S side of the choir aisle. Magnificent wooden **reredos** by *Gibbons*, executed by *Boulton & Sons*, perhaps even surpassing that of Temple Moore at St Michael (*see* p. 248). Heavily gilded with a blue background, it depicts incidents from the Book of Revelation. At its centre, God in Majesty with adoring figures at His feet in deep relief, set within an ogee-shaped frame with an exquisite traceried canopy. Four panels below with the symbols of the Evangelists. On the outermost parts, the leaves of the vine mingled with grotesque figures. Three **mosaics**, re-erected at the NE end of the choir aisle, depict the Crucifixion on a plain gold background; from the former reredos of 1887 by a *Signor Capello*. **Pulpit**: timber, octagonal with carving of St Chad holding a model of a church. **Choir stalls** with much carved foliage on the fronts. **Font**: sandstone with short clustered columns, the bowl carved with flowers. **Stained glass**: the E window (The Redemption of Creation) in Arts and Crafts style of 1922 by *Margaret Rope* [139] provides a glorious counterpoint to the reredos below. Of five lights with Adam and Eve in the centre, a variety of animals both domestic and exotic, and a deep blue expressing chaos at its base. More excellent glass in the chancel and the chancel clerestory, including figures of saints by *Hardman* of 1871–7, taken from the old chancel. In the s aisle from the E: one by *Hardman & Co.*, 1886, two windows of 1900 and 1908 by *Kayll & Co.*, one by *Clayton & Bell* of 1882, and two by *James Powell* of 1917 and 1904. In the N aisle, by *Powell Bros* of 1886, by *Wailes & Strang* of 1882 and by *Wailes* of 1871. N aisle w window by *James Powell*, 1904. N window of 1917 by *James Powell*.

N of the church on Otley Road, **St Chad's Day School** of 1891 by *Perkin & Bulmer* and opposite **St Chad's Gardens** (Nos. 114–120), a group of four Dutch-gabled brick and faience villas of 1885, built to display the products of Wilcock & Co.'s Burmantofts pottery, after its proprietor James Holroyd had come to live in Headingley. The houses have corner brackets with dragons and griffins and moulded string courses, probably the work of *Maurice B. Adams* who had been commissioned a few years earlier to design such details for the company to promote their architectural application.

Far Headingley still has a pleasant grouping of modest early C19 houses and cottages, few of them remarkable. In its centre on the corner of **Hollin Lane** and Weetwood Lane is the former **Hollin Lane School** of 1839–40, Neo-Tudor style, extended in 1872 and subsequently turned into an early working men's club. This part of Far Headingley was developed following the 1829 enclosure of the last 130 acres of Headingley Moor. In **Moor Road**, many cottages and some larger houses. Among them a simple former **Methodist Chapel** of 1860, its long elevation to the road with an ashlar façade and simple lancets. On **Cottage Road** to the right, **Cottage Road Cinema** appropriately flanked by small cottages. It was converted from a motor garage and opened as the Headingley Picture House in 1912. Refronted in the 1930s, it still retains its wood-panelled interior, a good example of an early back street cinema. At the top end of Castle Grove Drive is **Castle Grove**, built in 1831–4. Plain three-bay house embellished *c.* 1870 with bay windows, a porch and rear wings, and further enlarged in 1896 by *T. Butler Wilson*. Two wings flank the earlier work which was given a balustraded parapet and urns. An Italianate tower and a great copper dome over the staircase were also added. Wilson's interior is one of the most impressive in Leeds. Internally the dome coffered with coloured glass in the top light, circular windows with elaborate plaster cornucopias and masks. The double-height salon has a musicians' gallery, supported on Ionic piers, which also gives access to the bedrooms. Coffered ceiling

140. Kirkstall Grange, Beckett Park, by James Paine, 1752

and big fireplace in C17 style. The room to the left of the entrance has a heavy plaster ceiling with terms and a massive timber chimneypiece, that to the right is in early C18 style. The former billiard room has sumptuous panelling, a screen and another ornate plaster ceiling. To the s in **Claremont Drive** is an area developed with substantial middle-class houses in terraces and pairs including St Anne's Villas and St George's Terrace of the 1850s, and Woodbine Terrace (s of Claremont Road) of 1868. Down Claremont Road to **Shaw Lane** and more large villas in a gamut of styles on the N side, the most impressive No. 5 **Glebe House**, Gothic and gabled with blind tracery and quatrefoils in the tympana formed by wide pointed arches above the windows and a trac-eried staircase window.

Right into **Otley Road**. On the E side, **Hollydene**, the former par-sonage of the 1770s. Coursed stone with kneelers and stone slates with a much taller three-bay extension to the s, then **Fairfield** of *c.* 1875 and **Victoria Terrace** of *c.* 1850, built at right angles to the road, which share paired round-headed windows as a dominant motif.

A little s on the w side of Otley Road, a tiny picturesque Tudor **lodge** *c.* 1830 marks **St Chad's Drive**, which leads to **Beckett Park**. Formerly the grounds of Kirkstall Grange and in part occupied by Leeds Metropolitan University, the remainder is a public park. At its centre is **Kirkstall Grange**, rebuilt in 1752 by *James Paine* for Walter Wade [140].* It became the home of the Beckett family in the C19. The Grange is an important early example of the 'villa with wings' i.e. adopting a coun-try house form. It pre-dates Isaac Ware's Wrotham Park, Hertfordshire (1754). The inspiration was one of Colen Campbell's villa designs from the third volume of *Vitruvius Britannicus* (plate 29), itself based on Palladio's Villa Pisani, Montagnana. The main block has a giant den-tilled pediment across the entire width of the façade, the centre of

*It replaced New Grange of 1626, built for Benjamin Wade.

which is slightly recessed. A semicircular arch tops the recess which is carried through the base of the pediment. The three-bay façade has first-floor windows with pediments and splayed surrounds. The composition lacks grace, not helped by the demolition of one wing. The surviving wing echoes on a smaller scale the main block with a pediment but its bay window was added *c.* 1890 by *Chorley & Connon* who also enclosed the porch and added further bays on the exposed flank of the house. **Interior**. Top-lit main stair in the centre of the building, the staircase hall octagonal, a reference to the central saloon at Chiswick House. Gallery at first-floor level, stairs and gallery both with bow-fronted iron balustrades. Some original plasterwork to the staircase, elsewhere late C19 Rococo-style ceilings.

The Grange's estate was sold to the Corporation who laid out the public park but retained the mansion as part of the City of Leeds Training College. Impressively formal design, won in competition by *G.W. Atkinson* in 1911 with a main building **James Graham Hall** facing a rectangular green. Lifeless 350 ft (106.7 metre) frontage with the central part raised and brought forward with a pediment above four Corinthian columns *in antis* and segmental pediments to the raised end pavilions. Paired pilasters on the upper floors. It was planned with a central hall flanked by two quadrangles. Around the green are seven Neo-Georgian residential blocks. **E**-shaped of three storeys in red brick with modillion eaves, all similar but for the treatment of the central entrance bay. **Cavendish House** is a later addition of 1911–15 by *Sydney Kitson*. In Queen's Wood is the **Victoria Arch**, probably of 1766 but altered in 1858 to commemorate Queen Victoria's opening of the Town Hall. Possibly built as an eyecatcher, it has four giant Ionic columns supporting a pediment. The frieze of glazed tiles is later.

From the Park one can retrace one's steps along St Chad's Drive or continue along Church Wood Avenue to return to Otley Road.

Meanwood

Three important houses lie to the NE of Meanwood. Set in outer suburbia they are best visited by car. **Meanwood Hall**, off Woodlea Park, was built *c.* 1762 for Thomas Denison [142]. The N wing was added

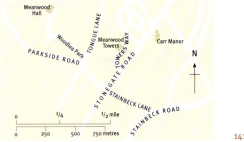

141. Meanwood

142. Meanwood Hall, remodelled by John Clark, *c.* 1834

in 1814 for Joseph Lees and the main block remodelled by *John Clark* for Christopher Beckett *c.* 1834. Clark's work is a precursor of the heavier classical decoration seen in the 1840s and 1850s. He employs channelled rustication to the ground floor, ornate hoods to the first-floor windows with scroll brackets, deep brackets below the eaves cornice and a heavy balustrade to the parapet. Bowed ends to the wings, porch with four Ionic fluted columns and original treatment of the chimneys which comprise four stacks linked at the top by a dentilled cornice, terminating in Soanian hoods. Grand entrance hall lit by a clerestory with a cantilevered divided staircase and a coffered ceiling. The house became part of a mental hospital in 1919 and, following its closure, is now surrounded by housing set within its former park.

Also set incongruously in a housing estate, **Meanwood Towers**, Towers Way, is a High Victorian Gothic fantasy of 1867 by *E.W. Pugin* for Thomas Kennedy, a partner in Fairbairns, textile engineers. It has remarkably tall ornamental chimneystacks (now cut down), oriels, gargoyles and gables. Cusped traceried windows and a heavy first-floor loggia above one of the many bay windows. In 1873 Pugin was bankrupt and *Norman Shaw* carried out internal decorative work, and rebuilt the top of the tower in a half-timbered, gabled manner, since truncated. Although converted for flats, the interior retains many fittings including a timber and painted glass screen in the hall, doors, panelling, medieval-style fireplaces, a black marble staircase and stained glass.

143. Carr Manor, Stonegate Road, by E.S. Prior, 1881; extended by Bedford & Kitson 1899–1900

There is no trace of the building put up in the grounds to house the Schulze organ now at St Bartholomew, Armley (*see* p. 209). **Lodge** on Stonegate Road.

Carr Manor, Stonegate Road of 1881, the first major work of *E.S. Prior* [143], for Thomas Albutt, a doctor, is much more relaxed, successfully aping the style of a C17 Yorkshire manor house. It was built on the site of Carr House, the home of the Oates family. The s front has five gables, those on the right are set back from the projecting centre, the two on the left additions of 1899–1900 by *Bedford & Kitson* for Col. F.W. Tannett-Walker, seamlessly blending with Prior's work. An arcade of three curious segmental arches connect this later w end with a n range, forming the entrance to a rear courtyard. The interior has much panelling, elaborate fireplaces and moulded plaster ceilings in C17 style. **Stables** by *Prior* with coved eaves to timber and roughcast panels, a dovecote in the gable and a re-set datestone of 1796. **Cottages** also by *Prior* to match the stables. In the grounds, a circular classical **Arbour** with fluted Ionic columns, topped by an open wrought-iron dome, probably by *Bedford & Kitson*. Opposite the Manor, the **Revolution Well**, a gritstone well-cover erected by Joseph Oates in 1788 to commemorate the centenary of the Glorious Revolution. Resembling an elegant dog kennel, it bears an inscription in incised lettering.

Excursions

St John the Baptist, Adel

5 miles N of the city centre, off Otley Road

St John the Baptist is one of the best and most complete Norman village churches in Yorkshire and is distinguished particularly by the rare survival of its decorative figure sculpture.

The church was built between 1150 and 1170. The neat w bellcote is by *R.D. Chantrell* who also rebuilt the w gable after the collapse of an earlier belfry in 1838. The roofs are also C19, having been lowered from their original steep pitch at an unknown, possibly pre-Reformation date. The chancel roof was rebuilt by *Chantrell* in 1844 to what was believed to be its original Norman form which he 'found was a difficult task, never having been certain what a Norman roof was . . .' The nave roof was raised in 1878–9 by *G.E. Street* as part of a comprehensive but sympathetic restoration. The church has a nave and lower chancel but lacks a tower or apse. The nave is of wide, comfortable proportions. The two lower windows in the w wall, which had been enlarged in the C18 to light a gallery, were renewed by Street who substituted Norman lancets. These were modelled on the remaining Norman window set centrally in the w gable. Very small windows, also largely the work of Street, in the N and S walls are placed high up above a string course. On the s wall a straight-headed two-light Dec window set low in the chancel, two straight-headed late Perp windows in the nave. Street also built a vestry in which he re-set the late Perp E window, which he had replaced by three small lancets. Corbel-frieze with seventy-eight faces and beasts all along the sides. A similar frieze in two diminishing tiers along the w gable: five heads below, three heads over. At the apex one more head. Small unmoulded priest's doorway in the chancel s wall.

In the nave s wall is the memorably sumptuous s **portal** [144], projecting and gabled so that it almost looks like a porch (cf. Kirkstall Abbey, *see* p. 271). Its sculpture was protected by a crude stone porch until *c.* 1816 but deteriorated badly following exposure. In 1982, the present minimal wooden porch was added to preserve what was left of the remarkable carving. In the gable, figures in box frames of Christ in Majesty, the Lamb over, the four symbols of the Evangelists to left and right (Revelations IV). In the spandrels, sculpture is squeezed into the available space, its forms now so weathered as to be indistinct: on the left, two serpents appear to be dividing into four to represent the Gospels. To the right is either a serpent dividing into four rivers or

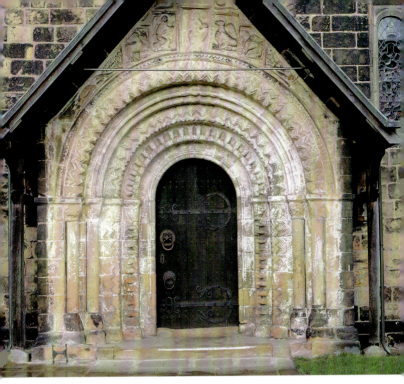

144. St John the Baptist, s portal, *c.* 1150–*c.* 1170

possibly the Tree of Life. On the apex of the gable, a beast's head. The door itself is arched and has four orders. The details are also badly preserved but it can still be seen that the capitals of the columns had intertwined bands and leaves. Inner order with beakheads up the shafts and along the arch. Second order zigzag on the wall surface and at right angles to it. Third order two rolls. Outer order with zigzag again on the wall surface as well as at right angles to it, but in the arch only. This arrangement of zigzag is typical of late Norman design after 1150. The door is a C19 copy of that discovered hidden behind a C18 panelled door in 1843. The Norman bronze **door ring**, probably made in York *c.* 1200 (cf. All Saints' Pavement, York), was of excellent quality (tragically stolen in 2002; it has been replaced in replica), with a monster's head, probably a lion, clasping the ring and a man's head protruding from its mouth.

The **interior** is much as Street restored it in the 1870s when he replaced box pews and a three-decker pulpit with choir and clergy stalls and refloored the nave. The key feature, however, is the splendid chancel arch [4]. Semicircular responds, two orders of shafts to the w, none to the e, though the carving of just two beakheads at the springing of the arch on the s side proves that at least one e order was projected. This detail is noteworthy proof that such sculptural detail was done *in situ*. The capitals are of special interest. The responds have on the N side the Baptism of Christ, on the S side the Crucifixion. The familiar motif of the mount of water round Christ's legs ought to be noticed, and the angel flying horizontally and holding a chrisom (medieval christening robe). The Devil (as a dragon) is trying to drink the water while John the Baptist and the ghost of King David, holding a branch of the Jesse Tree, stand on the bank. The Crucifixion has Joseph of Arimathaea supporting the arm of Christ while Nicodemus pulls the last nail from his feet. The middle capitals on both sides have dragon-like beasts, the outer capitals on the N side a centaur with bow, on the S side a horseman with lance. Arches with dogtooth, beakhead, a chain of box frames, and zigzag (on, and at right angles to, the wall). Beakheads carved with a variety of grotesques, principally devils, many of whom delight in devouring children. Plain stone **altar** from *Bodley*'s demolished St Edward, Holbeck of 1903–4. **Font**, simple octagonal bowl, possibly the original, recovered from the churchyard in 1858. **Font cover**, octagonal of 1921 by *Sydney Kitson*, carved with panels of the sacraments, reputedly by *Eric Gill*. Three **paintings** by *Van der Bank*, 1748: Crucifixion and Ascension and, much smaller, Gethsemane. **Hatchments**, two in the vestry. **Stained glass**, E windows of 1887. In the chancel, two windows of 1971 by *Henry Harvey*, central S window St Stephen, St Luke in N wall opposite. In SW corner memorial window by *Henry Gyles* of York to his friend Thomas Kirke d.1706. The former E window, removed to the vestry in 1879, has heraldic glass with prominent royal arms by the same, 1681. Nave: S side E two-light window by *F.C. Eden* 1933; in the small C12 window, Tubal-Cain instructs an apprentice next to a furnace and anvil. In memory of R.W. Eddison, a Leeds engineer d.1900; S side W, Virgin Mary and Infant, SS Michael and George of 1955 by *Harry Stammers*, pretty frieze with birds, rabbits, etc. on a foliage background.

Two **memorials**, both of 1884, in the churchyard; Suzannah Audus Hirst by *A. Welsh*, a young winged figure carrying a garland and Eliza and William Hill (the architect) by *Hodgson*, a cross in a Norman arch, flanked by angels.

Rectory (former). Externally, the rear part is entirely of coursed stone but it incorporates an L-shaped timber-framed house. A datestone suggests this was probably encased in 1652. A stately five-bay front range, pedimented over the central three bays, was built *c.* 1770, slightly S of the old work, and connected to it by a narrow passageway. Further work to the rear took place *c.* 1819. The space between the old and new parts was filled in and the porch added in 1858. Circular painted ceiling above the staircase. Late C18 **ice house** to the N of the house. Handsome **stables** with the centre part raised and gabled with a Diocletian window high up. Oval pitching eyes.

John Minnis

Kirkstall Abbey

3 miles NW of the city centre on the A65

Of all the Cistercian abbeys of England, Kirkstall is among those whose remaining buildings stand up highest. It requires little imagination to place roofs on the various parts of the church and the monastic buildings around the cloister. No imagination at all would have been required had C19 plans come to fruition to restore the church to sacred use, and to adapt the monastic buildings as a training college for clergy. Sir George Gilbert Scott published outline costs for the proposed restoration in 1873. The buildings and their precincts had been used for farming since the Dissolution, but by the 1880s were threatened by Leeds' urban growth. To secure their future in 1890, they were bought from the Cardigan Estate by Colonel John North who gave them to the Corporation of Leeds. Repairs were undertaken 1890–5 by *J. T. Micklethwaite*.

The Abbey was founded in 1147 at Barnoldswick in Craven by a group of Cistercian monks and lay brothers, who had left Fountains Abbey. Finding the place and its people inhospitable, in 1152 they obtained through the influence of their patron, the great magnate Henry de Lacy, an alternative secluded site in the Aire valley which they called Kirkstall. Their first dwellings here would have been of timber but these were soon replaced by the surviving buildings, constructed from local Bramley Fall gritstone and paid for by de Lacy. Kirkstall is an important exemplar of the Late Norman Transitional style. According to a late medieval account of the Abbey's foundation, the church and all the main buildings round the cloister were erected before the death of the first abbot, Alexander, in 1182. On the evidence of the structural sequence, it has been argued that the church itself had been completed by de Lacy's death in 1177.

Later building campaigns were few in number and limited in scope. A few new buildings can be assigned to the early C13 including the E part of the chapter house, the infirmary hall and the abbot's lodging. The late C15 and early C16 saw the building of new kitchens, a reconstruction of the refectory and a new belfry on the church crossing. At the time of its Dissolution in 1539 the community comprised an abbot and thirty monks.

The main losses have been the monastic infirmary buildings on the SE and a whole series of ancillary buildings – barn, corn mill, malthouse, bakehouse, guest-house – W of the abbey church. The foundations of

these were uncovered in 1893, when the abbey precincts were laid out as a public park by Leeds City Corporation labourers. The discoveries were interpreted and published by William St John Hope in 1907. Between 1950 and 1964 further excavations were conducted mainly in and around the buildings to the s of the cloister and in the infirmary. Between 1979 and 1986 the whole of the abbey's principal guest-house was excavated.

The A65 road passes close to the monastic church and cuts the former abbey precincts into two parts. The modern visitor begins in the N uphill part, where the only surviving medieval building is the C12 **Inner Gatehouse**, now incorporated in the Abbey House Museum which contains some displays of archaeological finds from the site. The gatehouse was converted into a farmhouse after 1539 and much extended thereafter. What is of the original building period of the abbey is the gateway itself, three bays deep and rib-vaulted. The arches to the N and s are round-headed and wide. Between the s and the middle bay is a division into a pointed arch for pedestrians and a wider round arch for horses and carts. Between this and the N bay is a wide pointed arch. The ribs have a tripartite roll moulding. There were evidently buildings on each side of the passage, as well as rooms above it. At the sw corner is a spiral staircase rebuilt in the C19.

The visitor no longer approaches the Abbey from the gatehouse but from the car park (built on the site of the medieval reservoir that supplied water to the Abbey's main drain before emptying itself into the River Aire near the SE corner of the precinct). This route provides much the same view of the buildings as would have greeted medieval visitors passing through the inner gatehouse. At some distance w of the abbey church are the remains of the principal **Guest-house**, used by patrons and other lords and their households. The foundations mark a typical medieval aisled hall of C13 date, with a two-storey solar block (with surviving latrines) at one end and services, kitchens and bakehouse at the other. On the far side, beyond the main drain, a subsidiary hall was converted in the later Middle Ages to stables and smithy. There would have been other lodgings for wayfarers, probably close to the outer gatehouse in the northern boundary of the precinct.

The **church** was arranged according to the typical Cistercian plan: nave and aisles, transepts with, along their E sides, three straight-ended chapels each and a farther-projecting straight-ended presbytery. Like the church at Fountains, begun soon after 1150, the transept chapels are covered with pointed tunnel vaults, derived from the Romanesque architecture of Burgundy, but the chancel and aisles have pointed rib-vaulting, in which John Bilson* saw the native influence of Durham where such vaulting had been created as early as *c.* 1095.

*J. Bilson and W.H. St John Hope, *Architectural Description of Kirkstall Abbey*, 1907.

145. Kirkstall Abbey, view into the s transept, 1152–*c.* 1177

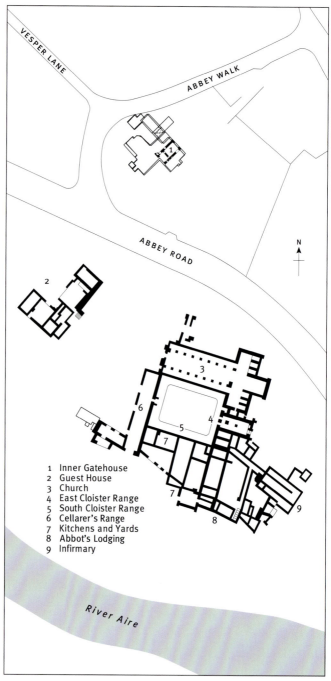

1 Inner Gatehouse
2 Guest House
3 Church
4 East Cloister Range
5 South Cloister Range
6 Cellarer's Range
7 Kitchens and Yards
8 Abbot's Lodging
9 Infirmary

146. Kirkstall Abbey, plan

147. Kirkstall Abbey, w portal, 1152–*c.* 1177

The **exterior** of the church is for its date comparatively plain: broad flat buttresses and round-arched windows, their hoodmoulds connected by a string course. The nave and aisles are divided by the buttresses into eight bays. The presbytery is similarly divided into three bays, though the rib-vaulting inside is in two, and this has caused some scholars to argue that the rib-vaulting was a late innovation, once work was well advanced. The transept gables contain vesica windows. On the s transept gable (but not the N) the buttresses are linked by semicircular arches to form arcading, a feature repeated in the w and s cloister ranges. The few later openings include two aisle windows (in the third bay from the crossing on each side), transept chapel windows and the vast Perp E **window** of the presbytery. This replaced an original large circular window with complex interlacing patterns of tracery and four flanking oculi, set above three tall round-headed windows.* Perp

*Loose fragments of tracery have been used to interpret the design of the rose window.

tracery was also inserted in some of the other original openings. The only additions to the original are the Perp square gable turrets with tiers of paired blank miniature arches and pyramid roofs, and more obviously the partially preserved belfry stage of the **tower**, added by Abbot Marshall between 1509 and 1528 (that is, when Fountains also received its great N tower), with one large window on each side. The stage below has clear evidence for windows and grooves for the original high-pitched roofs, showing that the C12 tower would have projected only a little above roof level, presumably in partial acknowledgement of the prohibition of stone bell-towers enacted by the Order's General Chapter in 1157. The additional weight of Marshall's belfry led to the collapse of the NW corner of the tower in 1779.

The most elaborate elevation is the **w front**, with its pair of larger windows (with traces of later tracery and moulded arches of two orders carried originally by detached shafts) and an impressive portal crowned by a gable, whose sides stand on wall-shafts. In the gable and above the portal proper are four intersecting blank arches. The portal [147] is round-arched and has five orders, whose capitals are many-scalloped, the arch orders moulded except for the middle one which has zigzag at right angles to the wall plane. Further important detail can be found on a second, smaller but no less ornate doorway near the w end of the N aisle wall, which has an opening framed by a very large crenellation motif. Within that, the capitals of the three orders are as before, the middle with zigzag also as before. The doorway seems, from excavated foundations and from the scars of walls to each side, to have provided access to the church from a long, narrow porch or passage projecting N. The porch had at some stage rooms attached to its E side.

Description of the **interior** is from E to W. All the constructive arches are pointed, while all the minor ones (e.g. for windows and doorways) are round, as at Fountains. In the **presbytery** the transverse arches and cross ribs have a broad rectangular section with big half-rolls. The N wall is bare but the s wall has round-arched recesses for the piscina, sedilia and credence, with mouldings of extreme simplicity. The sedilia niche is flanked by shafts, and these have the many-scalloped capitals which go on appearing throughout Kirkstall. Each of the tunnel-vaulted chapels leading off the **transepts** also has a piscina. The s transept [145] has the night stairs leading down from the monk's dormitory and a wall passage on the first floor, with heavy columns, originally connecting the same place with a chamber over the transept chapels. The N transept has a perfectly plain doorway, probably giving access to the monks' cemetery. The **crossing** has extremely lofty arches; that towards the E is far more heavily moulded than the others.

The eight-bay **nave** has heavy and complex piers, basically circular with shallow convex members and between them slim shafts or fillets, but the details vary from one pair to another [148]. The E responds and the first three pairs from the E have eight of the convex lobes with four shafts and four angle fillets between, the fourth pair of piers has angle fillets only, the fifth shafts only, the rest have lobes only. The capitals are many scalloped and the moulding of the pointed arches is of half-rolls and chamfers. The clerestory walls have no shafts and only small windows, below a nave roof which, as at Fountains, was of timber. Also like Fountains, the aisles are in contrast vaulted, similar to the presbytery vaults but here the rectangular projection is chamfered. The ribs and transverse arches rest against the aisle walls on corbels with many-scalloped capitals. Though these capitals recur throughout Kirkstall, there are also in the church other interesting types with upright leaves, and some with interlace ornament, which is also found on the presbytery piscina, along with knotwork on one of the nave pier bases. These may be minor echoes of the interlaced tracery in the original presbytery rose window.

s of the church's w doorway was the lay brother's range, with a small doorway giving access to the **cloister** garth. The cloister alleys have gone, but fragments of the limestone arcading remain, their waterleaf capitals proving that the arcades were built at the end of the initial construction phase, *c*. 1180. The arrangement of rooms around the cloister followed the Cistercian standard and is very similar to Fountains. At the E end of the N side is the monks' doorway into the church, round-headed and of three orders with scalloped capitals. On the E side, s of the transept, there is the arch of the book cupboard, then the library and vestry. After that follows the **chapter house**. This is clearly the work of two periods, its w part of the later C12, its E part of the C13. The w part

148. Nave, detail of pier base with knotwork

Decorative Tiles at Kirkstall Abbey

149. Kirkstall Abbey, reconstruction of mid-c13 floor tiles

The use of interlace design in various parts of the original church seems to have recurred in a floor of decorated tiles inserted around the mid c13. Some circular 'centrepiece' designs that would have occupied liturgical focal points have been reconstructed from the large numbers of loose tiles in the Leeds Museums collections, including one with an interlace border. They are almost identical to designs found at Jervaulx Abbey and were undoubtedly made by the same craftsmen.

has one of the Cistercians' elaborate façades with, unusually, a pair of large entrance arches flanked by smaller pairs. All the arches are round, the capitals scalloped as usual. Inside, the w part is square with one central circular pier surrounded by eight detached shafts, and four rib-vaulted bays, in which the profile of the ribs is round like those in the rest of the cloister ranges, not pointed as in the church. The e part is c. 1230 and has more elegant rib-mouldings that spring from very small corbels. In the e wall are two groups of three stepped lancets (restored with round heads), in the n and s walls pairs of pointed lancets. The walls of the rebuilt part are faced with a number of stone coffins, presumably disturbed during the works. Next is the parlour, of the same period as the w part of the chapter house, then the original stairs to the monks' dormitory that ran over the whole of this range. Beyond is a passage that gave access to the infirmary and abbot's lodging (*see* below), beyond that the monks' day room of five bays, its unribbed groin-vault (collapsed 1824) once supported on scalloped corbels and a central row of circular pillars. Beyond this is the main drain above which stood the monks' reredorter or latrines, attached to the s end of their dormitory.

In the s cloister range the e end doorway is c13 and marks a modified entrance to the dorter stairs. It was cut into the corner of the warming house which has a large c15 fireplace in the w wall. Between the entrances to the warming house and the refectory (or dining hall) to the w are the pointed trefoiled arches of a wall-mounted lavatorium, its hand-washing basins formerly furnished with a piped water supply. This c13 lavatorium replaced an earlier, free-standing one in this corner of the cloisters, its foundations revealed in excavations. The **refectory** was originally placed in the Benedictine tradition parallel with the s walk of the cloister, but was subsequently changed round to the preferred Cistercian position at right angles to the s walk. Reorientation enabled enlargement of the kitchens to the w; consequently the original refectory entrance, close to that of the kitchens, was blocked. Further changes were made in the later c15 to cater for the by then greater toleration among Cistercians of meat-eating. The refectory was divided horizontally to provide a meat refectory on the ground floor, served by a new meat kitchen at its se corner, while the old kitchen continued to serve the non-meat refectory on the first floor. Each dining hall had its own entrance from the cloister alley, represented by the two doorways just w of the lavatorium, one a rebuilt c12 opening with a c15 hoodmould.

As in other Cistercian abbeys, the facilities provided for the Kirkstall monks on the e and s sides of the cloister were to some extent replicated for the lay brothers in a series of buildings to the w and sw. The principal element within this group was the **w range**, now forming the w side of the cloister, from which it was originally cut off by a wall which bounded a wide lane running along the e side of the building. The scar of the wall (removed in c15) can be seen in the s wall of the church, e of the simple doorway that gave the lay brothers access to the nave. The s and w walls of the range are largely absent. Its ground floor of eleven bays was vaulted from end to end, the vaults supported by scalloped corbels in the walls and by a central row of columns (only one base of a pier is *in situ*). The n part contained the stores for the cellarer, while the five bays at the s end formed the lay brothers' refectory. Above was their **dormitory**, access from it to the church being provided by external steps descending into the lane. The doorway was itself

150. View from the sw of church and E range of the cloisters

evidently reached by steps within, and has a low arch with joggled voussoirs. Attached to the sw corner of the dormitory was the lay brothers'
reredorter, largely intact, standing obliquely to the w range but squarely
over the main drain. It is now a visitor centre for the Abbey. The original large archways into its ground floor, two to each side, are now
blocked and on the N partly destroyed by a C18 cart entrance. It was re-
roofed in the 1890s. Above the string course, narrow openings lit the
first-floor latrines themselves, accessed from the dormitory. The lay
brothers' infirmary would have been somewhere nearby, perhaps represented by wall foundations excavated just s of the reredorter in the
1960s.

The cloister lane originally continued beyond the s end of the w
range, with the kitchens that provided for both lay brothers and monks
on its E side. In the late C12 it was spanned by two archways that continued the line of the s range. Clearly not part of the original plan, these
left the ground floor open but allowed the adjacent buildings to be
linked at first-floor level. The arches were later walled up and the
ground floor between them seems to have become a **malthouse** in the
C15, with ovens in its E and w walls and a large stone vat attached to the
s wall. Along the s side of the malthouse, kitchen and refectory were
yards which contained various ancillary buildings whose foundations
have been revealed in excavations. To the E is the C15 **meat kitchen**,
attached to the SE corner of the refectory and on the E adjoining the

monks' reredorter. It blocked off the s end of the yard behind the warming house. Now very ruined, it contains fireplaces for roasting meat, and ovens for baking. Excavations uncovered large quantities of animal bone in the vicinity and, near its sw corner, a circular-plan building, probably a dovecote. s of the monks' reredorter a fishpond, originally perhaps one of a series, survived into the C18.

On the E side of the monks' reredorter stands the **abbot's lodging**, a three-storey, self-contained house, built *c.* 1230 and one of the earliest known examples of such residences. Its function is suggested by its location. Abbots were supposed to 'lie in the dorter', but before the end of the C12 they were starting to build separate living quarters (e.g. at Riveaulx and Fountains). The attachment of the house to the monks' reredorter, technically part of the dorter, may have made the new accommodation appear less in breach of the rule than it would otherwise have done. Its principal chamber was, effectively, a first-floor hall, set over a basement and reached by an external flight of steps from the yard on the N side, which led into a lobby lit by square-headed lights. The hall itself was originally lit by two large windows on each side, formed by pairs of lancet lights enclosed externally by a round-headed arch. The solar above the hall, of a similar size and reached by a wooden continuation of the spacious main staircase, was lit by similar windows to those in the hall, one in the s wall surviving complete. An oriel window also in the s wall seems to have lit the top of the main staircase. Fireplaces were inserted into the N wall of both hall and solar in the C15, one above the other. To the E is another oblong building, earlier than the abbot's lodging but also of the C13 and later connected to it. Little survives except parts of its gable walls. Scars in these walls indicate that the two rooms of the ground floor were covered by quadripartite vaulting. Above, the E gable wall contains the jambs of a lancet window. There is a pointed-oval window in the w gable. The building is thought to have contained a kitchen and cellar on the ground floor and a chapel above, originally serving the infirmary but later the abbot's lodging and the visiting abbot's lodging as well.

The **infirmary** buildings survive only a few courses high. The principal element is a C13 aisled hall of five bays, later developed into a series of private cubicles, some with fireplaces. Built at the same time, running s from the infirmary hall to the chapel and kitchen block, is a building which may have served as the **visiting abbot's lodging**. In the C15 it was furnished with a large, first-floor oriel window in its E wall, the base of which remains. N of the infirmary hall are the foundations of C15 kitchens and scullery. Excavation has revealed an earlier aisled hall, running N–s beneath these foundations and constructed with timber posts. It was probably the original infirmary hall, used during the late C12 and early C13.

Stuart Wrathmell

Temple Newsam House

4.6 miles E of the city, S of the A63 on Temple Newsam Road

The manor of Newsam was first recorded in the Domesday Book in 1086 (as *Neuhusū* or 'at the new houses'). In 1155 it became a property of the Knights Templar but after their suppression in the early C14 eventually passed to the Darcy family. Thomas Darcy – a courtier, mercenary and later crony of Thomas Wolsey – built the first house on the present site *c*. 1488–1521. Confiscated twice by the Crown (1537 and 1565) and subsequently neglected, it was bought in 1622 by Sir Arthur Ingram, a London merchant. He substantially altered the house leaving it as three wings around an open courtyard, much as now. Internally, his work was remodelled successively from 1702 by five of the nine sons of Arthur, third Viscount Irwin, who inherited the property; and from 1758 by their nephew Charles the 9th and last Viscount (d.1778) and his widow Frances (d.1807) who transformed the S wing from *c*. 1788. Her eldest daughter Isabella, Marchioness of Hertford, redecorated many interiors *c*. 1823–34; more fundamental changes were made by Emily Meynell Ingram *c*. 1877–97. Her nephew the Hon. Edward Wood (later Lord Halifax) sold Temple Newsam to Leeds Corporation in 1922 without its contents. Although developed as a country house museum of the fine and decorative arts from 1937, the house was used as the City's Art Gallery during the Second World War and the historic decoration of virtually every interior was destroyed. Most of the rooms have been restored since 1983.

The ideal way to approach Temple Newsam House is on foot from the E (past the site of *John Carr's* Gothick East Lodges, dem. 1946), for the undulations of the East Avenue – laid out by *William Etty* of York between 1710 and 1715, with bridges, cascades and fishponds – make the house rise up, vanish then reappear, closer and more impressive each time. Most visitors, however, approach from the NW, or the N, between **lodges** built 1742, perhaps to designs by *Sir Andrew Fountaine*. From any view the house presents a deceptively regular appearance, an austere grid of verticals and horizontals, mullions and transoms, of brick with stone dressings.

The Tudor House

Darcy's house enclosed a nearly square courtyard, with a gatehouse on the N side, but Ingram's demolition of the E wing created the present

151. Temple Newsam House, E front, early C16, remodelled after 1622

U-plan. The main entrance into the house itself was (and remains) in the s wing. Much of the C16 w wing remains visible: diaper-patterned brickwork, symmetrical arrangements of large polygonal and small rectangular bays. Sandstone dressings to the E face change to limestone with Gothic panelling. The bay windows would originally have looked much more Perp than they do today for the transoms are later (C17?) insertions. Excavations suggest that there were stair-towers at the inner angles of the three wings, and that the w face of the w wing had three central bays flanked by polygonal staircases or privy towers – blocked doorways survive inside. In the centre of the courtyard face of the N wing is a moulded stone doorway, truncated when the courtyard was raised in the C18. Excavations also revealed the foundations of the internal face of the demolished E wing, which may have contained lodgings. The s front was completely asymmetrical, the kitchens occupying the E end, with pantries etc in an extension at the SE corner.

The Present House

Much of what the visitor sees today appears to be Sir Arthur Ingram's work [151]. His house is called Carolean to be strictly accurate; in its style it is in fact still purely Jacobean, of the type of Hatfield, Blickling and Bramshill. He reorientated the house E–W by taking down the gatehouse in the N wing, demolishing the E wing (probably after a fire in 1636 which affected the s wing too) and replacing it with an entrance gate and lodges [152]. Large bay windows were added and the skyline unified by a stone balustrade. The loyal inscription on the courtyard side was set up in 1628 (and renewed with the present iron letters – cast by *Wigglesworth & Eyres & Co.* at Seacroft – in 1788). The porch in the s wing with round-arched entrance flanked by coupled Ionic columns must be Ingram's, but the panel and bust are of *c.* 1670–80. Limestone cladding above and *faux* quoins of the late C18, by *William Johnson* who made substantial alterations to this wing (*see* below). At the E end

152. Engraving, by Kip and Knyff (1701), showing early C17 alterations to the E front

of the N wing are basement windows with arched lights, for Sir Arthur's chapel. Originally square-headed, the arches are a contrivance. Otherwise windows were of the mullion and transom type, generally wider and lower than they are today.

The alteration of the windows to more classical proportions, with boldly moulded architraves and sliding sashes (as at Burton Agnes), came in a piecemeal campaign between *c.* 1719 and 1745, piecemeal because Rich, fifth Viscount, speculated recklessly in the South Sea Company and lost a fortune in 1720. In 1719 Rich had replaced Sir Arthur's entrance gates with a wall across the E side of courtyard, perhaps by *William Etty* of York who in 1726–7 constructed a series of 'out walls' and pavilions. These were presumably intended to link the house with projected stables and outbuildings, eventually built in the 1740s, *see* below. The N **front** of the house received a Palladian frontispiece – pedimented porch, Venetian window and Diocletian window – attributed to *Daniel Garrett*: it survived until *c.* 1897 when *C.E. Kempe* added the present façade in sandstone, reinstating mullions and transoms to the windows.

Major alterations to the exterior were considered in the 1760s and 70s when several distinguished architects were consulted, including *John Carr*, *Robert Adam*, *James Wyatt* and *Capability Brown* (who was already at work in the park, *see* below). *Wyatt* was paid £300 in 1777 for work including a new staircase but the transformation of the S **wing** was completed *c.* 1788–1807 by Wyatt's pupil *William Johnson*, a Leeds man, for Frances, Lady Irwin. (The plaque dated 1792–6 on the S front was attached retrospectively.) If only Adam's 1773 plans and elevations (in the Soane Museum) had been executed! The S façade would have been perfectly symmetrical, of two storeys above a basement, with

153. The Great Hall, as altered in the late C18 and 1820s

œil-de-bœuf windows in the attic; central bay with one at each end, string courses respecting those of the earlier fabric. Instead, Johnson's façade is asymmetrical and curiously ill-coordinated: limestone dressings, lintels with roundels and fluting, mullions with Gothick panels. The cupola (with a bell dated 1830) over the w wing is Johnson's too. Most of the Georgian sliding sash windows were transformed back to mullion and transom type in the 1890s – the scars where their classical architraves were hacked off can still be seen. Two sash windows survive in the N basement.

Interior

The description begins in the s wing, where visitors enter the house, then moves to the w and N wings.

The **s wing** is two storeys above a basement. The cellars (not open to the public) contain evidence of Darcy's early C16 house in the form of four-centred arches, an oak door frame and probably a buttery hatch guarding the kitchen. On the ground floor is the **Great Hall** of the Tudor and Jacobean house [153], formerly entered via a screens passage but altered in the later C18 by *William Johnson*, who made it the centre-piece of five new reception rooms. Panelling and ceiling with plaster ribs and cartouches in the 'Old English' style were added in the 1820s. Stained glass in the bay window is C16–C18 and was removed from the chapel (*see* below). At the E end, on the site of the buttery or pantry, is **Mr Wood's Library**, 1912, by *Ralph Freeman-Smith* of Lenygon's, a mostly convincing essay in the Early Georgian style. Next, the **Blue Drawing Room**, remodelled from the late C18 Best Dining Room in 1827–9 with imported *Régence* door architraves and hand-painted Chinese wallpaper (given by the Prince of Wales in 1806) embellished with birds cut from Audubon's *Birds of America*. W of the Great Hall is the **Terrace Room**, another Regency interior, hung with royal gifts of Brussels tapestries. It was adapted – by the insertion of its N wall and chimneypiece – from the ante-room created by *Wyatt* in *c*. 1777 for his new staircase (*see* below). Beyond the Terrace Room, the **Dining Room** (originally the Parlour) retains its 1630s plaster ceiling and frieze by *Francis Gunby* (who also worked at St John's New Briggate (*see* p. 48), Gawthorpe Hall, Lancashire and elsewhere), as well as much of its panelling. The room was remodelled in 1889–91 by *C.E. Kempe*, whose chimneypiece and overmantel were adapted from those in the hall at Hardwick, Derbyshire.

The rooms on the first floor of the S wing, reached via the **Little Gallery** (also by *Kempe*, 1889–91, with moulded plaster frieze) and Oak Staircase (*see* below), have a complex history. Where there are now a series of late C18 rooms was the 'Greate Chambr' (mentioned in the 1565 inventory), over the present Great Hall and Blue Drawing Room. Its entrance from the stairs is marked by a moulded stone jamb. The chamber was divided in the mid C18 into an 'Eating Room' and Drawing Room, and divided again by *Johnson* with trussed timber stud partitions to minimize the weight over the Great Hall. He created the **South Passage**, with little Gothick brackets under the cornice. Of the adjoining rooms, at the E end is the **Prince's Room** with a chimneypiece and doorcases rescued from Methley Hall in the 1950s; at the W end, the **Darnley Room** of *c*. 1897 by *Kempe*, panelled and fitted with plasterwork reproducing C17 originals elsewhere in the house. Much Jacobean plasterwork survives behind later decoration, including a complete ceiling beneath the floor of the **Grey Room**.

The link between the two floors of the S wing and the three of the W **wing** since 1894 has been *Kempe*'s **Oak Staircase** [154] which replaced *Wyatt's* top-lit classical staircase of *c*. 1777. The site must always have been unsatisfactory, for passages and rooms at three levels were shortened (leaving chimneypieces marooned in the corners of rooms) and worse, the staircase failed to link all the floor levels. Nevertheless Kempe's staircase, which continues the 'Old English' theme of the Great Hall and Dining Room, is very grand and archaeological. Plasterwork, perhaps by *Battiscombe & Harris*: the ceiling of West Country pattern, frieze aping Speke or Burton Agnes, soffits of stair-flights and landings adapted from the gallery ceiling at Hatfield. Joinery and carving by *Norman & Burt* of Burgess Hill, Sussex: the oak newel posts have carved decoration by *William Court*, some copied from the staircase from Slaugham Place, Sussex (now in Lewes Town Hall); the newel figures with heraldic shields were added in 1897. Evidence of *Wyatt's* chaste Neoclassical plasterwork, coved ceiling and glazed lantern survives behind the Victorian decoration.

The first floor of the W wing continues the grand processional route through the house that began in the Great Hall of the S wing and

154. Oak Staircase, by C.E. Kempe, 1894

culminates in the Picture Gallery in the N wing (*see* below). The **Gallery Passage**, with panelling and plasterwork designed by *Kempe*, 1889–91, was created in 1745 to link the s and N wings, perhaps by *Daniel Garrett*: plain C18 plasterwork concealed behind the panelling masks the corner piers of clustered shafts of the Tudor chamber which spanned the centre of this wing (carved oak lintels of the matching transverse chamber on the ground floor are visible in the Stone Passage and Still

Room). The rooms off this passage are mid C18 in character. The **Blue Striped Room** has a chimneypiece and bed alcove probably by *Wyatt*. The **Gothick Room** has a chimneypiece, virtuoso overmantel frame and Rococo plasterwork all of 1759 (the Gothic Revival 'stucco paper' was reprinted in 1993). Behind the **Boudoir** is a C18 servant's 'Dark Room' formed from a larger C16 interior: its brick fire arch and oak-ribbed plaster ceiling survive. The **Stone Staircase** linking the w and N wings is perhaps of *c.* 1788; it was given the elegant wrought-iron balustrade of Wyatt's main staircase in 1894.

The second floor of the w wing in the C16 contained important rooms including, perhaps, the chapel, but all were much altered in the C18. One room has late Gothic/early Renaissance panelling of 1542 brought from Bretton Hall, near Barnsley, in 1947: built-in cupboard with portraits of Sir Thomas Wentworth and his two wives; more carvings on the bed. Other rooms here had their C18 architectural features removed in an attempt to recapture their early Tudor character. A shallow niche has been revealed in one room together with a blocked fireplace and several blocked doors, one leading to what may have been a stair-turret. Several other C16 fire arches of moulded stone or brick survive, some behind later fabric. Arched timbers above one ceiling may be survivors of the earliest shallow-pitched, lead-covered roof.

In the basement and ground floor (not open to the public) of the N **wing** is the former **Servants' Hall** and an underground passage linking the N and s wings, both of *c.* 1718–19. At the E end from *c.* 1788 was the kitchen, converted from the C17 **chapel** now partly restored with some of its original decoration and furnishings, including *John Carleton's* painting of *The Supper at Emmaus* and his series of eighteen Old Testament figures (painted in 1636–7), together with *Thomas Ventris Jun.'s* carved oak pulpit of 1636, a small-panelled example of contemporary Leeds type (cf. St John's, New Briggate, 1634). The reredos by *Bodley* is from the 1877 chapel (*see* below). The ground floor contains the **Stone Passage** and **Steward's Room**, created *c.* 1719, and **North Hall** panelled by *Kempe* in 1897. Towards the E end one room, now at mezzanine level, has the best surviving length of moulded plaster frieze of the 1630s.

The first floor was occupied by Sir Arthur Ingram's Gallery (finished *c.* 1635) but this was reconstructed in 1738–46 as (from E to w) the Library, Picture Gallery and Crimson Bedroom. This was the major achievement of Henry, seventh Viscount Irwin. *Garrett* was almost certainly the architect throughout. The **Library** has a giant order derived from Palladio and lively proto-Rococo plasterwork of 1743 by *Thomas Perritt*. It was converted into a Chapel by *G.F. Bodley* in 1877: the organ by *Wordsworth & Maskell* of Leeds remains, otherwise his work has been obliterated.

The **Picture Gallery** [155] also has a *Perritt* ceiling with portrait medallions of George I, George II and other members of the royal

155. The Picture Gallery, probably by Daniel Garrett, 1738–46

family. *Richard Fisher* of York was the carver who decorated the joinery. Two fireplaces by *Robert Doe* of London after designs by *William Kent* published in 1735 have overmantel paintings by *Antonio Joli*. Original furniture by *James Pascall* and Grand Tour paintings by *Antonio Marini*. Behind the timber wall lining are blocked windows and fragments of the elaborate moulded plasterwork of Sir Arthur's Gallery. (An area of plaster stencilled in polychrome may be the decoration of one of the three 'lobbies' recorded in the early C18: one, at the E end, probably provided access via a winding staircase to the family gallery in the C17 chapel.) There are also patches of genuine stucco wall decoration from the early Tudor rooms that Sir Arthur destroyed in creating his Gallery – marbled grey and white (with traces of gilt leather-*mâché*) in one, white panels within black framing in another.

The Park

The historic park that Leeds bought in 1922 consisted of 917 acres. Its spatial and visual structure today is still recognizably that of *Capability Brown* who retained the C17 avenues to W and N, together with *Etty*'s East Avenue of *c.* 1710. The **Sphinx Gates** NE of the house are *Brown*'s, copying *Lord Burlington*'s at Chiswick: rusticated stone piers topped by lead sphinxes, gates cast by *Robert Johnson* in 1768. (Flanking walls of modern brick and incongruous cast-iron railings, N of the gates, rescued from Board Schools in Leeds in the 1970s.) Remains of *Brown*'s haha survive nearby and beyond the ponds is his little pedimented prostyle **Temple** with columns of clustered shafts. A domical Ice House of *c.* 1715 survived until the 1970s. The late C18 walled **Kitchen Garden** has lost its Victorian cast-iron glasshouses.

156. Stables, by Daniel Garrett, 1740s; extended by Capability Brown, 1760s

The **stables** [156] NE of the house – probably designed by *Daniel Garrett* in the 1740s and extended by *Capability Brown* in the 1760s – are of brick with stone dressings. Pretty cupola over w range with single-handed clock and weathervane in the form of a cock, the Ingram crest. The small two-room structure attached to the sw corner was built – perhaps by *William Johnson* – from the late C18 onwards as a **dairy** and appears to incorporate lengths of *William Etty*'s 'out walls' of *c.* 1726–7.

The **Great Barn** is the oldest building in the farm, built in 1694 (despite its incorrectly restored datestone). C18 **dovecote**, **farmhouse** and ancillary buildings, of brick and vernacular in character.

sw of the house is the **Mount**, only survivor of the Tudor park and gardens. The s garden preserves the fountain cast by *Andrew Handyside & Co.* of Derby *c.* 1875, the centrepiece of the handsome Italianate garden created by Mrs Meynell Ingram. The ha-ha beyond the bowling green w of the house was introduced after 1904. Open-cast coal mining during and after the Second World War affected most of the s of the estate and the historic tranquillity of the place has recently been destroyed by the new motorway that crosses the Aire Valley. This should be screened by landscaping and tree planting.

Anthony Wells-Cole

Roundhay Park

3 miles NE of the city centre, off Wetherby Road

Opened in 1872, at 373 acres Roundhay is the largest public park in the city although it remained outside the city boundaries until 1912. Its history dates back to the C12, when the land is first mentioned in a charter of 1153 as the deer park of the de Lacy family. Part of the original boundary ditch, 20 ft (6 metres) wide by 10 ft (3 metres) deep, survives at the NE corner. In the following century, the land was inherited by Alice de Lacy who married the Duke of Lancaster. It passed to the future Henry IV and became crown land; part of it remains so today. The rest passed through many changes of ownership from 1512 until 1803 when

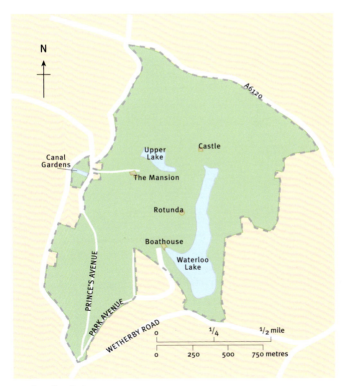

157. Roundhay Park

it was sold to Samuel Elam and Thomas Nicholson. The latter was a banker with shipping interests. They divided the estate, Elam taking the land s of the Wetherby Road for building and Nicholson that to the N for a residence set within a picturesque landscape of wooded belts, follies and two large lakes. A letter of July 1816 referred to the Nicholsons as 'completely settled' in their new house but Thomas died in 1821 and the estate was eventually auctioned in 1871. Sir John Barran, the Lord Mayor, and colleagues paid £139,000 to acquire it for use as a public park and sold it to the Corporation. In spite of his largesse, Barran was criticized for providing a park at such a distance from the city centre and therefore out of reach of Leeds' poorest citizens.

Three hundred acres of Nicholson's estate were reserved for the new Park, the competition for its landscaping won in 1873 by *George Corson* who proposed Swiss chalets, a pinetum and terraced croquet lawns. Little was done and the amenities necessary to serve trippers were slow to develop, causing the park to be dubbed 'The Great White Elephant'. A new entrance and approach road, Prince's Avenue, was created to improve access and a variety of proposals were considered to link the Park with the city, including an elevated monorail. Only with the opening of the electric tramway in 1891 did the Park enjoy great success. In 2004 the Park is undergoing an £8 million refurbishment (architectural work by *Purcell Miller Tritton*) to restore its decayed landscape features and buildings.

At the centre of the Park, close to the late C19 w entrance from Prince's Avenue is the **Mansion** (now empty). The design is probably by *Thomas Taylor*, the principal architect of early C19 Leeds. The house, raised on a slight eminence, is relatively modest in relation to the size of its park. Seven bays and two storeys with a spectacular s portico of four giant Ionic columns carrying a pediment. At the angles, Doric pilasters, repeated on the E and w façades where they flank bow windows. Large conservatory on the w side. Elegant imperial staircase with iron balustrade set in a semi-oval hall under a big oval lantern. The **stables**, complete by 1821, have a cupola above a clock tower. Nine bays, the central three projecting, and emphasized by a pediment. Ground-floor openings set in round-headed arches. N of these, **Park Cottages**, in coursed squared gritstone and of eleven bays divided by pilasters, the basement arcaded. Also a pair of classical **lodges** on Wetherby Road, built in 1811 after the road was opened as a turnpike.

From the entrance on Wetherby Road, Nicholson created a drive to lead N through the parkland, into a deep wooded valley and along the w side of the 33 acre **Waterloo Lake**: 'a miniature Windermere' completed in 1815. At its s end was a waterfall, popularly known as 'Lovers Leap', since destroyed. On the w side, a **boathouse** of 1902. The lake is fed at its N end by a series of cascades and two waterfalls, crossed by a rustic bridge, which flow through **The Ravine** from the 5 acre **Upper Lake**. Eyecatchers were placed picturesquely within this landscape,

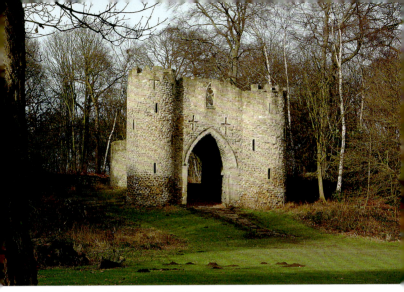

158. Sham Castle, possibly by George Nettleton, early C19

including, by the Upper Lake, a **Hermitage** of stone boulders with Gothic windows and an interior lined with hazel sticks (since destroyed). It had a boathouse underneath. When William Nicholson, step-nephew of Thomas, entertained visitors, he employed his gamekeeper to dress up in rags and moan as they passed by. E of the Mansion, stands a **Sham Castle** [158], reputedly designed by *George Nettleton*, with circular crenellated towers and a Gothic traceried window over a pointed archway. It was used by the family to take tea while viewing the lake.

Since 1891 the principal public approach to the mansion has been through the **main gates** on Prince's Avenue. The road separated the house from its former kitchen gardens. These are preserved on the W side of the road as **Canal Gardens** with a central rectangular canal, rustic bridges and a tall enclosing wall. Adjacent are kitchen gardens with hothouses and vineries. These were reused after 1872 with the addition of a glass conservatory. **Coronation House** was added in 1911 (now Tropical World) for the display of exotic tropical plants but is now rebuilt beyond recognition.

Stung by criticism of the park in its early days, John Barran responded by presenting, in 1882, at a personal cost of £3,000, the **Rotunda** [13], a classical domed drinking fountain designed by *Thomas Ambler*, Barran's favourite architect (*see* topic box, p. 21). Unfluted columns support a Corinthian entablature.

Sale of the estate's surplus land was needed to fund the development of the Park and was intended for the building of smart suburban villas by *George Corson*. Few were built initially but the estate of large houses on generous plots in an eclectic mixture of stone and half-timbering was largely complete by 1900.

John Minnis

Lawnswood Cemetery

4 miles NE of the city centre, off Otley Road

Lawnswood Cemetery, opened in 1875 on land purchased in 1874 by the Headingley-cum-Burley Burial Board, was created to cater for the expanding suburbs of Headingley and Far Headingley. The layout and most of the buildings were designed by *George Corson*, assisted by *William Gay*, the designer of Undercliffe Cemetery, Bradford. Corson's design was intended to be 'simple and unpretending and of a character to harmonize with the surrounding scenery'. This was achieved with an informal woodland setting, the trees forming a border around the cemetery. Entering the cemetery, a curving drive describes a gentle arc around a large clump of trees which screen the chapels and crematorium. Monuments line a mixture of straight and curving paths with clumps of trees and shrubs raised up on platforms forming islands around which the memorials are placed. The C19 monuments are mainly conventional Gothic and classical designs, few of great size or elaboration, but some of the early C20 monuments are spectacular. Lawnswood was extended in 1919 and 1965 and purchased by Leeds City Council in 1972.

The **Cemetery Lodge** on Otley Road, modified in 1907, is Tudor style and had a boardroom, a retiring room and a 'dead house'. The coursed gritstone **Cemetery Chapels** occupy a roughly central position, with the Anglican chapel to the N. It is linked by an open colonnade of three arches, the short columns of polished Aberdeen granite, to the Nonconformist chapel to the s which stands at right angles. The style is a muscular Gothic, lightened by a romantic octagonal turret with a louvred belfry and a tiled spire. **Stained glass** of 1893 in a side window and in the apsed chancel of the Anglican chapel. Attached to the s is the **Crematorium** of 1905 by *W.S. Braithwaite* in matching Gothic style. This was the first in Britain to use a gas cremator, initially supervised by French engineers who had developed the method. Before it came into service, it was opened to public viewing at 3*d.* per person. It has a tall square tower with an octagonal belfry disguising the flue.

The **Columbarium** by *Col. A.E. Kirk*, completed by *Kirk & Tomlinson*, was added sw of the crematorium in 1933, its setting more formal than the earlier parts of the cemetery. Refined Neo-Georgian of thin hand-made red bricks and Portland stone with a pantiled roof. Tall single-storey gabled chapel with a portico, continued as long L-shaped

159. Monument to Ethel Preston, d.1911

colonnaded wings with plain columns topped by Corinthian capitals. Under the groin-vaulted colonnade, tiers of tablets with urns. The **chapel** entrance is deeply recessed behind a large round-headed opening filled by a screen of two columns supporting an entablature, with two urns as finials above. The barrel-vaulted interior has the windows placed high, cutting into the vault. Recessed top-lit bays with shelves for the deposited ashes. Marble-clad walls with vertical brick bands raised across the vault, apsed E end.

Among the **Monuments**, the following, all located a short distance to the w of the Chapels, are of special interest: Arthur Currer Briggs, d.1906, of Henry Briggs & Son, owners of Whitwood Colliery near Normanton.* By *William Hamo Thornycroft*, a bronze relief of a sower (a popular subject for Thornycroft) watched by an angel set in a pedimented slab: – George Corson, architect, d.1910, a plain headstone: –

*Voysey built Broadleys, Windermere (1898) for Briggs and an institute and housing at Whitwood.

160. Monument to Sam Wilson, d.1918, by E. Caldwell Spruce

Ethel Preston, d.1911 [159], an extraordinary monument with a life-size statue wearing elegant Edwardian dress standing under a classical porch with Corinthian capitals and balustrade above, reputedly that of her home, The Grange, Beeston (dem.). It has a working panelled door left slightly ajar: – Charles Henry Johnson, d.1912 with an Art Nouveau surround: – Sam Wilson, d.1918 [160], worsted coating manufacturer and benefactor of the Leeds City Art Gallery. His memorial by *E. Caldwell Spruce*, a modeller for Burmantofts in the early c20, reflects Wilson's interest in Symbolist painting, displaying in its brooding intensity the influence of G.F. Watts. Black marble inset with a relief of a skull and snakes representing Death, with kneeling bronze figures of Faith and Benevolence flanking splayed plinths and surmounted by a tall bronze angel, holding a torch aloft. This develops themes also present in the somewhat macabre fireplace he commissioned from the sculptor Alfred Gilbert in 1908–14, now in Leeds City Art Gallery.

John Minnis

Further Reading

The following is a necessarily partial account of published and unpublished sources on Leeds architecture. Several of the works listed below include further bibliographies and the local studies library holds several books of old photographs and other titles of general historical interest.

The city's **architectural history** is described in the classic *West Yorkshire Architects and Architecture* by Derek Linstrum, 1978. Over four hundred Leeds buildings are listed in the index, and there is a select biographical list of Yorkshire architects (1550–1900). By the same author, *The Historic Architecture of Leeds*, 1969, is a short introduction with atmospheric photographs, while *Towers and Colonnades,* 1999, deals thoroughly with the architecture of Cuthbert Brodrick. Other Leeds **architects** are the subject of studies by T. Butler Wilson, *Two Leeds Architects,* 1937 (George Corson and Cuthbert Brodrick); C. Webster, 'R.D. Chantrell, Architect: His Life and Work in Leeds 1818–1847', Thoresby Society, second series, v.2, 1991 and D. Boswell, 'The Kitsons and the Arts: a Leeding (sic.) family in Sicily and the West Riding', PhD thesis York, 1995, which covers the local firm of Bedford & Kitson. Important works on architects who worked in Leeds include: J.M. Robinson, *Francis Johnson, Architect*, 2001; and A. Taylor, 'William Lindley of Doncaster', *Georgian Group Journal,* 4, 1994. B. Wragg's *Life and Works of John Carr of York*, ed. G. Worsley, 2000; P. Leach, *James Paine*, 1988. C. Cunningham & P. Waterhouse, *Alfred Waterhouse, 1830–1905: Biography of a Practice*, 1992, is important for the C19. Relevant to the restoration of St John is A. Saint, *Richard Norman Shaw¸* 1976. For the C20 there is N. Burton, 'Robert Lutyens and Marks & Spencer', *Thirties Society Journal*, 1985; and R.A. Fellowes, *Sir Reginald Blomfield: an Edwardian Architect*, 1985. B. Read, *Victorian Sculpture*, 1982, and S. Beattie, *The New Sculpture*, 1983, are informative on the public sculpture in City Square

Since the 1980s several publications have provided thematic **walks**. J. Douglas & K. Powell's *Leeds: Four Architectural Walks,* 1988 (Victorian Society West Yorkshire Group), was the first but has been followed by an excellent series published by the City Council and Leeds Civic Trust including P. Brears, *Briggate Yards and Arcades*, 1995, M. Hall, *Leeds Statues Trail*, 1995, and B. Godward, *Leeds Heritage Trail*,

2000. Peter Dyson and Kevin Grady, *Blue Plaques of Leeds*, 2001, also has much of value.

For **churches and religious buildings** good guides are Janet Douglas' *Leeds Places of Worship Trail*, 1996 and Terry Friedman's *Church Architecture in Leeds,* 1996. K. Powell, D. Chappell, and D. Bosomworth, *Leeds Churches, 1890–1940* (a typescript by the Victorian Society West Yorkshire Group), 1976, is at the public library. The *Ripon Diocesan Calendar* (in Leeds City Library) is particularly useful for c19 church furnishings. On individual churches and religious buildings, the important survivals at Kirkstall are covered by W.H. St John Hope & J. Bilson, *Architectural Description of Kirkstall Abbey*, 1907, B. Sitch, *Kirkstall Abbey,* 2000, and S. Wrathmell, *Kirkstall Abbey: The Guest House*, 1987. W.H. Draper, *Adel and its Norman Church*, 1909 remains an important source for St John, Adel. The Redundant Churches Fund published J. Douglas & K. Powell's *St John's Church Leeds* (revised 1993). For the c19: W.R.W. Stephens, *The Life and Letters of Walter Farquhar Hook*, 1879 (3rd ed.), D. Webster, *'Parish' Past and Present*, 1988, C. Webster, *The Rebuilding of Leeds Parish Church*, 1994. R.E. Finnigan, *The Cathedral Church of St Anne*, 1988, details ths history of the Roman Catholic church, while selected suburban churches are covered by B. Pepper, *A Goodly Heritage*, 1994, on St Aidan, Harehills, and informative guides to St Saviour by C. Tyne and St Hilda by S. Savage.

Of the **secular buildings,** Brodrick's Town Hall, Corn Exchange and Mechanics Institute are covered in detail by Linstrum (op. cit). The chief architectural periodicals are the principal resource for detail on new public and commercial buildings of the c19, c20 and c21. Articles on individual buildings or groups of buildings are rarer, although the following might be noted as particularly informative: S. Burt, 'Leeds Manor House', *Thoresby Society*, 5, 1995; F. Beckwith, *The Leeds Library*, 1994, which brings the building and c18 Leeds to life; D. Boswell's account of the School of Art in C. Miller (ed.), *Behind the Mosaic, One Hundred Years of Art Education*, 2003; and K. Powell, The Queen's Hotel, *Journal of the Victorian Society Yorkshire Group*, 1985. M. Parsons, *The General Infirmary at Leeds*, 2003 is a useful pictorial history of this major institution. For the University the relevant general accounts are P.H.J.H. Gosden & A. J. Taylor, *Studies in the History of a University*, 1974, and M. Beresford, *Walks around Red Brick*, 1980. Chamberlin, Powell & Bon's *University of Leeds Development Plan*, 1960 (revised 1963) details the major postwar expansion.

The significance of the **commercial and retail architecture** of Leeds up to the c21 is set in national context by K. Morrison's, *English Shops and Shopping*, 2004; J.F. Geist, *Arcades: The History of a Building Type,* 1983, and J. Schmiechen & K. Carls, *The British Market Hall: a social and architectural history*, 1999. S. Burt & K. Grady, *Kirkgate Market, An*

Illustrated History, 1992, also has an excellent account of trading in C19 Leeds. J. Chartres & K. Honeyman, *Leeds City Business 1893–1993*, 1993, covers Tetley's and Burton's.

For the **suburbs,** informative short walks include F. Matthews, *A Walk Round Little Woodhouse*, 1997 and J. Douglas, C. Hammond & K. Powell, *Leeds: Three Suburban Walks*, 1987 (Headingley and Roundhay). Also on Headingley, and **housing** generally: F. Trowell, Nineteenth Century Speculative Housing in Leeds with special reference to the suburb of Headingley 1838–1914 (PhD thesis, York), 1982; C. Treen, 'The process of suburban development in North Leeds 1870–1914', in F.M.L. Thompson, *The Rise of Suburbia*, 1982. D. Hall, *Far Headingley, Weetwood and West Park*, 2000, includes buildings information. G. Sheeran, *Brass Castles*, 1993 covers the city's large suburban houses, while the mansion at Temple Newsam is covered by its own guide book (Leeds City Council) and several articles in *Country Life* and the *Leeds Arts Calendar*. Also valuable is V.M.E. Lovell, 'Benjamin Gott of Armley House', *Thoresby Society Miscellany,* v.18, pt 2, 1986. S. Burt, *An Illustrated History of Roundhay Park*, 2000, is an expert account. Working class housing is set in a wider context by S.D. Chapman, *The History of Working Class housing*, 1971, and J.N.Tarn, *Five per cent philanthropy*, 1973. Among Alison Ravetz's important publications on this subject is *Model Estate – planned housing at Quarry Hill*, 1974.

Aspects of **industrial development** are detailed in *The Century's Progress*, 1893 (reprinted 1971), and C. Giles & I. Goodall, *Yorkshire Textile Mills*, 1992. The sources for the design of Temple Mills is analysed in J.S. Curl, *The Egyptian Revival*, 1982. On the Round Foundry: E. Kilburn Scott, *Matthew Murray Pioneer Engineer,* 1928, reprinted 1999. Gillian Gookson, 'Early Textile Engineers in Leeds, 1780–1850', *Thoresby Society* series 2, v.4, 1994 is based on her PhD thesis. For the waterways: Mike Clarke, *The Aire & Calder Navigation*, 1999, and *The Leeds & Liverpool Canal*, 1994.

The **earliest account** of the town is Ralph Thoresby's *Ducatus Leodensis*, 1715 (2nd ed. by T.D. Whitaker, 1816). A. Briggs, *Victorian Cities*, 1963, contains a compelling account of Leeds in the C19 but there are two classic **general histories**: M.W Beresford's scholarly *East End, West End*, 1988, covers the period 1684–1842 and Steven Burt & Kevin Grady, *The Illustrated History of Leeds*, 2002, contains a detailed bibliography. Also useful: Derek Fraser, *A History of Modern Leeds*, 1980; A. Heap & P. Brears, *Leeds Describ'd* covers documentary sources 1534–1905. Patrick Nuttgens' oddly-titled *Leeds, the back to front, inside out, upside down city*, 1979 was based on a television documentary. R. Unsworth & J. Stillwell, *Twentyfirst century Leeds, geographies of a regional city*, 2004 brings us up to date. **Archaeological evidence** is discussed in M. Faull & S.A. Moorhouse, *West Yorkshire: An Archaeological Survey to A.D. 1500*, 1981.

Geology and building materials are described in F. G. Dimes & M. Mitchell, *The Building Stone Heritage of Leeds,* 1996 (Leeds Philosophical & Literary Society). For the Leeds Fireclay Company: A. Garlick, *Burmantofts Pottery* (1984, ex. cat Bradford Galleries & Museums), and H. Van Lemmen, Burmantofts Marmo, 1984, *Journal of the Victorian Society West Yorkshire Branch*, 1983–4.

Maps of the city (over 300), are listed in K.J. Bonser & H. Nichols, *Printed Maps and Plans of Leeds 1711–1900*, Thoresby Society, 1958. Twelve are reproduced in Arthur Elton and Brett Harrison, *Leeds in Maps*, 1989; the 1905–8 O.S. maps (1:2500) republished by Alan Godfrey have informative commentaries by G.C. Dickinson. **Local guides and directories** include Edward Baines' directories of 1809, 1817 and 1822 and the various editions of White's and Kelly's directories. C20 changes are recorded in The Yorkshire Post's *Guide to the city of Leeds*, 1935, *The Industrial Capital of the North*, 1948 and 1954, and the City Council's publications: Stuart Hirst, *Leeds Tercentenary Official Handbook*, 1926 and *Guide to the City of Leeds*, 1961.

Websites: www.lookingatbuildings.org.uk – the Pevsner Architectural Guide's website – has further information on Leeds buildings and architects. The Leeds City Library's website, www.leodis.net has thousands of images of buildings.

Glossary

Acanthus: *see* [2D].

Acroterion: plinth for a statue on ornament on the apex or ends of a *pediment*.

Aedicule: architectural surround, usually a *pediment* on two columns or *pilasters*.

Ambulatory: aisle around the *sanctuary* of a church.

Anthemion: *see* [2D].

Apse: semicircular or polygonal end, especially in a church.

Arcade: series of arches supported by *piers* or columns (cf. *colonnade*).

Art Deco: a self-consciously up-to-date interwar style of bold simplified patterns, often derived from non-European art.

Ashlar: large rectangular masonry blocks wrought to even faces.

Atrium: a toplit covered court rising through several storeys.

Attic: small top storey within a roof. Also the storey above the main *entablature* of a classical façade.

Baldacchino: solid canopy, usually free-standing and over an altar.

Ballflower: globular flower of three petals enclosing a small ball.

Barrel vault: one with a simple arched profile.

Basilica: a Roman public hall; hence an aisled building with a clerestory.

Batter: intentional inward inclination of a wall face.

Bay: division of an elevation by regular vertical features such as columns, windows, etc.

Beaux-Arts: a French-derived approach to classical design, at its peak in the later c19–early c20, marked by strong axial planning and the grandiose use of the *orders*.

Broach spire: *see* [1].

Brutalist: used for later 1950s–70s Modernist architecture displaying rough or unfinished concrete, massive forms, and abrupt juxtapositions.

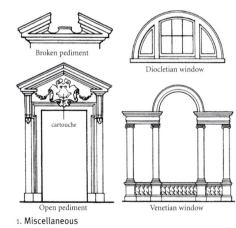

Broken pediment

Diocletian window

cartouche

Open pediment

Venetian window

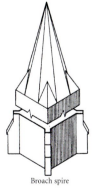

Broach spire

1. Miscellaneous

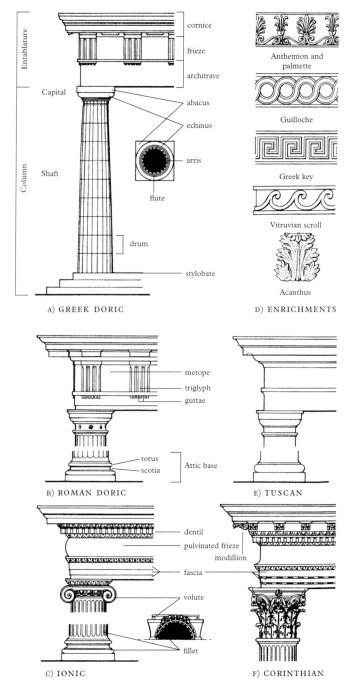

A) GREEK DORIC

- Entablature
  - cornice
  - frieze
  - architrave
- Column
  - Capital
  - Shaft
  - abacus
  - echinus
  - arris
  - flute
  - drum
  - stylobate

D) ENRICHMENTS

Anthemion and palmette

Guilloche

Greek key

Vitruvian scroll

Acanthus

B) ROMAN DORIC

- metope
- triglyph
- guttae
- torus
- scotia
- Attic base

E) TUSCAN

C) IONIC

- dentil
- pulvinated frieze
- modillion
- fascia
- volute
- fillet

F) CORINTHIAN

2. Classical orders and enrichments

Bucranium: ox skull used decoratively in classical friezes.

Cancelli: in early Christian architecture, a latticed screen or grille separating the choir from the main body of a church.

Capital: head feature of a column or *pilaster*; for classical types *see* [2].

Carding: passing blended wool between revolving cylinders with closely-set wire teeth to mingle the fibres. The process was originally undertaken with two hand-held wooden boards set with wires.

Cartouche: *see* [1].

Castellated: with battlements.

Chancel: the E part or end of a church, where the altar is placed.

Chapter house: place of assembly for the members of a monastery or cathedral.

Choir: the part of a great church where services are sung.

Clerestory: uppermost storey of an interior, pierced by windows.

Coffering: decorative arrangement of sunken panels.

Cogging: a decorative course of bricks laid diagonally.

Colonnade: range of columns supporting a flat *lintel* or *entablature* (cf. *arcade*).

Corbel: projecting block supporting something above.

Combing: dressing worsted fibres to separate the short (for the woollen trade) from the long, ready for spinning.

Composite: classical order with capitals combining Corinthian features (acanthus, *see* [2D]) with Ionic (volutes, *see* [2C]).

Corinthian; cornice: *see* [2F; 2A].

Cove: a broad concave moulding.

Crenellated: with battlements.

Crocket: leafy hooks decorating the edges of Gothic features

Cupola: a small dome used as a crowning feature.

Cyma recta and **Cyma reversa:** classical mouldings with double curves. Cf. Ogee.

Dado: finishing of the lower part of an internal wall.

Decorated (Dec): English Gothic architecture, late C13 to late C14.

Diaper: repetitive surface decoration of lozenges or squares flat or in relief. Achieved in brickwork with bricks of two colours.

Diocletian window: *see* [1].

Doric: *see* [2A, 2B].

Drum: circular or polygonal stage supporting a dome.

Dutch or Flemish gable: *see* [3].

Early English (E.E.): English Gothic architecture, late C12 to late C13.

Entablature: *see* [2A].

Faience: moulded *terracotta* that is glazed white or coloured.

Fleurons: carved flower or leaf.

Flying buttress: one transmitting thrust by means of an arch or half-arch.

Fulling: thickening and cleaning newly-woven cloth in soft water using a detergent. Originally done in tubs by walking, later fulling mills used water-powered machinery.

Frieze: middle member of a classical *entablature*, *see* [2A, 2C]. Also a horizontal band of ornament.

Geometrical: of *tracery*, a mid-C13–C14 type formed of circles and part-circles; *see* [4].

Giant order: a classical *order* that is two or more storeys high.

Gibbs surround: C18 treatment of an opening with blocked architraves, seen particularly in the work of James Gibbs (1682–1754).

Gothic: the style of the later Middle Ages, characterized by the pointed arch and *rib-vault*.

Groin vault: one composed of inter-secting *barrel vaults*.

Guilloche: *see* [2D].

Half-timbering: non-structural decorative timberwork.

Hipped roof: *see* [3].

Hoodmould: projecting moulding above arch or *lintel* to throw off water.

In antis: of columns, set in an opening (properly between simplified *pilasters* called *antae*).

Ionic: *see* [2C].

Italianate: a classical style derived from the palaces of Renaissance Italy.

Jamb: one of the vertical sides of an opening.

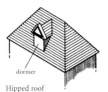 

dormer

Hipped roof   Mansard roof   Flemish or
Dutch gable

3. Roofs and gables

Jettied: with a projecting upper
storey, usually timber-framed.
Kingpost roof: one with vertical timbers set centrally on the *tie-beams*,
supporting the ridge.
Lancet: slender, single-light pointed-
arched window; *see* [4].
Lantern: a windowed turret crowning a roof, tower or dome.
Light: compartment of a window.
Lintel: horizontal beam or stone
bridging an opening.
Loggia: open gallery with arches or
columns.
Louvre: opening in a roof or wall to
allow air to escape.
Lunette: semicircular window or
panel.
Machicolation: openings between
corbels that support a projecting
parapet.
Mannerist: of classical architecture,
with motifs used in deliberate dis-
regard of original conventions or
contexts.
Mansard roof: *see* [3].
Mezzanine: low storey between two
higher ones.
Mihrab: the focus for prayer in a
mosque, usually a niche.
Moulding: shaped ornamental strip
of continuous section.
Mullion: vertical member between
window *lights*.
Narthex: enclosed vestibule or
porch at the main entrance to a
church.
Newel: central or corner post of a
staircase.
Norman: the C11–C12 English version
of the *Romanesque* style.
Oculus: circular opening.
Ogee: of an arch, dome, etc., with
double-curved pointed profile.
Opus Sectile: decorative mosaic-like
facing.
Orders (classical): for types *see* [2].

Oriel: window projecting above
ground level.
Palladian: following the examples
and classical principles of Andrea
Palladio (1508–80).
Parapet: wall for protection of a
sudden drop, e.g. on a bridge, or to
conceal a roof.
Pavilion: ornamental building for
occasional use; or a projecting subdivision of a larger building (hence
pavilion roof).
Pediment: a formalized gable,
derived from that of a classical
temple; also used over doors, windows, etc. For types *see* [1].
Pendentive: part-hemispherical surface between arches that meet at an
angle to support a *drum*, dome or
vault.
Penthouse: a separately roofed structure on top of a multi-storey block
of the C20 or later.
Perpendicular (Perp): English
Gothic architecture from the late
C14 to early C16.
Piano nobile (Italian): principal
floor of a classical building, above a
ground floor or basement and with
a lesser storey overhead.
Pier: a large masonry or brick support, often for an arch.
Pilaster: flat representation of a classical column in shallow relief.
Piscina: basin in a church or chapel
for washing mass vessels, usually
wall-set.
Polychromy: the use of contrasting
coloured materials such as
bricks as decoration, particularly
associated with mid-C19 Gothic
styles.
Porte cochère (French): porch large
enough to admit wheeled vehicles.
Portico: porch with roof and (frequently) *pediment* supported by a
row of columns.

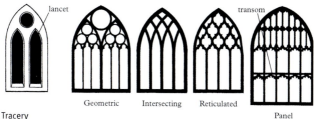

lancet | transom

Geometric | Intersecting | Reticulated | Panel

4. Tracery

Portland stone: a hard, durable white limestone from the Isle of Portland in Dorset.

Presbytery: a priest's residence.

Prostyle: of a *portico*, with freestanding columns.

Pulvinated: of bulging profile; *see* [2C].

Quatrefoil: opening with four lobes.

Queen Anne: the later Victorian revival of the mid-C17 domestic classical manner, usually in red brick or terracotta.

Quoins: dressed or otherwise emphasized stones at the angles of a building.

Rainwater head: container at a *parapet* into which rainwater runs from the gutters.

Render: a uniform covering for walls for protection from the weather, usually of cement or *stucco*.

Reredos: painted and/or sculpted screen behind and above an altar.

Rock-faced: masonry cleft to produce a natural, rugged appearance.

Romanesque: round-arched style of the C11 and C12.

Rood: crucifix flanked by the Virgin and St John, carved or painted.

Rubble: of masonry, with stones wholly or partly rough and unsquared.

Rustication: exaggerated treatment of masonry to give the effect of strength.

Sacristy: room in a church used for sacred vessels and vestments.

Saddleback roof: a pitched roof used on a tower.

Sanctuary: in a church, the area around the main altar.

Sedilia: seats for the priests in the *chancel* wall of a church or chapel.

Space frame: a three-dimensional framework in which all members are interconnected, designed to cover large areas.

Spandrel: space between an arch and its framing rectangle, or between adjacent arches.

Stanchion: upright structural member, of iron, steel or reinforced concrete.

Stiff-leaf: carved decoration in the form of thick uncurling foliage; originally late C12–early C13.

Stoup: vessel for holy water.

Stripped classicism: buildings whose proportions conform to classical precedent but where the usual classical decoration is implied or removed altogether.

Stucco: durable lime plaster, shaped into ornamental features or used externally as a protective coating.

System building: system of manufactured units assembled on site.

Term: pedestal or pilaster tapering downward, usually with the upper part of a human figure growing out of it.

Terracotta: moulded and fired clay ornament or cladding (cf. *faience*).

Tie-beam: main horizontal transverse timber in a roof structure.

Tracery: openwork pattern of masonry or timber in the upper part of an opening.

Transept: transverse portion of a church.

string course

channelled with glacial quoins

V-jointed with vermiculated quoins

5. Rustication

Transsom: horizontal member between window lights; *see* [4].

Trefoil: with three lobes or foils.

Triforium: middle storey of a church interior treated as an arcaded wall passage or blind arcade.

Truss: braced framework, spanning between supports.

Tunnel vault: one with a simple elongated-arched profile.

Tuscan: *see* [2E].

Tympanum: the area enclosed by an arch or *pediment*.

Undercroft: room(s), usually *vaulted*, beneath the main space of a building.

Venetian window: *see* [1].

Volutes: spiral scrolls, especially on Ionic columns; *see* [2C].

Voussoir: wedge-shaped stones forming an arch.

Willeying: cleaning and separating fibres to assist processing. Originally done by hand by beating with willow wands, the process was mechanised in the late C18.

Wrenaissance: early C20 work inspired by the architecture of Sir Christopher Wren (1632–1723), especially the E front of Hampton Court.

Ziggurat: a rectangular temple-tower in the form of a truncated pyramid.

Index
of Artists, Architects and Other Persons Mentioned

Names of artists, architects etc. working in Leeds are in *italic*; page references including relevant illustrations are in *italic*.

Aaron, Arthur 170
Abbey Hanson Rowe 38–9, 106, 119, 120, 134
Abbey Holford Rowe 40, 166, 260
Adam, Robert 284
Adams, Maurice Bingham 225, 262
Adams, Richard 29, 207, 238
Adams & Kelly 28, 123, 186, 209, 213, 229–30
Aedeas AHR 134
Airedale, Sir James Kitson, 1st Lord 107–8, 243, 244, 249, 253
Albert, Prince 30, 64, 195
Albutt, Thomas 266
Allan (James) & Son 121
Allen Tod Architects 38, 103, 143, 172, 232–3
Allford Hall Monaghan Morris 104
Alsop & Lyall 68
Ambler, Thomas 21, 25, 27, 36, 92, 93, 95, 96–7, 98, 103, 113, 121, 139, 148, 151, 293
Angus, Mark 179
Appleby, K. 109
Appleton Partnership 37, 170
Appleyard, John Wormald 77, 87, 98, 102, 120, 157, 158
Armitage, Kenneth 151
Armitage, William James 103
Arthington, John 112
Arup (Ove) & Partners 38, 143
Ash, Arthur S. 169
Austin-Smith:Lord 73
Athron (Joseph) & Henry Walker 28
Atkinson, G.W. 164, 168, 169, 170, 264
Atkinson, John (C18) 10
Atkinson, John (C19) 149, 184, 189, 190
Atkinson, Moses 145
Atkinson & Shaw 169
Austin, Joseph 258
Austin & Paley 196
AXIS Architecture 149

Bacon, Percy C. 221
Bacon (Percy) & Bros 236
Bage, Charles 206

Bagshaw (J.) & Sons 101–2
Bagshawe, Commander Bernal 242
Baguley, G.J. 220
Baines, Sir Edward 176
Baines, Edward Jun. 192
Bakewell, William 26, 102, 106, 116, 129–31, 152, 167
Bankart, George 249
Barlow, W.H. 90
Barnett, F. 95
Barran, Sir John 21, 25, 28, 92, 93, 97, 113, 194, 223, 241, 292, 293
Barran, John Jun. 21
Barry, Sir Charles 60–1, 62, 67
Barry, E.M. 17, 46, 196–7
Battiscombe & Harris 286
Bauman Lyons Architects 40, 232, 241
BDP see Building Design Partnership
Beckett family 16, 21–2, 245, 260, 263
Beckett, Christopher 13, 149, 265
Beckett, Edmund Jun. 83
Beckett, Edmund Sen. 16, 158
Beckett, John 21
Beckett, William 47, 83, 223
Beckwith & Webster 213
Bedford family 249
Bedford, Francis W. 248–9, 252–3
Bedford, James 195, 249
Bedford & Kitson 26, 29, 152, 162, 241–2, 249, 250, 258–9, 266
Beevers, W.H. 234
Behnes, William 30, 198, 255
Bell, Quentin 182
Bellman, Ivey & Carter 81
Bennett (T.P.) & Son 109
Bentley, J.F. 54, 58
Benyon, Thomas and Benjamin 206
Berry, Mr 134
Billington, William 252
Bilson, John 273
Birchall, Edward 136–7, 187, 253
Birchall & Kelly 29, 153–4
Bischoff, John & George 201
Blayds, John 60
Blenkinsop, John 15
Blomfield, Sir Reginald 32, 156, 168, 169, 170, 224

Index
of Localities, Streets and Buildings

Principal references are in **bold** type; page references including relevant illustrations are in *italic*. 'dem.' = 'demolished'

Illustration Acknowledgements

Every effort has been made to contact or trace all copyright holders. The publishers will be glad to make good any errors or omissions brought to our attention in future editions.

A special debt of gratitude is owed to English Heritage and its photographers, particularly Tony Perry, who took many of the photographs for this volume and also to the following for permission to reproduce illustrative material:

Paul Barker/Country Life Picture Library: 151, 154, 155
The Builder: 40, 58, 135
Carey Jones Architects: 67, 105
Dixon Jones Architects (Richard Bryant): 86
DLA Design Group: 89
DLG Architects: 85
English Heritage/NMR: 2, 4, 5, 8, 9, 10, 12, 13, 14, 15, 16, 17, 18, 23, 25, 26, 27, 30, 32, 33, 35, 36, 37, 39, 41, 42, 45, 46, 47, 48, 49, 51, 54, 55, 59, 60, 61, 63, 64, 68, 70, 71, 72, 73, 76, 77, 78, 79, 81, 82, 83, 84, 87, 92, 93, 94, 96, 98, 100, 101, 102, 103, 104, 106, 108, 109, 112, 113, 114, 115, 117, 119, 120, 121, 123, 124, 126, 127, 128, 129, 130, 131, 133, 134, 136, 137, 138, 139, 140, 142, 144, 145, 147, 148, 150, 158, 159, 160

Alan Fagan: 146
Paul Gwilliam © West Yorkshire Archaeology Service: 149
Leeds City Council: 7, 65, 125, 143
© Leeds Museums and Galleries (City Art Gallery) www.bridgeman.co.uk: 11, 44
Leeds Library and Information Services: 56
Leeds Library and Information Services (The Thoresby Society): 52
Leeds Museums and Galleries (Temple Newsam): 152, 153, 156
Derek Linstrum: 31
Les McLean: 97
John Minnis: 116
The Penny Magazine, 1843 (Leeds Central Library, Reference Department): 66
Tony Quinn © Red Door VR Ltd, Images of Leeds: 20, 21, 28, 38 (Reproduced by permission of the Henry Moore Foundation), 34, 53, 57, 75, 111
R. Thoresby, Ducatus Leodiensis, 1715 (second edition edited by Rev. T.D. Whitaker, 1816): 6
Touchmedia: 1, 22, 43, 50, 62, 69, 74, 80, 90, 99, 107, 110, 118, 122, 132, 141, 157
University of Leeds Media Services: 19, 29, 91, 95
C.H. Wood Ltd.: 88